Ageing in
Developing Countries

Ageing in
Developing Countries

KEN TOUT

Published by
OXFORD UNIVERSITY PRESS
for
HELPAGE INTERNATIONAL
1989

Oxford University Press, Walton Street, Oxford OX2 6DP

Oxford New York Toronto
Delhi Bombay Calcutta Madras Karachi
Petaling Jaya Singapore Hong Kong Tokyo
Nairobi Dar es Salaam Cape Town
Melbourne Auckland

and associated companies in
Berlin Ibadan

Oxford is a trade mark of Oxford University Press

Published in the United States
by Oxford University Press, New York

British Library Cataloguing in Publication Data
Tout, Ken, 1924–
Ageing in developing countries.
1. Developing countries. Old persons. Social aspects
I. Title II. Helpage International
305.2'6'091724
ISBN 0–19–827279–0
ISBN 0–19–827276–6 (pbk.)

Library of Congress Cataloging-in-Publication Data
Tout, Ken.
Ageing in developing countries / Ken Tout.
Bibliography: p.   Includes index.
1. Aged—Services for—Developing countries.
2. Aged—Developing countries—Social conditions.
I. HelpAge International. II. Title.
HV1494.T68 1989   362.6'09172'4—dc19   88–39187
ISBN 0–19–827279–0
ISBN 0–19–827276–6 (pbk.)

Set by Hope Services, Abingdon
Printed in Great Britain by
Biddles Ltd., Guildford and King's Lynn

This book is dedicated to Sister Pacifica
McKenna, working for forty years in the Beni,
Bolivia, and others like her, who have taken the
first steps in meeting the unfamiliar modern
phenomenon of Ageing in Developing Countries.

FOREWORD

Ageing in Developing Countries elegantly separates fact from fiction, while sorting out salient problems from the many issues arising out of humankind's booming Third Age of Life. In a compendious and deft manner, the reader is guided through the tangle of consequences and concomitants of modernization, industrialization, and urbanization affecting the greying generation. As we journey from Fiji to Ghana, from Belize to Malta, from Bolivia to Bangladesh and other nations on the globe, we begin to understand Ken Tout's call to action to overcome the unexpected and unplanned coming of 'ageing and abandonment' in the developing world.

The book does not allow us to gloss over the current and foreseeable negative cultural context within which change and hope in the lives of older persons must start. We are given the human detail of how much developing countries have become dislocated socially and economically in their quest for modernity, and how this has not allowed them to deal well with the greying of their people.

Especially dramatic is the negative impact of non-support and non-remittance of funds on the extended family, a happening which is linked with mass migration to the city and large-scale emigration of family members of so-called working age. Equally important is the connection between a pervasive paralysis of public effort on behalf of 'the elders' and governmental preoccupation with international debt and maintaining domestic political tranquillity. Moreover, we acquire a better grasp of how lack of public awareness of the grey revolution is abetted by the persisting tradition of divisive functioning between health, social service, welfare, and educational institutions, as well as by the near absence of meaningful pension plans.

Having sensitized us to seemingly intractable negatives of ageing in developing countries, Ken Tout weaves a neat tapestry of human inventiveness in building natural continuities across abandoned extended family supports into new voluntary older person networks of profitable enterprise and ageing well. We are treated to a series of case histories affirming workable local and regional experiments of shared income generation and renewed, self-directed living.

For instance, we learn about a bakery owned and operated by the grandparent generation which funds a walk-in clinic for the indigent and also distributes free baked goods among those with the least sustenance. Other self-help responses backed by newly formed voluntary infrastructures include a cottage weaving industry which brings together the younger and older generation in a joint effort. A further notable local initiative involves a governess-training programme—'Grandma crèches' for old persons left behind by younger relatives in the village. It has led to assured employment by well-to-do city dwellers, and to a rebirth of hope and family respect.

A major theme throughout this treatise on solving old problems of ageing in new ways is that we must ensure a complementarity of 'action with ideas' and of 'ideas with action' before we can move ahead and remain in step with the unfolding capabilities of the older person. Indeed, mobilizing 'local responses and experimenting with model projects of a low key nature which can be replicated' works when it is quite out of step with the common view that to be old is doing and being less, and having a monopoly on institutions and death.

In practical terms, Ken Tout invites us to engage much more in knowledge-sharing and in participatory planning and implementation, whether in the city or in rural areas. It means that we must learn to focus clearly on feasible action which moves the older and the younger person towards becoming co-agents in educational, social, and economic development.

Most important, this book tells all that is needed to retire transcultural predictions of a prolonged shelf-life of destitution, decrepitude, and dependency in our Third Age. The very nearness of the third millennium AD, with its projected huge increases in elderly population, beckons us to practice better group solutions towards individual well-being and economic productivity, and to form lasting partnerships in self health care, mutual support, and personal service.

Professor Otto von Mering
Director

Center for Gerontological Studies
University of Florida, USA

ACKNOWLEDGEMENTS

THIS book was prepared with access to files of HelpAge (Help the Aged UK and HelpAge International), which in many cases are confidential. On occasions it has therefore been impossible to give a clear quotation of a source. At the same time HelpAge did not wish this book to become what might seem a propaganda exercise on behalf of a charitable organization. As in many areas of developing countries HelpAge is the only external agency involved in stimulating and supporting both basic research and practical projects, the HelpAge contribution is in fact underplayed rather than overemphasized.

My thanks go in the first place to HelpAge's Director of Overseas Operations, Dr Christopher Beer; he was to have been co-author, but his unenviable overseas travel programme made concentration on a book almost impossible. However, Chris's influence on the book has been substantial.

Among those whose advice or work has contributed greatly are Gary Andrews, Elias Anzola-Pérez, Nana Apt, Farley Braithwaite, Larry Coppard, Denise Eldemire, Sybil Francis, Eduardo and Rita García, Joaquín González-Aragón, Joe Hampson, Jorge Jiménez Gandica, Alex Kalache, Katie Kelly, Sir Leslie Kirkley, Esther de Lehr, Diane Loughran, David McFadyen, John Mayo, Meredith Minkler, Charlotte Nusberg, J. D. Pathak, Margaret Peil, Luis Ramos, Ann Rose, Peter Strachan, Otto von Mering, Tony Warnes, Douglas Williams, and the staff of HelpAge. The experts of Oxford University Press have remedied many a typographical or stylistic blemish.

Thanks also to my secretary, Jackie Shaw, who will probably never want to see another bibliography or subject-index. And finally, thanks to my wife Jai, who shared one of my research assignments, tolerated bedrooms blocked with ageing documents, and also offered advice based on her experience with local authority services for the elderly.

CONTENTS

LIST OF TABLES

ABBREVIATIONS

AAIA	American Association for International Aging (Washington, DC)
AWARE	Action for Welfare and Awakening in Rural Environment (India)
BMA	Blind Men's Association (India)
CEC	Commission of European Communities
CEPAL	Comisión Económica para América Latina (UN)
CEWA	Centre for the Welfare of the Aged (India)
CIGAL	Centro Internacional de Gerontología para América Latina (Colombia)
DIF	Desarrollo Integral de la Familia (Mexico)
HAI	HelpAge International (London)
HtA	Help the Aged (London)
ICHP	International Conference on Health Policy
IDESPO	Instituto de Estudios Sociales en Población (Costa Rica)
IFA	International Federation on Aging (Washington DC)
ILO	International Labour Organization
LDC/LDR	Least Developed Country/Region
OECD	Organisation for Economic Co-operation and Development
PAHO	Panamerican Health Organization (WHO)
PAMI	Programme for Integrated Medical Attention (Argentina)
UNCTAD	UN Commission for Trade and Development
UN DIESA	UN Department of International Economic and Social Affairs
UNFPA	UN Fund for Population Activities
UNRWA	UN Relief and Works Agency

WAA	World Assembly on Aging, 1982 (UN)
VIPAA	Vienna International Plan of Action on Aging (WAA)
WHO	World Health Organization (UN)

INTRODUCTION

A WORLD now accustomed to planning in terms of 'baby bulges' may find it difficult to adjust to the new phenomenon of a 'greying population'. United Nations estimates confidently predict that over 20 years the number of people aged 60 and over will double, from about 300 million to about 600 million. Some of the most rapid increases will occur in developing countries.

This new factor will distort the present population pyramid, which tends to show vast numbers of children, slightly lesser numbers of adolescents, and so on up to a very tiny representation of people over 70 years of age. The new population pyramid will probably reveal much smaller numbers of children, but considerably more people surviving into extreme old age.

One expert commentator, Alfred Sauvy, has said that 'the twenty-first century will be the century of the aging of mankind'. Other commentators have been greatly disturbed at the thought of many more millions of unproductive old people making huge additional demands on health and social services paid for by dwindling numbers of working people in nations, developed and devloping, whose economies are already strained to a frightening degree.

The World Assembly on Aging, called by the United Nations in Vienna in 1982, awakened considerable awareness of the new problem, but subsequent action was disappointing. Observers tend to take a pessimistic view of the effects of increased survival of unproductive people at a time when unemployment of working age people is a massive problem.

This book endeavours first of all to set out the available facts about the forecast increases in longevity. It attempts to present a positive view, based on a number of pilot programmes that appear to point to ways in which potential problems associated with ageing can be met. As F. W. Notestein argues 'viewed as a whole the "problem of aging" is no problem at all . . . It is only a pessimistic way of looking at a great triumph of civilization . . . With a perversity that is strictly human, we insist on considering

INTRODUCTION

the aggregate result of our individual success (achieving our goal of individual survival) as a "problem".'

As will be seen, the severity of the 'problem' of a greying population varies: in certain developed countries the 'age boom' is already being experienced in full force, in certain developing countries its effects are beginning to emerge as matters for national concern, while in other, lesser developed, countries the problem is restricted to relatively few individual cases. The developing world of the late 1980s and 1990s has the golden opportunity of moving towards solution of a major problem before that problem has reached full development in too many countries. Policies on ageing, such as setting up universal governmental pension schemes, require a considerable period before their full impact is felt, while many old people have only a brief life expectancy during which they will be able to benefit from effective action. This world 'problem' therefore demands urgency both in consideration and in action.

At the individual level the urgency is extreme, as in a case I experienced in one developing country. A tiny shack in a shanty town was occupied by an old woman almost 80 years of age. Also living in the shack were her nine small grandchildren. The old woman had sole responsibility for caring for the children on an income of little more than a dollar a week. The two parent couples to whom the children belonged had emigrated to the United States, leaving the children behind in order to facilitate their own migration and, no doubt, with every intention of sending money home to assist the grandmother. The parents, being unqualified and unprepared for the transition to United States society, had apparently been able to obtain only the humblest of jobs, with wages inadequate even to maintain themselves in any comfort in their new homes. No remittances were ever sent home to the grandmother. Whether out of shame, incompetence, or a more selfish preoccupation with their own fate, the two couples had severed contact, leaving the grand-mother and nine infants to their fate.

It might be argued that the world at large has no responsibility for repairing the personal ills caused by the absence and neglect shown by those two parent couples. It is equally arguable that the parents were themselves victims of circumstances beyond their own comprehension, that a more sensibly organized world could have avoided the more distressing aspects of the case, and certainly that the grandmother and the infants are now a responsibility of those who have a duty to care.

The 'greying of the population' constitutes a major problem for the entire world, and in that sense requires the most serious economic and political attention. It also involves severe physical and psychological suffering for many old people and their dependants, and in that sense the world bears a moral responsibility for action within the life-span of the sufferers.

This book therefore proposes a new approach to the problems of older people in developing countries, rather than advocating mere 'do-gooding' or alleviation of the immediate sufferings of a relative few of the most needy. Instead, the intention is to build structures for the future, when there will be so many more elderly people in every country. This means stimulating awareness of this incipient but rapidly developing problem, and providing local communities with the resources to take their own action; and mobilizing and maximizing the many talents and the wealth of experience of the elderly themselves into productive programmes. Most important, it means supplying skills in matters such as management, fund-raising, financial control, training, information, and similar day-to-day activities without which the spontaneous flame of enthusiasm and volunteer response may so quickly dim and die out.

As my own work currently lies with HelpAge, and as the organizations operating under this umbrella serve as pathfinders in this new field of activity, it would seem appropriate to say a word or two here about the organizations involved. Help the Aged (UK) commenced as a fund-raising, grant-making organization in the 1960s, raising money by public appeal (which it still does) and sending grants to caring bodies working with the elderly in developing countries. Over the course of two decades, several developing countries developed their own agencies, similar to Help the Aged and sometimes even borrowing the name, but all working towards self-sufficiency with indigenous leadership and their own local fund-raising programmes.

Fourteen of those organizations, mainly from developing countries, now form HelpAge International, which has undertaken the specific role of helping to initiate and support other, similar national age-care agencies throughout the developing world. HelpAge International is therefore the supporting frame of a non-governmental structure that can quickly initiate pilot projects and experiment with new methods, until such time as the armies of inter-governmental and governmental organizations are able to make a sufficient response to the phenomenon of a greying world.

I

WHAT IS AGEING?

A SIGNIFICANT factor emerging from the World Assembly on Aging[1] was the lack of standardization of concepts and terminology on ageing, which resulted in a special Expert Group being formed on the subject.[2] It appears that it is not possible to take the basic concept of 'ageing' as a universally understood term.

This chapter queries what is meant by ageing, and then goes on to examine arguments which are frequently encountered when reference is made to problems of ageing in the developing world. Firstly, that ageing is normally a kind of prolonged terminal illness which has no remedy during its process. Secondly, that traditionally the elder was revered, and that the sufferings of older people are entirely the result of modernization effects. Thirdly, that the extended family always cares for the old person in the Third World.

The implications of the first argument are often developed in general conversation in terms like 'the old are going to die soon anyway. Give them a little bit of comfort. Then let them die as quickly as possible and save us problems.'

---

[1] The World Assembly on Aging held in Vienna from 26 July to 6 August 1982 was a United Nations assembly of governmental representatives, but non-governmental organizations (NGOs) were invited to participate.

The assembly was preceded by a Forum of NGOs from 29 March to 2 April 1982, also in Vienna, which made recommendations to the main assembly. I attended both and prepared the submissions published as Assembly Paper No. A/Conf 113/NGO/19 (UN WAA 1982a).

[2] Recognition of the need for codification of systems was included in the Vienna International Plan of Action on Aging issued by the World Assembly (UN WAA 1982e, Recommendation 52). I participated in the somewhat inconclusive Expert Group Meeting on Standardization of Definitions, Terms, and Research Methodologies in the Field of Aging held subsequently in Vienna (25–29 Mar. 1985).

What is 'ageing'?

An American sociologist has suggested that 'old age may be
defined functionally as a substantial change in the individual's
capacity to contribute to the work and protection of the group'.[3]
The frequency with which ageing is taken to have adverse
connotations is indicated by a Colombian psycho-geriatrician
who asks, 'let us seek to change the idea of age as being passive,
useless, dependent and isolated into an ageing that is active,
autonomous and socially participative'.[4] Russell A. Ward quotes
Simone de Beauvoir as finding that age is generally associated
with ideas like 'tragic, ludicrous, revolting or some combination
of these', while other terms cited by the same writer include
'mentally slower, grouchy, unproductive, feeling sorry for themselves, withdrawn', and so on.[5]

Another commentator states that old age is seen as a
pathological state—a time of sickness and strangeness and
'falling-apartness'.[6] A Brazilian professor speaks of 'taboos'
relating to ageing, including educational taboos which impede
the true knowledge of the subject.[7]

The World Health Organization emphatically refutes these
ideas. None of the above conditions is inevitable. It is true that
elderly people may be more prone to chronic illnesses than
younger people. But even the most chronically disabled have
been found to be able to perform much of their own self-care and
rehabilitation. The World Health Organization characterizes the
use of the single word 'ageing' to embrace all the phenomena of
growing old as 'unproductively simplistic'.[8] The Argentine
geriatrician Mira y López is emphatic that lack of health is not
an exclusive factor of ageing, and that most frequently when an
older person is ill he is simply suffering from the development of a
condition which has been present from a much earlier age.[9]
Epidemiologists studying people over 65 years of age have
calculated that 95% have a normal ageing pattern (that is, no

[3] R. A. Ward 1979, p. 9.   [4] Dulcey-Ruiz 1985, frontispiece.
[5] R. A. Ward 1979, p. 160.   [6] Kalish 1979.
[7] Jordão Netto 1982b.   [8] UN WAA, 1982f.
[9] Mira y López, 1962, repr. in Carbal Prieto 1980, p. 17.

excessive increase in illness); only 5% are classified as exhibiting 'pathological ageing'.[10]

Alan A. Anderson's investigations demonstrated a minimal deterioration of reaction in ageing persons. Using the test of pushing a button when a red light came on, the average time delays were:

> Persons aged 55—0.212 seconds
> Persons aged 65—0.217 seconds
> Persons aged 75—0.245 seconds[11]

A similar test in India showed a variation from 0.198 seconds for persons in their 20s to 0.279 seconds for a group of average age 65.[12]

Mexican Joaquín González-Aragón feels that it has been adequately demonstrated that 'psychological factors are more decisive than age itself, as much in the ageing process as in the quality of life during old age'.[13] Far from approving the view that to move into old age is to move into dementia, a Seattle longitudinal study suggested that intelligence may even increase into the 70s.[14]

Nor does the physiological picture differ so much from the psychological. The Baltimore longitudinal study was a 27-year study of 1,000 volunteers as they aged. Within this study, Dr Edward Lakatta's team found that cardiac output does not decrease with age but only with specific disease. Although the heart rate may slow slightly, the heart muscle may enlarge to maintain a constant flow of pumping right into extreme age.[15] Dr Paul Costa, in the same study, failed to find any significant evidence of change of personality due to ageing.

A survey of over-60s in the Western Pacific covered activities of daily living such as dressing, walking, taking a bath, shopping, and handling money. In Fiji only 8% had difficulty with one activity, and 10% with more than one; 82% could accomplish all the activities adequately. In the Philippines only 9% had problems with one or more of the activities, and in Malaysia only 10%.[16]

---

[10] Adolfson *et al.* in Gilmore *et al.* 1981, p. 139.
[11] A. A. Anderson Jr. 1981.   [12] Pathak 1978.
[13] González-Aragón 1984.   [14] Schaie 1982.
[15] T. F. Williams 1985, p. 29.   [16] Andrews *et al.* 1986.

Relevant to the study of ageing in many developing regions are the findings of Dr T. A. Lambo of Nigeria on the tendency of endemic tropical diseases to trigger or exacerbate psychiatric disorders in old age. Conditions such as typhoid, malaria, trypanosomiasis, diseases transmitted by intestinal parasites, and even simple malnutrition and anaemia, can account for 'acute . . . and chronic brain syndromes in advancing age groups' which may be mistaken for what are termed 'senile dementias' by practitioners who fail to recognize the true condition.[17]

An Age for Ageing?

A debate is also current about the 'age of ageing', or at what average age the individual passes the invisible frontier of failure to cope with the expected work load or responsibilities of the indigenous culture. The question also arises as to whether there can be such a standard age.[18] One observer in the United States considered 35 to be the crucial age of onset of deterioration, inadaptability, and unproductiveness.[19] My own work in Potosi suggests 30 as a lower limit for ageing in that area.[20] This is very different to the legally established retirement age in, say, Britain where eligibility for the state old age pension starts at 65 for a man and 60 for a woman.

A Nigerian study found that some people equated 'old' in a female with the menopause. Yet in the same areas men were not regarded as old until 80. The Nigerian research team also found older people generally at work or wanting to work. Having studied conditions for retirement also in Sierra Leone and the Gambia, they concluded that their studies show 'the artificiality of official retirement at 60, except for its function of clearing jobs for the younger generation'.[21]

In 1976 the gerontologist B. L. Neugarten pointed out that, with increased survival rates and improved health, it was becoming apparent that there were two, rather than one, strata of ageing population, which she distinguished as the 'Young–Old' and the 'Old–Old', a distinction based on the intellectual

[17] Lambo 1981, p. 78.
[18] A topic at the Expert Group Meeting cited in n. 2 above.
[19] Chinoy 1955. See also Cambridge 1964.
[20] See ch. 4.   [21] Ekpenyong et al. 1986.

awareness and physical ability of the individual rather than on a chronological age categorization.[22] In Mexico, González-Aragón has perceived the same division, although he tends to give a vague chronological label to the phases. He notes the young, healthy, old person, who is independent or partially independent, as likely to be between 60 and 75 years of age. The chronically infirm or invalid old person who is totally dependent is more likely to be over 75 years of age.[23]

An Ecuadorian Ministry of Social Welfare study lowers the age brackets and talks of a pre-senile or critical age group from 40 to 60 years of age and a *senil* group of more than 60. However it must be remembered that the Spanish word *senil* is not as weighted with connotations of dementia as the English term 'senile'.[24] Arabic has one word, *ajouz*, for a chronologically old man but another, *musen*, for a dependent old man.

The Indian geriatrician J. D. Pathak distinguishes between *ageing*, or normal deceleration of activity, and *senescence*, which is age debility accelerated by disease, malnutrition, stress, and strain. Pathak's distinction is not between young–old and old–old but between normally ageing and traumatically ageing.[25]

Another important distinction is that drawn by Professor Roy Walford between *ageing rate* and *longevity* or survival. Studying survival curves from various countries and comparing them with data from ancient Rome he concludes that the ageing rate—that is, the decrease in the individual's physical reserves—is roughly the same. What has changed is the ability to preserve life and combat disease. His conclusion seems to suggest that there is a limit of biological longevity at somewhere around 100 years of age.[26] It must be remarked, however, that such studies tend to ignore, or dismiss as unreliable or not proven, any reports, ancient or modern, of people living for substantially more than 100 years. A Maltese statistic showing down-trends within the up-trends of longevity is quoted in Chapter 4, and may support Walford's contention.

A last general point on ageing is that a number of students of ageing have detected in cross-national observations a fair similarity in the processes and effects of the aged in diverse

[22] Neugarten 1976.   [23] González-Aragón 1984, p. 25.
[24] Merchan 1984.   [25] Pathak 1978.
[26] Walford, in Danon *et al.* 1981, p. 302.

cultures—although with varying chronological patterns of onset
and deterioration—as also in the basic social needs of the older
person. One published work which supports this view bears the
imprint of the Pan-American Health Organization, PAHO.[27]

Historic Ageing

In studying present attitudes to ageing, it is of interest to have a
brief background on historic attitudes to ageing. Modern
attitudes can then be judged as similar, improved, or deteriorating. Direct historic references to questions of ageing are
infrequent, but some factors can be deduced. One of the earliest
indications of the elderly as a revered class is found in inscriptions
at Tihuanacu, an ancient site in Bolivia. There, in the Reza–
Lipichis language, the symbol Achachi, written Ӿ, is used both
for God and Old Man, as well as Father.[28]

A somewhat more recent commentator, the seventeenth-
century Jesuit Martin Dobrizhoffer, lived for two years among
the Abipone Indians of the Chaco. He reported that even in
extreme age the Abipones could hardly be called 'old'. He cites
men of 100 who could leap on a fiery horse like a boy of 12 and sit
it for hours. Such men could easily retain their status in society.[29]
However, an early eighteenth-century report from a nearby area
gave age as a reason for divorce among Guarani chiefs. And
Padre Sepp, also writing at that time, stated that not many
people lived beyond 50, there being high mortality due to worms
from eating ill-cooked meat in excessive amounts.[30]

Equally ambivalent reports remain from the Maya era.
According to some sources, the aged were favoured by reduced
tax liability, communal help, and food and stores from the royal
store house. Other records suggest that the aged and crippled
were thrown into the pool sacred to the rain God Chac at
Chichen Itza. But select families also spent life advancing in
status so that in late life they achieved high priestly or secular
posts.[31]

[27] Tapia Videla and Parrish 1981, pp. 6, 7.
[28] Posnansky 1896 pl. lxix*b*, pp. 160–1.
[29] Dobrizhoffer 1704–32, vol. vi, p. 50.   [30] Sepp 1975.
[31] Burland 1976, pp. 110, 129, 226.

A study of pre-industrial tribes by Leo Simmons found that 56 out of 71 tribes had old people serving as chiefs. In some Himalayan tribes the greatest compliment possible was to call a person an 'old man'. An African tribe described its old people as the 'Great Ones', while in other African areas older people used their acquired knowledge of magic to impress younger people. In Ghana the aged became a 'symbol of deity'. Yet in 50% of pre-industrial tribes Simmons found neglect of the elderly. The Eskimo people abandoned their aged to die on an ice floe. Some Amerinds held a feast for the aged one, smoked the pipe of peace, and then the son killed the father with one blow.[32]

Nomadic peoples tended to consider the aged as a burden (understandably enough when constant mobility was required); agricultural communities, in contrast, valued the older person's years of experience in planting and cultivating the essential crops. Recent studies in Asia and Africa reveal that within historical memory the old person was more revered and cared for than at present. Certainly where the elder was able to contribute something of value to the community, although not always in terms of physical resources, the community responded by according respect and dignity.[33]

The detrimental effects that education has had for the status of the elderly have been pointed out by a number of commentators; it has been suggested that as society moves 'from gerontocracy to franchise' the elderly are excluded by lack of formal education, political know-how, and other aspects of 'modern sector education'.[34] Now, in the words of a Brazilian, there are many institutions, groups, and social sectors which have turned against the elderly person, or which tolerate him in a manner with little respect, or which apply a form of aggression, subtle or cruel.[35]

In Tanzania 'modern education' has been identified as 'fostering individualism to the detriment of community ties', and in Cameroon 'traditional values are seen to be eroded by mass media transmission of ideas from greatly differing cultures'.[36]

Another factor which traditionally affected the older man's status was his ability to control land tenure, and thereby the (mainly agricultural) commerce of yesteryear. The development

[32] Simmons 1945.   [33] Light with Keller 1982, p. 132.
[34] Warnes 1986a, p. 10.   [35] Jordão Netto 1982b, p. 3.
[36] CIGS 1/84, p. 7. Tanzania's own recent education seeks to remedy this.

of land sales and industrial commerce has transferred much of
that power to the young person, who has the training to
understand real estate finance and the physical strength to
operate within industry and the commercial activities that are its
by-product.[37]

Whether the elder was *always* more respected and cared for in
the past or not, the transition has *often* been radical in the
extreme. This is illustrated in the following description of a
journey which took me to Cuzco. An old woman could be seen
sitting penniless, hungry, ragged, and abjectly miserable on the
steps of a glorious Christian church. The church was built on
a still-visible base of massive stones hewn by the Inca that the
early Christian builders were unable to demolish. The Incas who
built the original pagan Temple of the Serpent cared for their
aged and gave them a gentle role in society. The ostensibly
Christian culture superimposed upon the pagan has been unable
to provide the same system of care,[38] not even the basic Inca
system of providing free sufficient foodstuffs for each elderly
person.

Breakdown of Family

This breakdown in care systems has nowhere been more cruel
and tragic than in the collapse of the traditional, extended family
system, in which the elder remained always part of a stable
community unit ordered by blood ties. The extended family unit
has been defined as 'a patriarchal organization of parents,
unmarried children, married sons and their families, and
occasionally brothers and their families, who lived together
under the authority of the extended family'.[39] A United Nations
population document describes this extended family as 'the first
line of defence' for older people who cannot defend or support
themselves.[40]

Evidence as to the breakdown of the traditional system comes
from many places. From Costa Rica comes the comment that
modernization has created institutions which have assumed the

[37] UN World Assembly on Aging Preparatory Meeting, Haifa, 1982, p. 411.
[38] Tout 1983, p. 13.   [39] R. A. Ward 1979, p. 293.
[40] Petri, P., in Binstock *et al.* 1982, p. 104.

functions, tasks, and duties which previously the children fulfilled. The residential segregation of generations is an effect both of the ambitions of young people to live within the new urban societies and of the built environment of the urban sector itself, with its prioritizing of nuclear accommodation. Fertility and family size are other factors identified by a Costa Rican writer, for as these indicators descend, the single nuclear family becomes more common. This is part of an evolutionary process in which kinship systems disintegrate and the living patterns of agrarian societies disappear.[41]

A Mexican declares proudly, 'We Mexicans look after our elders and it is a question of honour not to abandon them,' yet he sees on all sides social change, industrialization, urbanism and 'progress' (*his* quotation marks) causing material, economic, spatial, and domiciliary problems which are overcoming the strong, elemental, emotional ties and causing inter-generational catastrophe.[42] From Ecuador comes a similar message: aged people 'drink solitude' because the patriarchal family, centred on grandfather or father, has dwindled *hasta casi su desaparación* (until almost its disappearance).[43] In a survey in Peru, the Social Worker responsible reported that 58% of old people were abandoned by the family and had no place within an extended family unit. From Colombia an experienced worker, Mother Provincial of her Catholic order, informed a conference that the family today tends to disintegrate, giving more importance to young than to old, and obliging the aged person sadly to request admission to some asylum.[44]

A 1962 study in Ghana, a land proud of its traditional family life, found that older people in some 18% of the rural households interviewed had 'come close to having lost contact with their educated children who migrated to the towns'. Of all children born to those surveyed, only 35% had become what their parents considered 'good providers' for their old age. In a ninth of rural families and a sixth of urban families, 'no help had been forthcoming in old age'.[45] (Other Ghana studies were less pessimistic.)

[41] Denton and Acuña 1985, pp. 29, 117.
[42] González-Aragón 1984, p. 1.   [43] Merchan 1980, p. 17.
[44] Reports to Help the Aged, London, on projects.
[45] Apt 1981.

In Kenya similar trends have been observed. As one worker described it, 'with the growth of towns and boarding institutions far from home, a tendency of neglecting the aged has grown'. In a conference of 40 African countries this trend was described in varying terms. In Malawi, the new division of labour puts 'emphasis on the individual rather than the community'. In the Congo 'a new type of social relations has emerged'. In Zaire the rural exodus leaves a void of those who 'would have been able to provide for the essential needs of the aging population'. Guinea's representative referred to 'the bursting of the framework of traditional life'. But in Africa these new factors are still only marginal trends; in many countries the extended family still survives, and indeed in some areas still flourishes.[46]

J. D. Pathak, an Indian geriatrician already quoted, summarizes the situation thus: 'the joint family system in the East, now shows signs of cracking very fast, with the advent of industrialisation and consequent urbanisation'. A recent study in the Western Pacific has shown that statistically the extended family is still very important. In Fiji 75% of older people surveyed lived with their children, in Malaysia 69%, and in the Philippines 77%. However, there was a discrepancy between the proportion of extended family households in rural areas as compared with urban areas. The researchers believed that one reason for this lay in the tendency for young people to leave the rural areas to seek their fortune in the towns, a kind of migration which, if it continues (or worse, increases), will leave more old people isolated. They say, 'the trend away from rural and towards urban living may affect young people selectively, so that aged parents remained in villages while their children move to cities. In this situation, extended family support would be minimal.'[47]

In South Korea, where research has been more detailed than in many other major developing countries, over the 10 years between 1960 and 1970 the percentage of three-generation extended family households dropped from 27.62% to 22.06% of all households. And the percentage of households comprising more than three generations fell from 1.63% to 1.15%.

A United Nations population study indicates that increased longevity, generally good news, also exacerbates the effects of the

[46] CIGS. 1/84.   [47] Andrews et al. 1986.

breakdown of the family, with more old people suffering abandonment for longer periods.[48] A more graphic statement emanates from Brazil, to the effect that today the extended family is 'a museum piece', certainly in large urban areas.[49] This tendency is a new problem in many lands. Even in Argentina, a considerably developed country, the problem has been traced back only to about 1965.[50]

The deterioration of the family gives rise to what has been described in a Brazilian commentary as the 5 'DIS' factors translatable as: distancing, disrespect, disbelief in, disdain, and discourtesy (or probably, active persecution).[51] It should, however, be observed that this may not be the end of the story, for gerontologists in developed countries have suggested that improved communications make it possible for an extended family relationship to be sustained, in spite of physical dispersion, where technical facilities such as fast roads, frequent air transport, universal telephones, aids for the disabled, two-way radio, and micro-chip transmitters are available.[52]

One researcher concluded that the breakdown of the extended family affects the male more than the female. She found that housewives were able to continue living with, and rendering service to, the younger generations, even when widowed, because of the continued usefulness of this service. But the widowed male was generally seen as unproductive, of little service to the younger generation, and indeed an increasingly heavy and unwelcome burden upon family resources and loyalties.[53] The United Nations Fund for Population Activities observes that as the extended family generally disintegrates, there is a marked proportional increase in the number of female-headed families. These are often elderly widows with dependent children in the lowest socio-economic strata of their societies.[54]

The closeness of family ties and the traditional sanctity of marriage in countries with strong religious traditions cannot necessarily be relied upon to stay the processes of disintegration. In a country of such devout Catholicism as Malta, the same trend of family disintegration is evident. During 1985, in that

[48] Giele, in Binstock 1982, p. 43.
[50] Carbal Prieto 1980, p. 138.
[52] Litwak 1960, p. 385.
[54] Giele, in Binstock 1982, p. 44.

[49] Jordão Netto 1982a, p. 3.
[51] Jordão Netto 1982a, p. 4.
[53] Denton and Acuña 1982, p. 4.

country where divorce was at one time unthinkable, a record
level for nullity of marriages was registered, and by May of 1986
the total for 1986 was already higher than for the whole of 1985.[55]
The secularizing effect of modernization in Catholic Latin
America is equally obvious although not so clearly recorded.

The effect of migration on the extended family is felt in a
number of Muslim countries. In Bangladesh, with large rural
Islamic communities, the elderly traditionally enjoy the role of
murubbi, or guardians of the extended family. But even this
traditional support base is becoming shaky due to changes in the
social structure and the deterioration of economic conditions and
in the relative status of the elderly.[56]

Hinduism also requires its followers to care for the aged:
'woman is to be protected by father in childhood, by husband in
youth, by sons in old age'. But urbanization can affect the settled
support system. As one Indian woman professor so graphically
warns, 'when societies are unstable, and the rate of social change
assumes a galloping pace, the aged are riding for an early fall,
while the younger members take their seats on the saddle'.[57]

[55] *The Times* (Malta), 7 May 1986, p. 24.
[56] Ibrahim 1985.
[57] Dastur, in Pathak 1975, p. 20.

2

POPULATION FORECASTS

I t is estimated that between 1950 and 2000, the number of persons over 60 years of age in the world will have risen from about 200 million to 590 million. The elderly will then constitute 13.7% of the world's population. These demographic trends will have major effects on society, some potentially detrimental. Such were the predictions of the United Nations World Assembly on Aging held in 1982 and subsequently confirmed by United Nations demographers in 1985.[1]

It is only since the Second World War that the majority of industrialized countries have been affected by significant 'greying' of their population. While the effect is already being felt in many developing countries, the full impact in those countries is yet to come.[2] Whether this is considered good news or bad, the world is now faced with what one writer has called 'the demographic imperative' of an ageing population, that is, a population in which proportionately more people live longer.[3]

Ageing in Demography

If some observers should be tempted to doubt the imminence and inevitability of this ageing process, Sauvy, quoted in the introduction to this book, has said of demographic ageing that 'of all contemporary phenomena this is the least doubted, the best measured, the most regular in its effects and the easiest to forecast well ahead, as well as the most influential . . . ' In basic human terms, the people who constitute this demographic ageing

---

[1] UN WAA 1982e, p. 14, I, A, 7, and follow-up report UN WAA ECOSOC 1984.
[2] Myers 1982, p. 1.
[3] Swensen 1983, p. 327.

bulge are already alive and the majority of them will fight to stay alive as long as possible.[4]

The eminent demographer George C. Myers bases his certainty about demographic ageing on the interaction of mortality and fertility levels. High mortality combined with high fertility produces a population with a high proportion of young people. Many of the younger population will die early, thus reducing average life expectancy. As long as the fertility rate exceeds the mortality rate, even though the mortality rate is in decline, the median age of the population will become still lower.[5]

It is when the fertility rate begins to decline that the youth dependency section of the population (children under working age) becomes proportionately less. At this point the median age of the population begins to rise, and the demographer regards the population as 'ageing'. As disease and mortality are further reduced, the survival rate is likely to increase at all age levels, including among the aged themselves. A further effect of such survival is the proportionate increase in females beyond the age of child-bearing, which again reduces the fertility rate in relation to total population.

From a demographic point of view, 'population ageing' is simply the *proportionate* relationship of age groups. However, the phenomenon which now concerns the demographer goes beyond the classic factor of proportionate ageing within the overall population pyramid. The demographer now forecasts a huge increase in *gross* numbers of elderly people, unprecedented in history. This is caused by dramatic falls in both mortality and fertility rates.[6]

Myers and others also point to ways in which the 'population ageing' in today's developing countries differs from the 'greying' of developed nations in the past. Many of the developing countries commence their 'ageing' from a start point of very high gross population (India, Brazil, Mexico, and others—including China, although records for the latter are not complete), rather than the long-term ageing of more modest populations of developed countries in the nineteenth and early twentieth centuries. The pace of change is much more rapid in today's developing countries. And some of the factors that have

[4] Sauvy 1948, p. 115.   [5] Myers 1982, p. 5.
[6] Binstock *et al.* 1982, p. Ii.

contributed to this are clearly attributable to resources and methods transferred from developed countries (medical and pharmaceutical treatments, for instance) rather than to developments that evolved organically out of the local culture over a long period of time.[7]

World Population Increase

To clothe these demographic principles with statistical data, Table 2.1 gives the prospect for the ageing of the world's population as presented to the World Assembly on Aging in Vienna in 1982 and subsequently confirmed. In percentage terms, while the total population of the world is expected to increase by 37.6% between 1980 and 2000, the over-60s population will increase by 60.5%. Likewise, while the total population of the least developed regions (LDRs) is expected to increase by 46.2%, the over-60s population of the LDRs will increase by 82.5%.

TABLE 2.1 *Population, World Regions, 1980 and 2000 (millions)*

Region	Year	Total pop'n	Pop'n aged 60+	
			Number	%
World total	1980	4,453	371	8.3
	2000	6,127	595	9.7
Developed regions	1980	1,136	173	15.2
	2000	1,276	234	18.3
Developing regions	1980	3,317	198	5.9
	2000	4,851	362	7.5

Source: UN DIESA.

Table 2.2 shows the projected increase in the numbers of people over 80 in the period 1980–2000–2020. It can be seen that the rate of increase forecast for the over-80s population of

[7] Ibid., p. iii; Myers pp. 14–24.

TABLE 2.2   *Over-80s Population, World Regions, 1980, 2000, and 2020 (millions)*

Region	Population aged 80+			% increase
	1980	2000	2020	1980–2020
World	34.2	58.2	103.9	204
Developed	22.0	30.5	45.8	108
Developing	12.2	27.7	58.1	377

Source: UN DIESA.

developing countries is over three times the forecast for developed countries. The contrast is even more extreme between Tropical South America, with a 405% increase, and Northern America, with 60%, or South-eastern Asia with 408%, and Europe with 90%. Whilst the economically developed countries of Northern America are having to organize for just over 3 million additional people over 80, Africa will have to accommodate nearer 5 million extra.

Factors and Effects

Having regard to the importance placed by Myers and others on the effect of the fertility rate on 'population greying', it might be relevant briefly to recall the reasons usually put forward for a high fertility rate, which in many areas are now observed to be in a state of reversal. They include:

1. Children seen as a labour pool in an agrarian society structured in families or clans
2. Children seen as insurance against parents' old age problems
3. The acceptance of machismo—the creed of dominant masculinity, with woman as a largely subservient child-bearer
4. Religious doctrinal opposition to birth control methods of a mechanical or chemical nature
5. Early marriage age
6. Sexual activities seen as a life fulfilment where few other non-work options exist

7. Large number of women of child-bearing age
8. Lack of education and population awareness
9. Lack of interest on the part of governments.[8]

Another important factor in the changing age balance, this time affecting mortality rate, is the improvement in health knowledge and services. This aspect includes improved nutrition, housing, sanitation, and information methods, as well as the prophylactic, clinical, and surgical achievements in the medical world.[9] An indicator of the extent to which medical achievements affect the age balance is provided by Hayflick's calculation that maintaining the present rate of prevention of early deaths from vascular disease and cancer could lead to a net increase in life expectancy of as much as 21 years.[10]

An apparently new factor tending towards longevity has been pointed out in a World Bank report. Because of the success of medical science, especially in controlling infectious diseases, the traditional demographic links between income/GNP and health/life expectancy are breaking down. It is no longer true that less wealthy countries will be relatively less healthy than more developed economies. Life expectancy in Africa in 1980 was about equal to that of Americans of African descent in the 1930s, although the latter had incomes four times as great as the 1980 African. Life expectancy today in India is higher than it was in France in the 1920s, although the average Frenchman of those days enjoyed infinitely higher standards of income, nutrition, and education than the average Indian of today.[11]

This factor augurs well for a continued increase in life expectancy in poorer countries, although the same World Bank report reminds urban man that he has created his own additional sources of morbidity and fatality, such as traffic accidents, crimes, and environmental pollution, while in rural areas improvement in irrigation have encouraged snails that carry schistosomiasis.

A UNFPA summary suggests that as the economy of a country progresses, the proportion of the aged increases in urban areas compared with rural areas, partly due to physical migration and partly due to there generally being better medical and water

---

[8] Smith and Thomas 1973, p. 63.   [9] Kalache 1986.
[10] Hayflick in Danon 1981, p. 178.   [11] Golladay and Liese 1980, p. 22.

facilities in urban areas. Another apparently surprising global factor, given the general predominance of aged females, is that rural areas in developing countries do not have relatively more females than aged males. Often there is a clear majority of aged males.[12] Reasons given include the high mortality of rural women in child-bearing due to primitive conditions, and the tendency of the older woman to accompany the younger generations migrating to the city. The older man tends to remain on his rural plot of ground as long as possible.

Ageing amid Poverty

Perhaps this ageing of the world's population would be considered a general blessing if good economic conditions were the lot of every nation. However, the ageing factor must be set in the context of the present prevalence of absolute poverty in many countries or regions. By Robert McNamara's definition, 'absolute poverty' is a 'condition of life so degraded . . . as to deny its victims basic human necessities'.[13]

In one of his speeches, McNamara painted a picture of the absolute poverty which can be identified in the world at present, probably affecting 40% of the people of developing countries and causing much suffering or deprivation:

1. One-third or more of the two billion people in developing countries suffer from hunger or malnutrition

2. More than 20% of children die before their fifth birthdays, and many more are stunted for life

3. Life expectancy is 20 years less than in the developed world, denying '*them*' of 30% of the life span which '*we*' enjoy (McNamara's emphasis)

4. 800 million are illiterate and many of their children will also be illiterate.[14]

Migration and Ageing

The combined effect of migration of younger workers in search of urban affluence and the actual demographic ageing of societies had a specific impact on rural economic conditions. Loss of the

[12] Myers 1982, p. 32.   [13] McNamara 1973, p. 6.
[14] Ibid., p. 7.

major manpower source places an additional and insufferable burden on the remaining population of women, children, and elderly. The migratory confusion also leads to conflict, as shown in an analysis of 45 cases in developing countries demonstrating that problems caused by the population dynamic go beyond the particular problems which derive directly from increased or decreased numbers only.[15] In this prolonged conflict in modernized conditions, the advantage is now always with the younger population.[16]

The new imbalance also affects services, especially in rural areas where the elderly, incapacitated, and otherwise dependent are left behind. Though demographically categorized as 'dependent', they can depend neither on the informal, traditional network, which is rapidly breaking down, if not extinct, nor on the formal provision of essential personal social services, which is yet to be established.[17]

Another factor which will have world-wide impact is the great increase both proportionally and numerically of the 'old-old', or to use the French term, the 'Fourth Age'. (Many gerontologists define this group as the over-80s.) It is the main risk group subject to episodes of acute illness and suffers a higher percentage of chronic illness than other age groups, and consequently requires greater inputs of medical care. Such illness will often cause dislocation of the individual family's routine, requiring some state support. Rising need for total care will hold back the campaign to reduce present institutional levels and to increase domiciliary services.[18] Hopes that budget provisions for social programme growth might be found from economies resulting from a decrease in expensive institutional care are likely to be frustrated by the high cost of the high risk, high increase Fourth Age group.[19]

Developing Country Forecasts

Developing countries can anticipate similar age increase variations to those anticipated in the world regional statistics. In some cases

[15] Choucri 1974, ch. 12.
[16] Ibid., ch. 9. [17] Iliovici 1982. [18] Myers 1982, p. 24.
[19] Ibid., Golladay and Liese 1980, p. 46.

this increase is expected to be gentle in the immediate future but in almost every case a steep rise in the proportionate and gross numbers of older people is projected by 2020. This trend is illustrated by Table 2.3, covering selected developing countries. (The selection was made by me in the interests of clarity and brevity and has no demographic judgemental basis, except that examples of both gentle and steep increases are included, various regions are represented, and the smallest countries are excluded.)

Some countries, such as Barbados and Jamaica, can expect a gradual rise in their numbers of aged up to 2000 but after that a very steep increase up to 2020. Others, such as Argentina and China, will have exceptionally high relative numbers of people over 70 by 2000. However, the general trend, for countries as different as Ethiopia and Argentina, or China and Lesotho, is for very large relative increases. The time-scale may be slightly different, but the gross result is constant to all types and sizes of country.

This future population shape becomes even more relevant in considerations of future national economic and social strategies if translated into a percentage of the total population. The data of Table 2.3 then take the form illustrated in Table 2.4. It can be seen that some countries are already bearing the responsibility of a higher percentage of older people, as in the case of Argentina and China, while in African countries, less developed American countries, and elsewhere, the elderly are not such a relatively significant section of the population from a demographic point of view. Against the national figures must also be set such facts as that in urban Buenos Aires in 1987 the percentage of population over 60 was already 22%!

In some countries the continuing high fertility rate, combined with higher infant survival, will continue to hold down the *relative* significance of the upper age bulge—as in Bolivia, Bangladesh, and many African countries—but reference to Table 2.3 will show that in fact the *gross numbers* of older people are increasing rapidly.

African countries generally appear to be confronting a less rapid increase, and in some cases there is even a temporary decrease of 'age dependency'. It must be remembered that one of the relevant factors is the high fertility rate still experienced in

TABLE 2.3 *Over-60s Population by Broad Age Group, Selected Countries, 1980, 2000, and 2020 (thousands)*

Country	1980		2000		2020	
	60–9	70+	60–9	70+	60–9	70+
Ethiopia	905	471	1,687	849	3,165	1,699
Kenya	332	176	760	388	1,760	1,015
Mozambique	429	218	730	426	1,238	800
Chad	173	87	258	146	434	247
Algeria	613	465	1,095	658	2,321	1,277
Lesotho	49	26	84	47	140	92
China	45,695	27,120	75,587	51,801	147,706	86,326
Burma	1,315	711	2,137	1,313	3,981	2,234
Philippines	1,472	764	3,019	1,751	7,132	4,015
Bangladesh	2,867	1,700	4,321	2,314	8,421	4,136
India	25,001	11,719	48,180	25,638	83,100	49,188
Sri Lanka	584	374	1,146	703	2,145	1,354
Papua New Guinea	115	55	196	111	363	214
Jamaica	105	80	111	106	270	130
Haiti	205	119	299	177	545	304
Costa Rica	76	48	153	110	365	224
Argentina	1,958	1,420	2,546	2,367	3,549	3,158
Colombia	930	503	1,560	1,030	3,428	1,979
Bolivia	189	101	309	179	575	335

Source: UN DIESA.

TABLE 2.4   *Over-60s as Percentage of Total Population, Selected Countries, 1980, 2000, and 2020*

Country	1980	2000	2020
Ethiopia	4.3	4.3	4.8
Kenya	3.0	3.0	3.7
Mozambique	5.4	5.3	5.6
Chad	5.8	5.5	5.7
Algeria	5.8	5.0	6.7
Lesotho	5.7	5.8	6.3
China	7.3	10.1	16.4
Burma	5.9	6.4	8.0
Philippines	4.6	6.4	11.4
Bangladesh	5.2	4.6	6.1
India	5.3	7.7	11.4
Sri Lanka	6.4	8.9	13.8
Papua New Guinea	5.3	5.8	7.6
Jamaica	8.5	7.6	11.4
Haiti	5.6	4.8	5.2
Costa Rica	5.5	7.3	12.2
Argentina	12.0	13.2	14.7
Colombia	5.6	6.8	11.0
Bolivia	5.2	5.0	5.5

Source: UN DIESA.

many African countries. And, as elsewhere, but at a somewhat later date, this 'baby bulge' carries the menace of an 'age bulge'; this is already evident in the gross statistics of Table 2.4.

In many instances, cross-cultural comparisons are difficult in developing countries because of the scarcity of comparable data. It is often feasible to illustrate certain factors only by reference to a particular country that has assembled the relevant type of data as typical of a number of countries where no accurate data exists. A set of data available from Colombia (Table 2.5) illustrates the relentless upward trend of age statistics over a period of 11 years.

To illustrate another aspect of ageing population it is useful to study a Belizean projection which takes 50 years old as its 'ageing' limit (Table 2.6). This projection is of interest in illustrating how survivability is expected to increase. The 1985 cohort aged 50–4 becomes the 1990 cohort aged 55–9 and then the 2000 cohort aged 65–9. Extracting the corresponding data from Table 2.6 in order to check the survival of the cohort of 4,635 people aged 50–4 in 1985, we find the following:

Year	Cohort	Size
1985	50–4	4,635
1990	55–9	3,615
1995	60–4	3,546 (mean value)
2000	65–9	3,477

By this comparison, 78% of the 1985 cohort will survive to 1990, whereas 98% of the 1995 cohort will survive to the year 2000.

As in most developing countries, the fall in mortality levels in Brazil is attributed to improvement in health, which in turn is attributed to the introduction of antibiotics, residual action insecticides (reducing malaria and other diseases), chemotherapeutics, new kinds of vaccines, and simplified methods of diagnosis. Even so, there is still scope for further radical lowering of morbidity and mortality rates in the country in general, and in

TABLE 2.5 *Colombia: Over-60s Population, 1970–1986 and 1993*

Year	Total pop'n	Over-60s	
	('000)	No.	%
1970	21,329	914	4.28
1971	21,837	950	4.35
1972	22,324	995	4.45
1973	22,774	1,042	4.57
1974	23,185	1,072	4.62
1975	23,467	1,093	4.65
1976	23,935	1,092	4.56
1977	24,390	1,118	4.58
1978	24,924	1,160	4.65
1979	25,697	1,227	4.77
1980	26,263	1,305	4.96
1981	26,794	1,351	5.04
1986[a]	30,241	1,650	5.46
1993[b]	32,996	1,996	5.96

Source: Colombia Ministry of Health (1981).
[a] Estimate.
[b] Projected.

TABLE 2.6   *Belize: Over-50s Population, to 2020*

Age group	1985	1990	2000	2020
50–4	4,635	5,006	6,558	11,876
55–9	3,361	3,615	4,736	8,421
60–4	2,865	3,051	3,966	6,663
65–9	2,542	2,695	3,477	5,633
70+	4,377	4,626	5,968	9,668

Source: Tout and Tout (1985).

the north-east in particular. In the latter region, out of a total population of 36 million, some 4 million are suffering from bilharzia, and 3 million from Chaga's disease, while 17,000 new cases of tuberculosis are diagnosed each year.[20]

Another way in which the ageing of the population can be very graphically illustrated is by calculating the median age. Obviously, if there are comparatively large numbers of young age groups, the median age will be low, whereas if there are relatively less younger people and more older people, the median will be higher. To illustrate the trend, Table 2.7 gives median ages for the countries referred to in previous tables. It shows that the 'baby bulge' years had an effect on the median age of some countries between 1960 and 1980, and will continue to do so until 2000. However, in a number of countries, such as India, Sri Lanka, China, and the more developed Latin American countries, even during the 'baby bulge' years the population was gradually ageing.

In the African countries generally, the 'baby bulge' effect is projected to have longer duration, but once the ageing trend takes effect it will have rapid and significant impact, as revealed by the increase in median age for more rapidly developing countries, like Algeria, Egypt, and Nigeria, between 2000 and 2020, and in all African countries during the further five years to 2025.

In all countries of Asia and Oceania (except East Timor), an increase in median age is projected during the remainder of the twentieth century. In a number of countries, apart from those

[20] Bishops of Brazil 1986, p. 6.

quoted in the table (e.g. Malaysia, Indonesia, and Fiji), the increase in median age between 1980 and 2000 will exceed five years. In Singapore it is expected to increase in this period from 24.5 to 34.6, and on to 41.8 in 2025.

Life Expectancy

Reference has been made to increased life expectancy at 60 or 65. In fact, the individual's life expectancy may vary from age to age as various danger points, like infant mortality, are survived, and as the body builds up immunity. This can be seen from the results of a Mexican survey (Table 2.8).

These variations in life expectancy at varying ages mean that life expectancy statistics can be misleading. The life expectancy

TABLE 2.7   *Median Age for Selected Countries, 1960–2025*

Country	1960	1980	2000	2020	2025
Ethiopia	18.0	17.2	16.7	18.9	20.0
Kenya	15.1	14.2	14.3	18.6	20.1
Mozambique	19.6	17.9	17.7	20.5	22.0
Chad	20.6	19.0	18.3	19.9	21.1
Algeria	18.2	16.6	18.1	24.9	26.0
Lesotho	19.7	19.0	18.8	20.7	21.9
China	21.0	21.7	30.2	37.7	38.1
Burma	21.0	19.1	21.1	26.5	28.0
Philippines	16.6	19.1	23.7	30.7	32.0
Bangladesh	19.9	16.8	19.3	24.9	26.0
India	19.3	19.9	25.0	31.9	33.0
Sri Lanka	19.1	20.9	27.0	33.7	35.0
Papua New Guinea	19.8	18.7	20.2	25.6	27.1
Jamaica	19.6	18.5	25.8	33.1	34.9
Haiti	19.6	18.1	18.1	20.2	21.2
Costa Rica	16.4	19.7	24.2	29.9	31.3
Argentina	26.8	27.4	27.5	31.2	32.1
Colombia	16.9	19.4	24.1	29.6	30.9
Bolivia	18.6	18.2	18.1	20.3	21.4
Cyprus	23.0	28.7	23.0	36.3	37.1
Jordan	17.6	15.3	15.6	19.9	21.6

Source: UN DIESA.

TABLE 2.8   *Mexico: Life Expectancy by Age and Sex, 1980*

Age	Male		Female	
	Crude	Gross	Crude	Gross
At birth	63.6	63.6	67.4	67.4
At 5 years old	64.2	69.2	67.6	72.6
At 20 years	50.3	70.3	53.6	73.6
At 40 years	33.1	73.1	35.6	75.6
At 60 years	18.0	78.0	19.3	79.3
At 70 years	11.9	81.9	12.6	82.6

Source: Contreras de Lehr (1986).
Note: Crude = total life span remaining; gross = total life span from birth.

statistic most usually quoted is 'at birth', is therefore quickly affected by variations in infant mortality, such as those produced by successful prophylactic campaigns among infants, than by the more gradual improvements in health of the aged. But having stated these reservations about 'life expectancy at birth' as an indicator, the projections shown in Table 2.9 none the less bear out the ageing trends revealed by other statistics already quoted.

One of the extraordinary factors arising from the ageing tendency in many developing countries is the increase in four- and even five-generation families, so that a married couple of working age may have not only their own children as dependents but also their own parents, grandparents, and even a great-grandparent. Whereas such a situation was until recently a social freak, it is now becoming increasingly frequent.[21]

Regional Variations

Within a particular country there can, of course, be a considerable disparity between regions, even between regions of a same environmental type and cultural tradition. An example of this is quoted from Panama where, in three quite similar rural, tropical provinces, Cocle has 13.9% people over 60 years of age, Los Santos has 20.12%, and Herrera 14.51%, compared with an average of 13.44% for the whole of Panama.[22]

[21] Jiménez Gandica 1986, p. 28.
[22] Club de Leones, Panama, unpublished report to Help the Aged 1986.

An Ecuadorian gerontologist has pointed out that there can be wide variations according to region, social strata, or other factors. When the life expectancy in Ecuador stood at 45, there were several centenarians in the small community of Vilcabamba,[23] which region will be treated in Chapter 4. In north-east Brazil life expectancy is currently eight years less than the average for the country.[24] Another researcher found that in Guatemala and Honduras, life expectancy in villages is much lower than the

TABLE 2.9   *Life Expectancy at Birth, Selected Countries, 1960–2025*

Country	1960–5	1980–5	2000–5	2020–5
Ethiopia	36.9	42.9	50.9	58.9
Kenya	43.0	52.9	61.6	68.1
Mozambique	41.1	49.4	57.4	65.4
Chad	35.5	43.0	51.0	59.0
Algeria	48.3	57.8	67.2	72.5
Lesotho	41.3	49.3	57.3	65.2
China	44.1	67.4	71.9	75.0
Burma	45.0	55.0	63.9	70.1
Philippines	54.5	64.5	71.4	75.2
Bangladesh	43.9	47.8	55.2	62.5
India	43.7	52.5	60.7	67.9
Sri Lanka	63.5	67.5	72.9	75.3
Papua New Guinea	42.7	53.3	63.8	70.9
Jamaica	64.3	70.3	74.2	76.5
Haiti	43.6	52.7	60.3	66.0
Costa Rica	63.0	73.0	74.6	75.2
Argentina	65.5	69.7	72.6	74.0
Colombia	56.2	63.6	67.9	71.3
Bolivia	43.4	50.7	61.6	67.2
Cyprus	69.2	74.3	76.6	77.9
Jordan	48.2	64.2	71.2	75.0
France	71.0	74.5	76.6	77.6
United Kingdom	70.8	73.7	76.4	77.4
United States	70.0	74.0	76.4	77.4
Australia	70.9	74.4	76.6	77.6

Source: UN DIESA.

[23] Merchan 1984, p. 5.   [24] Bishops of Brazil 1986, p. 6.

national average, as is also the case with indigenous groups. Very few people of Indian blood live beyond 60 'to enjoy the pre-rogatives of an older person in an Indian village'.[25]

It is possible that racial traits may be a factor in some morbidity variations in developing countries, although little concrete evidence appears to be available on this point. My own study in Belize discovered a small pointer to this effect in a survey of the incidence of hypertension in people over 40 (counted as 'elderly' in some areas) with the majority of the survey covering persons over 50. The survey had not been broken down by race, but details were available and revealed a striking racial difference.

Nine racial groups were identified, and an incidence rate was worked out on the basis of the percentage of a racial group's over-40 population diagnosed as suffering from hypertension. Whites (English- and Spanish-speaking) had a rate of 6.6, Chinese were rated at 2.5, Garifuna 1.7, Creole 0.55, 'East Indian' (from the Indian sub-continent) 0.4, with no incidence at all among mestizos or pure Indian Maya and Ketchi people.[26]

A series of surveys in the Western Pacific found country-by-country variations in health problems of the elderly. In Malaysia, 57% of old people examined showed evidence of cataract, compared to 22% in the Philippines and only 10% in South Korea; but 25% of the elderly in the Philippines had hearing problems, compared to 22% in Fiji and only 16% in Malaysia. In a study of Malaysian elderly, it was discovered that 7.15% of people of Chinese origin were over 60, compared with only 5.18% of Malaysian origin and 5.17% of Indian origin. However, comparative studies of the aged in developing countries broken down by race and nationality are so few and so lacking in detail that no clear deductions can be hazarded on this point, other than to indicate it as an area for future research.[27]

Sex ratios

Another important datum for the socio-economist is the relation of numbers of elderly males to elderly females. This is of prime importance to service planners, for demographers assume that

[25] Denton 1982, p. 117.   [26] Tout and Tout 1985, p. 24.
[27] Andrews *et al.* 1986.

elderly women are more likely to be living with their daughters and thus to be less in need of medical and social services than men living alone.

World-wide, there is a slight majority of females compared with males at age 60. This tends to increase with age, as shown in Table 2.10. Demographers expect these ratios to continue, within about 1%, through 2025.

TABLE 2.10 *Males and Females per 100 Population, Less Developed Regions, 1980*

Age	Males	Females
60–9	49.12	50.88
70–9	45.91	54.09
80+	41.83	58.17

Source: PAHO.

There is no general consistency in these figures, however, with sex ratios sometimes varying greatly between apparently similar countries, between regions of countries, and between urban and rural environments. Some relevant comparisons appear in Tables 2.11 and 2.12.

TABLE 2.11 *Males and Females per 100 Population Over 60, Selected Countries, 1980*

Country	Males	Females
Cuba	51.82	48.17
El Salvador	44.90	55.10
Somalia	34.88	65.12
Tunisia	55.53	44.47
Bangladesh	54.94	45.06
Burma	47.38	52.62
Qatar	66.67	33.33
Yemen	47.48	52.62

Source: UN DIESA.

TABLE 2.12   *Sex ratios, persons over 60 in Urban and Rural Areas, South American Regional Groupings, 1980 and 2000*

Region	1980		2000	
	Urban	Rural	Urban	Rural
Caribbean	45.05	53.05	43.18	52.60
Middle America	43.18	51.45	44.44	53.65
Temperate South America	43.82	54.54	43.18	53.42
Tropical South America	45.95	53.44	46.52	54.13

Source: PAHO.
Note: Sex ratio = number of males per 100 females.

A preponderance of older men in rural populations, compared with a majority of older women in urban populations, appears to be a general phenomenon throughout American developing countries, as Table 2.12 demonstrates. This may well be true in other developing regions.

A further indicator is that of marital status, for in many developing countries there appear to be great numbers of aged widows. Older men, by comparison, are more frequently cared for by a wife. Where the extended family holds together, the older widow can expect support. Where, as so often, the extended family is breaking up, the increasing number of elderly widows represent a significant potential problem. The South-east Asian four-country comparative survey produced the data summarized in Table 2.13, revealing the percentage of elderly women who are widows to be as much as four times the corresponding percentage for elderly men.

Table 2.14 shows how a straight comparison of rural and urban populations in American developing countries highlights the urban preponderance which already exists. When the figures are projected to the year 2000, that preponderance becomes even more marked in all regions. A significant figure in Table 2.14, representing a continent of increasing populations, is the projected *decrease* in the rural over-60 population of Temperate South America.

TABLE 2.13   *Percentage of Married and Widowed People, by Sex, among Over-60s in Urban and Rural Areas, Four Western Pacific Countries, 1984/5*

Country	Marital status	Urban		Rural	
		Male	Female	Male	Female
Fiji	Married	82	45	77	48
	Widowed	14	52	19	48
Korea (South)	Married	66	41	82	45
	Widowed	13	59	18	55
Malaysia	Married	85	38	88	48
	Widowed	13	61	10	52
Philippines	Married	82	47	86	50
	Widowed	12	47	14	45

Source: Andrews *et al.* (1986).

TABLE 2.14   *Urban–Rural Distribution of Over-60s, South American Regional Groupings, 1980 and 2000 (thousands)*

Region	1980		2000	
	Urban	Rural	Urban	Rural
Caribbean	1,360	1,031	2,491	1,209
Middle America	2,901	1,782	6,424	2,442
Temperate South America	4,085	682	6,209	677
Tropical South America	7,839	3,645	17,079	4,460

Source: PAHO.

Continuing high trends

While the projected rate of ageing may appear to be very high, some observers have suggested that the actual increases may well be even higher, especially in view of the increase in life expectancy in many lands for people already aged over 60.[28] Demographers have tended to err on the side of conservatism,

[28] Guerra de Macedo in PAHO 1985, pp. 165–8.

assuming that present trends in such areas as medical advances, sanitary improvements, health education, and so on will continue rather than intensify. One factor, difficult to quantify, which has not come into some demographic calculations is the pacifying effect of ageing upon a population. One expert has pointed out that the age composition of a population is a powerful element in tendencies to violence. The younger the population, the greater the propensities for violence, including war, civil riot, crime, and various migratory disturbances which affect standards of life, health, and longevity. An 'older' world with less violence would almost certainly see another upward trend in the longevity pattern.[29] Reinforcement of this view comes from a psychologist. The positive aspects of ageing which might be universalized in an older population include emotional stability, serenity, objectivity, loyalty, discipline, honour, and patience, whereas typically more youthful traits would include impatience, indocility, rivalry, lack of awareness of dangers personal and communal, and so on.[30]

Before terminating this chapter on demographic data and population forecasts it is necessary to point out elementary dangers which occur when reading apparently simple and straightforward statistics, such as those quoted above which give certain countries a static age dependency ratio over a period of 45 years. Percentages of a country's population may not be accurate reflections of gross figures. In Ecuador the number of people over 60 represent 3.3% of the total population in both 1980 and 2000, but when reference is made to gross figures this constant percentage in fact hides a gross increase in the over 60s from 424,000 to 779,000. Over the same period, the aged population of Barbados shows a *proportional* decrease, from 13% to 11.4%, but the gross numbers constitute a slight increase.

The same caveat applies to facile comparisons. The proportion of over-60s is expected to increase by 1.2% in both Argentina and Venezuela (from 12% to 13.2% and from 4.5% to 5.7% respectively), but whereas Argentina's increase represents a 45.6% increase in the gross number of over-60s, Venezuela's represents a 124% increase in the gross. Yet numerically the same data represent 1,538,000 additional older people in Argentina as against only 866,000 more in Venezuela.

[29] Choucri 1974, ch. 9.
[30] Flores Colombino 1982, p. 20.

Reference must therefore be had to the base data and the comparability of data. Also, as already indicated, life expectancy at birth is not an indicator of eventual longevity. Venezuela's life expectancy is higher than Chile's, but relatively more Chileans than Venezuelans (10.3% compared to 7.2%) survive from 60 to beyond 80 years of age.[31]

[31] UN DIESA, *Periodical on Aging* (1984), Tables 22–4, 28.

3

SOCIO-ECONOMIC FACTORS

THE increase in the relative numbers of older people in the developing countries of America coincides with another modern phenomenon which has been called 'stagflation'. This is the combination of recession and excessive inflation which is stated to have constituted an economic crisis in the higher developing countries even worse than in the Great Depression of the 1930s.[1]

Stress of Modernization

Within the developing countries themselves there is an inequality of benefits accruing from modernization. The situation is most succinctly summarized by an Argentine psychogeriatrician, who says:

In the last decade it has no longer been possible for so-called 'developing countries' to be defined in linear terms solely on the basis of their socioeconomic and political characteristics. Their relations with the 'developed' world have become more complex. Within each individual region and country, the conditions and quality of life differ. There are small areas more developed than in 1970, urban areas inhabited by well-to-do classes (which create an 'ecological pocket' of high medical technology) and poor suburbs, created almost always by unorganized country-to-town migration of people driven from their place of origin by lack of work.

The great majority of this last population is submerged in poverty and hunger, and lacks safe drinking water and sewage disposal, medical care, education, and even elementary knowledge of hygiene . . . In this underdeveloped underworld, where hunger, the harshness of the elements, endemic diseases, and illiteracy reign, to reach old age is an achieve-

[1] PAHO 1985, p. 90.

ment reserved for those best endowed genetically—and occasionally is the result of luck.[2]

An African gerontologist continues the story in a similar strain:

Modernization with increased physical and social mobility is shifting people from the traditional patterns of family and clan settings. New factors of social stratification based on new forms of political leadership, modern up-to-date skills, education, occupation and income have taken precedence over traditional ones . . . This is made worse by urbanization which is widely discussed as one of the most serious factors of social change in Africa today.[3]

Even from one of the less developed Asian countries the same trend is described:

However, modern developmental thrust—appropriate or inappropriate —has introduced considerable stress and disorganisation in the traditional society. In Bangladesh it is manifested in rural–urban migration especially of the youth and the able-bodied . . . over the last three decades or so [development] has rendered landlessness to grow from 20% to over 50% of the population, without any major economic or industrial transformation.[4]

Of the 19 countries in the Latin American region for which comparable data are available, 17 experienced a downturn in economic growth in 1981–3, and the 2 which retained some positive growth, the Dominican Republic and Panama, experienced a considerably lower growth than in the previous decade.[5]

Deeper into Debt

While in previous years the increase in oil prices had adversely affected several countries, the 1986 oil price drop meant that Mexico stood to lose US$8 billion a year on top of an existing debt of US$97 billion. Venezuela and Ecuador suffered similarly.[6] Moves to abandon the Coffee Accord and other agreements on primary materials added to the economic disequilibrium of Kenya, Colombia, Costa Rica, Guatemala, Brazil, and others.[7]

[2] Ibid., p. 91.   [3] Apt 1981, p. 4.
[4] Ibrahim 1985, p. 2.   [5] PAHO 1985, p. 91.
[6] *Financial Times* 28 May 1986, p. 10.
[7] *Le Nouvel Economiste* 28 Mar. 1986, p. 534.

OECD (developed countries') restrictions on imports, saving those countries just over 2% in their total of unemployed, hit exports from the Third World. Between 1980 and 1983, tariff obstacles to imports into the United States rose from 6% to 13% of imports, and in the European Community countries from 11% to 15%.[8]

Meanwhile within these countries themselves there was lack of equity in economic impact. In Argentina 50% of registered taxpayers found ways of refraining from paying tax. Over the last decade, 18 of the American developing countries experienced a 'capital flight' (largely, illegal export of personal monies) of $198 billion, almost a half of the total borrowing power of those nations.[9] With the sole exception of coffee, commodity prices are now as low in real terms as in the Great Depression. For many countries minerals are the only major natural resource and excess capacity keeps prices low, a situation likely to continue for years to come.[10]

In 1982 the cash flow on all external debts for Mexico—that is, annual interest and principal repayments for the year on all debts in proportion to the year's exports of goods and services—stood at 129%, for Brazil at 122%, and for Venezuela at 118%. In other words, those nations were producing and exporting throughout the year in order to cover, if they could, the year's due repayments.[11] The developing countries were also held in thrall to interest movements in highly industrialized economies. Sir Geoffrey Howe calculated in 1983 that a 1% general rise in interest rates added at least US$3.5 billion a year to Third World interest due on debts.[12] Whilst debt repayments from other countries were not as immense as those of Mexico or Brazil, in most developing countries debt repayment proved to be excessive loads on infant economies.

One commentator described the 'tyranny of technology' and the unhappy choice left to developing countries between expensive adaptation of their economies 'to avoid significant social and economic distortions', or the relatively cheap transplantation

[8] *Le Nouvel Economiste* 11 Apr. 1986, p. 536.
[9] Morgan Guaranty Tust Co., statement in *Wall Street Journal* 28 May 1986, p. 11.
[10] *Standard Charter Review* Mar. 1986, p. 4.
[11] World Bank 1982, tables.
[12] Sir G. Howe, quoted in Belize Ministry of Education 1984, p. 75.

into their industries of inappropriate technology.[13] Others summed up the helplessness of the developing countries in the phrase 'dependent development in which the periphery grows less rapidly in the margin of the capitalist vortex'. A non-political writer looked at the situation with pessimism, for he saw the only solutions as reform, revolution, or incorporation into the existing economic empires: reform would require unavailable solidarity on a world scale, revolution would lead to the fragmentation of the world economy, and incorporation had been tried in the past and found wanting.[14]

As though this picture were not gloomy enough, there can also be discerned a growing diversity in development, leading to the possible *marginalizacao* (dropping out of the race) of the lesser developed countries. Another factor which exacerbates the worsening situation is that foreign capital tends to dominate strategic sectors of industry; in Brazil, for example, external capital provides only 10% of all investment, but that 10% 'dominates the dynamic sectors of the economy' and makes the country ever more dependent.[15]

Whilst gross national product (GNP) per capita is only an approximate indicator of a country's economic state or of the average individual's wealth, a comparison of selected countries reveals drastic differences. Table 3.1 illustrates two clear points. Firstly, that the disparity in wealth between countries like Mali and Bangladesh on the one hand and Singapore and Venezuela on the other is immense, while the leap to the level of the developed economies is likewise large. Secondly, there is an almost unbelievably regular relationship still obtaining, at least in other than the smallest countries, between GNP per capita and life expectancy, although some projections suggest an eventual narrowing of the longevity gap between rich and poor. For the immediate future, the World Bank projection for developing countries throughout the world is for 'fragile' economies.[16]

---

[13] Lietaer 1979, p. 36.
[14] Hill and Tomassini (eds.) 1979, p. 6.
[15] Grunwald (ed.) 1978, p. 13.
[16] World Bank 1985, p. 138.

TABLE 3.1　*GNP per Capita and Life Expectancy at Birth, Selected Countries, 1985*

Country	GNP per capita (US$)	Life expectancy at birth (%)
Mali	100	45
Ethiopia	120	43
Bangladesh	130	50
Zaire	170	51
Burkina Faso	180	44
Burma	180	55
Uganda	220	49
India	260	55
Haiti	300	54
Kenya	340	57
Egypt	700	58
Papua New Guinea	760	54
Philippines	760	64
Jamaica	1,300	70
Colombia	1,430	64
Jordan	1,640	64
Korea	2,070	67
Argentina	2,070	70
Venezuela	3,840	68
Singapore	6,020	73
Trinidad and Tobago	6,850	68
United Kingdom	9,200	74
USA	14,110	75
Switzerland	16,290	79

Source: World Bank (1987).

The Disaster Factor

World Bank projections such as that just cited assume the continuation of 'normal' conditions. It so happens that in many developing countries normality is often disrupted by disasters, natural or man-provoked. The attention of the entire world has recently been focused on the immense drought problem affecting vast areas of Africa and millions of people from a number of countries. Other natural disasters have been reported of through modern history, often in localized disasters which caused little international reaction.

In the Americas, Kingston, capital of Jamaica, was entirely destroyed by earthquake and tidal wave in 1907. Belize City was destroyed in 1931 and again in 1961 by hurricanes. Grenada's entire nutmeg crop was lost in 1955. St Lucia lost 97% of its banana crops to hurricanes in 1979,[17] and St Vincent 95%. Nicaragua suffered nine major disasters in a decade to 1980, including hurricanes, drought, earthquake, volcanic eruption, civil war, and floods. In 1985 Mexico City experienced a savage earthquake, and an area of Colombia was totally obliterated by volcanic mudslide. Several vast floods devastated areas of Bolivia in 1979 but failed to make news headlines in the European media.

The Indian subcontinent is among the regions most subject to such natural disasters, as well as to epidemics of diseases like cholera. While leprosy is no longer the dreaded disease it once was, it has left its mark on many populations in India and elsewhere, requiring special care in old age for those disabled or debilitated by the impact of that and other tropical diseases.

Man contributes his own disasters. In 1985 the mountain of Guazapa in El Salvador was razed in three days by 80,000 pounds of aerial bombs concentrated on an area of 12 square kilometres. Not far away, an old refugee woman lost 56 members of her family—sons, daughters, grandchildren, brothers and their children—in the Sumpul River guerrilla area.[18] Kampuchea, Mozambique, and many other developing countries have been desolated in recent wars. During the 1980s millions of refugees have fled from disrupted economies, often to the detriment of some other developing country which has the misfortune to become the first host nation of a new refugee flood, as in 1987 Zimbabwe and Malawi receiving refugees from Mozambique.

Reference should also be made to regional differences, as when the perpetual disaster of endemic poverty affects a whole segment within a national population. The north-east of Brazil is a case in point, where 45% of the people have an income of less than

[17] Griffiths 1984, p. 4.
[18] Cortina 1986, p. 5.

US$25 a year. In that region the distribution of 'wealth' has deteriorated generally since 1970.[19] .Often rural areas suffer in comparison with urban. Malaysia has one of the highest levels of income per capita in Asia, yet in 1980 29% of its inhabitants, mainly in the rural areas, were below the poverty line.

The national economies of some nations in Oceania and the Caribbean suffer from minuscule labour and capital pools due to small populations. Of 27 Caribbean countries or territories, 10 have less than 100,000 inhabitants, 20 have less than a quarter of a million, and only one, Cuba, has a population as large as New York or London. In 1985, 17 of those nations had a GNP per capita of under US$2,000.

Where industrialization is able to proceed, social thinkers point to the phenomenon of 'massification of the job market', with the congregating together of people to serve the needs of industry, often in locations which are convenient for industry but inappropriate for mass human settlement.[20] Some part of the problem is undoubtedly due to human ambition in migrating towards the apparently greater opportunity, but a basic cause is the need of industries themselves to concentrate into compact, élite geographical locations. Further reference will be made to the problem of migration later in this chapter.

The 'modernization' process has been identified as moving from traditional technology (folklore) to scientific knowledge; from subsistence agriculture to cash crops; from human and animal power to fossil fuels; from rural life to urban settlements, each tendency being to the eventual disadvantage of the elderly. A sociologist has described this as a 'built-in system of obsolescence', whereby the skills and the knowledge of older people become inappropriate to the modern requirement which therefore favours the young.[21] In and around the new cities, land becomes available for those who can afford to buy it; those who can afford to buy it are the young, whose education, or ability to train and adapt, enable them to earn the city wages.

In this climate of economic depression and technological discrimination against the aged, an important regional con-ference of Opera Pia at Villa Leyva in Colombia in 1981 could pronounce that 'poverty is the gravest problem in developing

---

[19] Bishops of Brazil 1986, p. 6.   [20] UN WAA 1982d, p. 6.
[21] Light with Keller 1982, p. 552.

countries and the aged form the worst affected s
population . . . In the consumer society the basic need
tion, health, dwelling, clothing, recreation, education—
on the economic factor'.[22]

Inadequate Age Provision

Given the prevalence of modern pension, social security, and
general insurance provision in developed countries, it is perhaps
necessary biefly to mention the inadequacy and often complete
absence of retirement or old age pensions and social security in
most developing countries. One United Nations report states
that 'at present retirement benefits are not generally high enough
in developing countries to have widespread retirement effects'.[23]
Further reference will be made to the non-availability of pensions
in Chapter 6, but the absence of state economic provision,
combined with increased ageing and 'development', will cause
considerable problems for very many elderly people until such
time as major reform has been effected.[24]

The world renown of Mother Teresa's order of nuns in India is
related to the presence on city streets of numbers of people, a
large proportion of them elderly, who were totally destitute of
traditional family support. Father Luis Ruiz of Macao, Major
Dudley Gardiner of Calcutta and Sister Pacifica of the Beni,
Bolivia were also notable among the many others who have
improvised interim relief solutions.

An African report covering Nigeria, Sierra Leone, The
Gambia, and Ghana, noticed the way in which elderly women
and farmers face dependency on children, relatives and/or the
local community: 'Almost all of them get help . . . but some are
unlucky.'[25]

González-Aragón, commenting generally on the economic
situation of older people in his own country, Mexico, states that
there are hundreds of thousands who must work in order to
survive, but that, in addition, there are 'thousands who live
by public charity begging in the streets'.[26] When visiting a

---

[22] UN WAA 1982b.   [23] Binstock et al. 1982, p. 106.
[24] Warnes 1986a, p. 15.   [25] Ekpenyong et al. 1986.
[26] González-Aragón 1984, p. 41.

t in a rural district of Ecuador, I saw
ls plead for scraps of offal from open-
mall change from blond tourists. And
I saw nuns going out at midnight to
're sleeping in city gutters.[27]

ven further for older people, another
istrialization was taking root the new
g pressure to bear on employers in
rs in favour of younger entrants. He
of the *ladinos*, the Central American
Indians who make the migration into the city with little success,
returning to their village in their later years only to find that they
are no longer accepted by the community. They are outcasts in a
cultural limbo, unsuccessful in the urban setting and rejected as
defecting traitors by their own race.[28]

The lack of educational provision, due initially to lack of state
finance, also militates against the involvement of older people in
the modern society. In a survey in Fiji, 36% of older women and
19% of older men had never attended school. These figures rose
in Korea to 78% of older women and 49% of older men, and in
Malaysia to 89% of aged rural females and 36% of aged rural
men.[29] Similar results emerged from African surveys. A Peruvian
survey found that half the people between 45 and 64 years of age
had no education at all, while among the over-65s, more than
56% had no education and 36% had one year or less of studies.

Where low-cost social programmes have been introduced by
governments there is frequently 'a discrepancy between promise
and achievement', largely due to underdeveloped administrative
machinery, again because of inadequate state financial resources.
Indeed, some authorities are beginning to question the 'ability of
sociopolitical fabrics' in higher developing countries to withstand
the continuing conflicting pressures of rapid development,
population ageing, demand for social services, and financial
dearth.[30]

[27] Tout 1983, p. 12.
[28] Denton 1982, pp. 108, 118.
[29] Andrews *et al.* 1986.
[30] World Bank 1985, p. 141.

Rural Decline

Arising often, although not exclusively, out of economic pressures, migration has helped to turn the economic modernization
of developing countries into a social nightmare for older people.
Not all commentators take a negative attitude to urbanization.
Some emphasize the importance of the attraction of the cities,
suggesting that there is plenty of space in all developing countries
for internal migration to new cities with plenty of land still
available for development. Social services are more accessible in
urban developments.[31]

Economic disparity between urban and rural areas is certainly
easy to identify and in many rural areas living conditions are
inhuman. Examples of rural deprivation are quoted from the
north-east of Brazil. In the Mata region, as sugar became the
prime export crop, tenants were stripped of their subsistence
plots so that the landlords could extend sugar cultivation. The
tenants either became wage-labourers or migrated. In the Sertao
region a condition of tenure was that during drought the
landowner's cattle might feed on the tenants' crops, thus
bankrupting or starving the tenants out. In Agreste region,
share-croppers plant palma cactus for cattle-feed for the landowner but are allowed to cultivate their own inter-row crops
during the four years of the palma's maturing period. Then the
share-cropper must move on.[32]

There are several reasons for peasants leaving their rural home
districts. Ecological problems, such as drought and earthquake,
often provide a trigger. Lack of capital in rural districts retards
development. When capital is available the large landowner is
often encouraged to cut the labour force by using advanced
mechanical devices, thus saving wages in order to repay his
capital loans, but leaving many labourers without income. Often
no alternative industries are available to take up excess population
caused by the high birth rate. The repeated division of land
inheritances in order to accommodate many heirs leads to
overworked soil. In some areas the climate permits agricultural

---

[31] Bourne 1969, p. 287.
[32] Levy 1973, p. 173.

work only in a minority of months of the year and there is no income-producing alternative for the rest of the year.[33]

An assessment by the Institute of Economic Affairs in London blamed protective systems which were set up in developing countries to encourage industry. These had the effect of increasing the cost to agricultural sectors of industrial inputs, such as machinery, tools, and artificial fertilizers; and of services at a time when agricultural prices were not increasing to the same extent. Many countries had assumed that agriculture could be left to stagnate financially and that industry was the 'engine of growth'. However, the same source points out that historically industrial development has always been preceded or accompanied by an agricultural revolution. Only in the present century has fiscal tinkering upset the balance.[34]

Among the indirect incentives to migration have been the improvements in transport since the Second World War, making it possible for masses of people to travel (especially the new rural bus services). The cheap transistor radio has also made communications much more rapid and awakened remote rural peoples to the supposed delights and opulence of city life, as well as to means of getting there. Often however, the means of communication has been the family network, so that once one migrant has become installed in the city, family and friends follow. This movement unfortunately often continues even after the frequency of opportunities in the new area has diminished and its relative advantages have declined. In this respect, the family intercommunication system has proved economically disadvantageous at times.[35]

As people began to move in larger groups from country to town, another social phenomenon came into play which has been described as 'group momentum'. The decision to move was no longer taken by an individual, a married couple, or an extended family. There was a mass decision which carried entire communities of people into migratory action with little objective individual consideration of the odds.[36] In Peru, for example, such movements of people were so large as to be termed 'invasions',

[33] *Revista*, Departamento de Investigaciones Socioeconomicas, Universidad de Loja, Ecuador, Feb. 1982, p. 35.
[34] Lal 1983, p. 94.
[35] Wilkening 1982, p. 144.   [36] Mangin 1982, p. 183.

which were eventually tolerated by the helpless authorities to the extent of providing basic services for the new incoming group where it 'squatted' along the desert perimeter of Lima's existing shanty towns. Some maps of Lima have identified entire peripheral districts as 'Invasion 1980' or 'Invasion 1982' rather than by a more common type of place name.

A lesser known factor of migration is that the migrant often moves by steps, through a series of moves and stays, and not always directly from the original rural home to the eventual urban settling place. They move often through rural areas into provincial towns before making their way to the national capital or the new industrial megacity. This makes it even harder for an old person to follow younger, earlier migrants. Accordingly, a specific study of households in a Lima *barriada* revealed a preponderance of single-family households with a median age of 16, compared with the median age of 30 in the United States at the same date. Most of the households included another peer relative, but very few grandparents had accompanied the migrants. Residents of grandparent status had become grand-parents while in the shanty town.[37]

Migration Crises

Migration from an Indian village to Bombay, or from the slopes of Kilimanjaro to Nairobi, or from the Andes Mountains down to Lima, or from the Sertao of north-east Brazil to São Paulo, can be critical for the grandparent generation. But the seriousness of the crisis may be increased where the emigration is away from the home country altogether. The generations are even more removed in terms of distance, communications, currency, and cultural environment. Integration of unskilled young workers from a distinct socio-economic environment may be much more difficult when the immigrant is seeking fortune in Miami or London or Johannesburg than when seeking El Dorado in a larger town of the person's own nation, culture, and wage standards.

One demographer has calculated that between 1962 and 1976, a quarter of a million people entered the United States as illegal

[37] Andrews and Phillips 1982, p. 178.

immigrants from Jamaica, Trinidad, Guyana, and Barbados. Others migrated legally to North America, and yet others moved by one means or another, to Britain, Canada, France, Holland, and Australia.[38] Emigration of their children out of the country has been suggested as the main cause of ill health in old people in Barbados. I found the same situation in Belize, where the population resident within the country is 150,000, while nearly 50,000 Belizeans, mostly of working age, now live permanently in the United States.

Some impression may be gained of the rapidity of this urban-to-rural migration process from Colombian data which show that 50 years ago the country's urban population was 37% of the whole, and the rural population 63%. Today that proportion has been precisely reversed. A similar situation is found in many other countries, as indicated by the data in Table 3.2, which covers some of the countries where change has been rapid in the last 20 years. Whether migration has already peaked or not, an international conference meeting held in Asunción, Paraguay, in March 1986 to consider the subject confirms the continued mass migration of workers from developing countries, both within

TABLE 3.2   *Urbanization in Selected South American Countries: Urban Population as Percentage of Total, 1965 and 1983, and Number of Cities with Half a Million Inhabitants or More, 1960 and 1980*

Country	% Urban		Cities of 0.5 million+	
	1965	1983	1960	1980
Bolivia	26	43	0	1
Peru	52	67	1	2
Jamaica	36	52	0	1
Ecuador	37	46	0	2
Brazil	51	71	6	14
Argentina	76	84	3	5
Mexico	55	69	3	7
Venezuela	72	85	1	4

Source: World Bank (1985).

[38] Griffiths 1984, p. 50.

their own countries and between countries at differing stages of development.[39]

What are the direct effects upon the elderly of such high levels of migration? One source has calculated that between 1950 and 1970 around 29 million people migrated from rural to urban areas in 20 Latin American countries, with a consequent increase of 40% in the size of cities. The vast majority of the immigrants— and a disproportionately large majority at that—consisted of young people with comparatively high educational standards by rural norms.[40] Yet despite their education, most of the migrants achieved little more than to swell the ranks of the unemployed and underemployed; they were accordingly unable to send much, if anything, back to their families at home, nor could they form an adequate urban base in which to receive the extended family unit.[41]

Researchers for a classic study of migration in India looked closely at the ability and willingness of migrants to send remittances to those left at home. Out of 4,700 migrants surveyed, only 56.7% had ever sent remittances home. Strangely, the number of remittances sent tended to increase according to the distance of migration. A significant factor was that remittances tended to be sent most frequently by husbands to wives, then by older generations to younger generations, and least frequently by younger to older. This has considerable negative significance for older people left behind and hoping for financial support from the out-migrant, especially when it is discovered that 55% of out-migrants were young workers aged 15–24, and no less than 86% fell within the age group 15–39. The fact that less than 6% were aged less than 15 or more than 50 suggests that a considerable number of children were left behind with grandparents.[42]

Slum Environment

A brief reference is necessary here as to the general environmental conditions in the new slums. In Guayaquil, Ecuador, 60% of

[39] *ICMC Newsletter* (International Catholic Migration Commission, Geneva) (1986), 1–2.
[40] UN CEPAL 1982, (microfiche).
[41] *Revista* (see n. 33 above), p. 25.
[42] Oberai and Manmohan Singh 1983, ch. 4.

squatter communities are built over tidal swamps. In some areas, solid land is a 40-minute walk away. In Chile, dry river beds are inhabited for more than 11 months of the year and then reinhabited after the inevitable annual flash flood has destroyed all the dwellings. In El Salvador 63% of *total* housing is illegal or informal; 9% is in river beds, steep gullies, or public rights of way.[43] In Lima there are 300 *barriadas,* euphemistically termed by the official demographers *pueblos jóvenes* (young towns) or *invasiones*, but a number of them are built on or over public garbage dumps. In Mexico landowners sell illegal subdivisions of property, contrary to land use laws.

Researchers have discovered in the new urban zones a 'negative image' of the elderly, based on the older person's lack of preparation for, and function in, the urban setting. In the family unit itself there is an increase of 'distancing'. The normal process of cultural, educational, and economic distances between the generations is exacerbated and expedited by the exceptional circumstances of migration.[44] The stress and confusion of the shanty town existence often means that, whereas the extended family system is beneficial to the older person in rural areas, the close proximity in the slum shanty, wedged among many similar dwellings, turns the older person into an unwelcome and unproductive extra burden on space and basic services, especially where, for example, water for every purpose has to be purchased instead of fetched by the elder from copious mountain streams. This leads to the dual disadvantage that the normal spatial family unit of the city becomes nuclear in capacity, while the old are seen as objects to be cared for by official services rather than being the prime concern of the family.[45] The old become marginalized in respect of work opportunities, education, leisure, specialist health care, and basic services.

Another aspect that should be addressed by researchers especially of the extended family unit in urban areas but also of the extended family and clan in pre-industrial areas is this: if the old person *is* cared for within the extended family, just *what quality* of care is provided? Is extended family care indeed a preferable option? Or a myth perpetuated by political apologists and over-enthusiastic sociologists?

[43] UN CEPAL 1982.   [44] Warnes 1986a, p. 14.
[45] UN CEPAL 1982.

Aggression is a factor always present in the new urban zones where primitive systems of control have broken down, modern systems of control have not yet fully evolved, and the 'law of the strongest still reigns'.[46] Fatality causes include homicide, suicide, motor vehicle accidents, and 'incompatibility accidents' due to lack of familiarity with new facilities. The homicide figures for over-65s in the middle America subregion (Mexico through Panama) are high.

Distorted Economies

Looking back from the new urban settlements to the rural areas of emigration, in many Third World rural areas high densities of older persons distort the normal population profile. This distortion also affects the entire economic equilibrium of such areas if the skills and resources of the elderly are not fully utilized. In certain cases this economic disadvantage will affect the whole region, and in some of the smaller countries of Oceania and the Caribbean, the entire nation. For the individual who remains behind in the villages—and such individuals will be mainly women, children, and older people—must fight for subsistence, adopting informal types of agriculture or commerce, of lesser profit potential, in order to meet their own individual needs. And the children who have emigrated will frequently fail to remit any financial support to families which, in effect, they have abandoned. Psychogeriatricians are in no doubt as to the impact on the elderly of migration on the present scale. Helplessness and abandonment have been experienced by many hundreds of thousands, and in such cases 'the health and well-being of elderly displaced persons are far more compromised than in the case of youths and adults', says PAHO.

Little detailed research is available linking mental health with migration, so assumptions are based on individual cases treated rather than on a systematic research sample of an entire population. In the four-country study of the Western Pacific already cited, the question of mental health problems was studied in some detail but migration was not one of the

---

[46] Morelli *et al.* 1982, p. 34.

socio-economic variables applied. Aspects such as 'lost interest' and 'depressed' scored very high incidence (up to 65%) in some countries but scored low in the Philippines. Among Filipinos, only about 4% have migrated inter-province and 3% inter-municipality. So the very low relative incidence of mental problems in a low-migratory population may be significant.[47]

Although much of what has been said may appear condemnatory of the urban trend, there are certain advantages to be found in the new settlements as compared with the primitive village style. For many workers the slums are a stepping stone or a graduation stage in urban and technical skills. In the shanty environment there are little or no rent and service costs in comparison with the normal built-street environment, allowing the new immigrant to make weekly savings from arrival. Health and education conditions are generally better than in the rural setting, although still poor. Higher specialization is immediately attainable both in personal training and in public services. In the urban areas life expectancy is often higher than in the villages, due to sanitary campaigns, improved maternal care, pre-school nutrition, and access to medical and surgical services.

Age Discrimination

The 1985 meeting of UNCTAD forecast that at least for the next 10 years, 'hunger, unemployment and emigration will continue to be major problems' throughout the developing countries. The greatest problem for the older person without a pension or social security recourse is undoubtedly that he or she has to work to live. But a study in São Paulo revealed that the only group in which unemployment was increasing rapidly was among older workers, because employers preferred the greater physical potential of the younger worker.[48]

A pre-World Assembly on Aging technical meeting referred to the 'increasing informational and social obsolescence' of the older person in the modern work-place. Another commentator underlined the rapidity of changing labour requirements due to the frenzied modernization of industry, and pointed out the

[47] Andrews et al. 1986.
[48] Mahar 1979, p. 170.

extent to which the older worker was at a disadvantage in the constant need for re-education. A researcher working in Brazil saw a similar rejection of older labourers in the mainly agricultural area of Rio Grande do Norte, where 'when you leave off producing you lie around like an outcast till you die . . . The old man after a certain age no longer finds work, nobody wants to give him any work.'[49] I have met many similar cases, such as the 83-year-old waiter still keen on working, but who said he spent most of his time in queues just 'waiting to wait'.

Yet another Brazilian study found that workers over 40 years of age could expect to be discriminated against because of their 'ageing', but, perhaps surprisingly, this factor was found mainly in qualified and semi-qualified older workers and not unqualified labourers.

This discrimination has been condemned as an infringement of the right to work. Likewise, the way in which society categorizes the older person as socially useless is an attack on the right to dignity at any age. Yet it has been pointed out that a person's work often improves with the years, especially in craftwork, with quantity of output being replaced by quality. Russell A. Ward, dismissing the idea of automatic deterioration in work ability through ageing, quotes eight authoritative studies which have shown either a lack of deterioration with age or ample compensation for diminished powers in the increase of other aptitudes. Leo Simmons, in his work with 71 pre-industrial tribes, also remarked on the usefulness of the elder in agriculture and 'the economic value of knowledge and experience relative to physical prowess' as being very high in stable agricultural societies.

However, many of the tasks available for workers in developing countries are heavy and arduous. For example, a porter in Bolivia may have to carry a load of 500 oranges for 50 miles on a 6,000-foot climb over a 14,000-foot pass from the Yungas to La Paz.[50] Such a task emphasizes the physical prowess of the younger labourer to the disadvantage of the older. The older widow seeking to maintain herself by physical labour is at an even greater disadvantage. Many of the poorest rural women marry early and are totally worn out physically by excessive child-bearing as well as hard work in the fields and in the home.

[49] CERIS 1981, p. 15.
[50] *Daily Mail* 27 May 1986, p. 18.

They are also unlikely to have the educational basis to adapt to
other than the most menial toil.

Malnutrition Circle

A problem interacting with age unemployment is malnutrition.
This is part of the vicious circle of ageing life: underemployment
means that the worker never has enough to eat. Lack of
sustenance means that the worker is unable to exert the physical
force needed to keep him from the trap of unemployment. A
Bangladesh survey quoted 85% of older workers subsisting
beneath the minimum requirements of 2,000 calories daily.[51] A
study of 230 elderly people in Jamaica revealed protein energy
malnutrition in 24% of men and 18% of women. Triceps skin-
fold values were less than 60% of standard. Thiamine and
vitamin C were particularly deficient.[52]

A Peruvian report states that the elderly are the main sufferers
from 'subnutrition', with a diet seriously lacking in necessary
vitamins. The report points out that this leads to another vicious
circle whereby the constant malnutrition renders an old person
depressed or even acutely mentally confused, so that the person
becomes indifferent to feeding requirements, or forgets to provide
food, or is unable to judge the daily balance of nutrition and
prepare the daily menu. This in turn impinges on the work cycle
and makes the person even less able to offer reliable service. The
report also singles out the often desperate need of elderly
widowers who, in such communities, have never been involved in
catering. In fact, in some societies the macho image would
prevent a man from becoming so involved. Then, in a moment,
he is widowed and has to assume an unfamiliar, distasteful task
without means of learning. A further reference in the same report
refers to the effect which malnutrition at an early age—that is, in
infancy and youth—has in causing early ageing.[53]

The seriousness of the malnutrition problem can be assessed
from the fact that in a number of American developing countries

---

[51] Ibrahim 1985.

[52] *Medical Needs of the Elderly*, report to the Commonwealth Caribbean Medical
Research Council, Barbados, 1982.

[53] Report by Caritas Arequipa to Help the Aged, 1981.

TABLE 3.3 *Daily Calorie Intake per Capita, Selected Countries, 1982*

Country	Calorie intake	% of requirement
Haiti	1,903	84
Bolivia	2,158	90
El Salvador	2,060	90
Peru	2,114	90
Ecuador	2,072	91
Uruguay	2,754	103
United States	3,616	137

Source: World Bank (1985).

the average calorie intake per capita for the entire nation is well below requirements (see Table 3.3). In a number of African countries the malnutrition problem is even more extreme. In Ibrahim's 1985 Bangladesh study 80% of the population had nutrition levels below 2,000 calories. But calorie intake data does not, of course, provide the whole picture: it does not indicate deficiency in the quality or balance of calorie intake, or deficiencies in vitamins and other essential ingredients of diet.

In terminating this chapter on socio-economic factors, it is timely to record the growing recognition of the effects that adverse socio-economic conditions can have on some elderly people's health. The World Health Organization blames socio-economic causes for many of the intractable health problems of older people in poorer countries and cites premature death from malignant neoplasms, hypothermia, alcoholism, suicides, and accidents. These causes present considerable differentials between economic classes of workers. Also, many illnesses leading to disability go undiagnosed or untreated for economic reasons.[54]

[54] Lindgren 1981, p. 232.

4

REGIONAL STUDIES OF AGEING

THE next two chapters will review findings from some specific studies of ageing. In this chapter the emphasis will be on wider, regional studies of a scientific nature. Chapter 5 will narrow the consideration down to individual cases and themes, some of them treated in a more narrative style.

The first major world focus on the global problem of the 'greying population' was the World Assembly on Aging called by the United Nations in 1982. In that year non-governmental organizations met in Vienna during late March and April in a Pre-Assembly Conference to discuss this new world phenomenon. In August of the same year, governmental representatives gathered in Vienna, together with non-governmental organizations for the full Assembly. These world meetings had been preceded in 1980 and 1981 by regional and sectoral preparatory meetings, and subsequent to the World Assembly the United Nations General Assembly ratified the report now known as the Vienna International Plan of Action on Aging.

The studies preparatory to the World Assembly constituted the first somewhat co-ordinated attempt to present the realities of the global problem. Prior to those preparatory studies any surveys of ageing in the Third World had been unco-ordinated, fragmentary, and localized. Even since the 1982 World Assembly the study of ageing in developing countries has not been on a scale comparable with the studies carried out on almost any other subject.

In 1984 I attended a Vienna United Nations meeting on the standardization of research methodologies and terminology of ageing. Probably the major outcome of this meeting was a fuller recognition of the vast differences in concepts and terms, as well as the vacuum in the field of research related to developing countries.

An excellent study of ageing in the Western Pacific, published in 1986, covered only four countries; similar studies for other regions are virtually non-existent.[1] A PAHO/HelpAge International study of 13 countries was completed in 1988. In some countries this was restricted to urban ageing only and did not fully address other aspects of ageing. Some country studies of varying profundity and authority exist but are rarely comparable as to data selected. A number of recent regional conferences have produced some consensus of assumptions on ageing,[2] such as the increasing impact of the breakdown of the extended family and the reduced prestige of the elder.

In view of these limitations, the studies quoted in this chapter were selected mainly because of their availability, but none the less they should be of some value in indicating situations, phenomena and trends which may be similar for a group of developing countries and occasionally for all.

Major Factors in Ageing Patterns

Before detailing some of the data emerging from some studies in which I have been involved in Latin America, it may be pertinent to identify six major effects or factors which illustrate the varying circumstances of older people according to region. While each of the six effects is encountered in a number of regions throughout the Americas, and indeed in many developing countries, they are categorized here according to particular locations where the author found the specific tendency to be extremely marked, for one reason or another. This variation underlines the fallacy of generalizing about any developing country or region. The effects have not previously been categorized in this way.

These are described in some detail in the next pages but may be briefly differentiated thus:

1. *The Vilcabamba effect*: extraordinary longevity related to environmental conditions. An unpolluted, temperate environment

---

[1] Andrews *et al.* 1986.
[2] For example, International Centre of Social Gerontology conferences in Dakar and Bogotá, WHO meetings in Hyderabad and Singapore, and various HelpAge International meetings.

and unpressured rural culture are particularly conducive to survival. Persons in their late 60s and 70s are not considered *anciano*. Many people of 90 and 100 are still active and lucid. Retirement is a totally unknown concept.

2. *The Potosi effect*: a remarkably low survival rate, combined with early disability. Various factors, such as high altitude, endemic malnutrition, industrial diseases, and excessively heavy labour cause debility. Many people in their late 30s are physically unable to continue working as the only type of labour available locally is mining.

3. *The Beni effect*: characterizing a geographically remote and isolated area where older indigenous people have little or no access to health and social services. The small central town forms a kind of microcosm of the immigrant reception areas more usually associated with mega-cities, but, because of its isolation there are no further service or migration possibilities for the older person.

4. *The Bogotá effect*: found in metropolitan settings in which a certain measure of social services infrastructure has already been created. The necessary complementary voluntary agency services already exist, but have yet to be organized in terms responsive to the massive need. Opportunities for rapid development are afforded by a fairly developed commercial sector of the city.

5. *The Lima effect*: the reception focus of extraordinary migratory movements of large numbers of population. One of the classic examples of mega-city magnetism, along with Mexico, São Paulo, Bombay, Lagos, and others, Lima's type of shanty towns tend to visible identification and geographic segregation, making small research projects easier to mount than in some other similar cities. Examples of abandonment of the elderly, both in the rural hinterland and in new shanty towns.

6. *The Belize effect*: a classic example of out-of-country emigration which tends to precipitate problems of a somewhat different, and frequently more critical, nature than the within-country type of migration.

Where abandonment of the elderly takes place, the younger generation has normally moved to a remote foreign country where the costs and styles of living further complicate the problems of the migrant and reduce the possibility of aid to those remaining at home.

This brief description of six major factors affecting the elderly reveals both the extremes of situations which must be considered in developing countries and also the prevalence of the 'ageing problem' across various environmental scenarios.

The oldest of the old: the Vilcabamba effect

The Vilcabamba Valley is situated in Loja province of Ecuador, not far from the Peruvian border. Known locally as the 'Valle de la Ancianidad' (valley of old age) or 'Isla de Imunidad' (island of immunity), it is famous among anthropologists, biologists, and others as one of perhaps three sites in the world where people live longest (the others being in Soviet Georgia and in Pakistan). Experts have suggested that longevity in the valley is due to one or other or a combination of the following: ideal altitude (1,200–1,500 metres); a mainly vegetable diet; a tension-free culture; hard but not intolerable work conditions; the extraordinary air-recycling capacity of the huilco tree in this thickly wooded area; isolation from contacts with other groups of population; and various unexplained natural phenomena, such as the low incidence of serious snakebite in a district populated by snakes similar to those which can tender fatal bites in surrounding districts; but it is not the intention here to develop this biological argument.

International attention was first drawn to the valley by an article in the *Reader's Digest* in 1959 by Dr Eugene H. Payne, while in 1971 Dr Alexander Leaf noticed low cholesterol levels in the valley and made the link between cholesterol and heart disease.[3] Using baptismal records, Dr Leaf calculated that there were many very aged people, the oldest of them aged 131. He also found that the calorie intake was 1,700 with only 153 calories of fat (compared with USA intake at the time of 2,600 calories with 500 calories of fat). In 1972, Trujillo and Moreta encountered a man aged 120 with 48 living great-grandchildren. They also calculated that the percentage of inhabitants of the valley aged over 60 was 20%, compared with a 4.6 average for Ecuador as a whole.[4] In 1982 I found that the man who in 1972 was aged 120 years had only recently died, and the oldest inhabitant met was

[3] Leaf, *New York Times*, 21 Apr. 1971.
[4] Trujillo and Moreta 1972.

118 years old. Some commentators doubt the accuracy of these ages, but baptismal records are still in the possession of the village priest.

The director of the local medical centre is Dr Guillermo del Pozo Veintemilla, himself a cardiac specialist and a researcher into cardiovascular illnesses. Dr del Pozo is collaborating with the WHO in a world comparative study of cardiovascular incidence and environmental variants. On first contact with me, Dr del Pozo commented that, while many scientists had visited Vilcabamba to investigate the reasons for the longevity of the inhabitants, none had ever enquired as to whether old age was happy and fulfilling in the valley, or whether the aged people themselves might have aspirations to other styles of life.

It was therefore agreed that I should instigate a research project to look at the social and economic aspects of ageing in the valley. Instead of being mere biological curiosities or anthropological freaks, the *ancianos* should be considered as sensitive human beings. The University of Loja therefore provided a small group of young researchers who would live with the *ancianos* for three weeks and gain their confidence in order to complete a comprehensive socio-economic questionnaire. To date the results have never been published in full, although the research has been used as the basis of project planning and co-funding submissions to governmental and international funding sources.

Preliminary interviews were conducted in 16 sites throughout the valley, as a result of which 135 persons were selected for in-depth interviews representing all areas and aspects of the valley's over-70 population. Of these, 49.6% were male and 50.4% female, in keeping with the current sex ratio. The main findings were as follows:

1. *Personal status*: 57% were married, 29.6% widowed, and 13.4% single or divorced.
2. *Home ownership*: 70.4% were home owners, 22.9% lived with their families. 3.7% rented a house, 1.5% lived with friends, and 1.5% were without settled abode.
3. *Building materials*: 48.9% of the houses had mud-brick walls, 20.7% were adobe (lime or plaster over mud brick), 16.3% of wattle type, 10.4% a mixture of bricks and cement, with 3.7%

being a composition of various materials such as wood and cement.

4. *Number of rooms*: inside the houses 35.6% had only one room 37.8% two rooms, 14.1% three rooms, 6.7% four rooms. The remainder had five, six, or nine rooms, although some of the rooms had uses like storage or space for animals.

5. *Water and sanitation*: 58.5% had running water on the property, with the remainder carrying water from local streams. 11.1% had WCs, 2.2% had dry privies, 3% had septic tanks, but 83.7% had no form of lavatory at all and had to use nearby fields or river banks.

6. *Lighting*: 45.9% had some electric light and the remainder used candles or other fuel-ignited lights.

7. *Education*: 33.3% had received 'elementary education' amounting to two or three years, 31.1% had only one year or part of the year, 35.6% were completely illiterate. Only 19 out of the 135 interviewees had completed the full four-year course of primary education.

8. *Occupations*: 48.1% were engaged in agricultural pursuits, with 53% owning their own plot of land. Some 19.3% gained their livelihood from crafts, mainly rope-making, wood-carving, sewing, or making cigars or cigarettes by hand. A further 20% were involved in miscellaneous activities such as casual laundering, casual hired labour, or petty selling. Only 12.6% said they did not work because of their age. Those in some kind of work were engaged for an average of five hours a day.

9. *Supplementary sources of livelihood*: when not working at their main source of livelihood, 65.2% sought some other activity, mainly productive of a little additional income (although often the entire 'income' consisted of subsistence products and some surplus for barter). Additional activities included breeding domestic animals (goats, pigs, donkeys, dogs, a few cows), knitting, bird-rearing (also for food), tobacco-growing, handicrafts, flower growing, other optional agricultural tasks, growing of medicinal herbs, and domestic help.

10. *Nutrition*: basic foods were black beans, green beans, corn, green bananas, manioc root, rice, and pasta, and the meals tended to be very similar day by day. The available basics were not used with any degree of variation in the preparation. About 54% claimed to eat meat probably about once a month, the

remainder less often; 16.3% ate eggs. Only 8.9% drank milk, but 77% drank coffee every day. Also 39.2% took a daily herbal drink to which they attributed medical value.

11. *Health*: 39.3% said they never suffered illness, 34.2% complained of rheumatic problems, 8.9% suffered from malaria, 9.6% had liver complaints, 9.6% did not seek medical aid because of fears of modern medicine. Treatable ophthalmic conditions troubled 60% of respondents, 46% had bad hearing, often due to lack of hygiene. Almost 15% had been operated on at some time for tumours, prostate, gall bladder, ulcers, removal of a bullet, abscesses, ophthalmic diseases, ovaries and appendicitis. Mental problems afflicted 16.3%.

12. *Participation in social activities*: 8.9% belonged to some club or co-operative and the rest to no social organization. Fully 82.2% took part in the civic religious holidays which are a feature of the region and include music and dancing, although 17.8% could not afford to take part in such events. The majority (64.4%) owned 'some kind of instrument which transmits music', including primitive flutes, home-made guitar type instruments, and drums.

13. *Access to the media*: 64.4% owned radios of the cheap transistor type, but the preference was universally for folk music rather than modern or pop music, 26.7% did not like music at all. Books, mainly of a religious nature, were read by 26.7%, other popular subjects being history, grammar, medicine, and classical Spanish literature. But of those who could read, 20.7% did not read at all. Daily or other newspapers were rarely seen.

The main complaints, almost universal, were that the work task at present undertaken was insufficient to provide reasonable basics of life, such as a variation of diet, changes of clothing, a few home comforts, etc.; and that the agricultural tasks in particular were becoming excessive burdens in an environment where most people had to walk and climb considerable distances to reach their place of work. There was no request for total relief from toil, but simply the option of a less arduous type of work, or a workplace more accessible than the mountain slopes.

It was suggested that a centre or series of small centres for the elderly might one day be set up. There is no old people's home in the valley and the concept was strange to those interviewed, but 100% agreed that this would be a good thing; 95.6% wanted to be associated with such centres and 4.4% did not want to be associated, although supporting the idea. The idea of living and working in such a centre appealed to 58.2%, 26.7% saw it as a centre where they might work but not live, while 10.4% said they would like to live and be taken care of in such a centre.

When asked what type of productive activity they might wish to be associated in if a work programme were set up, 27.4% favoured some kind of work tilling the land, 18.25% proposed poultry farming, 4.4% handicrafts, 9.6% tobacco growing, and 3.7% medicinal plant growing. A further 9.6% expressed a miscellany of ideas, including tablet making, the production of herbal medicines from plants, collecting wild grains, flower-growing, and domestic work, 14% did not think that they would be able to work in such a programme.

After the research project had been concluded, I had several meetings in Vilcabamba, including one attended by 180 people over 70 years of age. In the course of the meetings a *Comité pro defensa del anciano* (committee for the defence of the old person) was set up with a majority membership of the *ancianos* themselves. The first projects put into operation were a small rural bakery and a sewing room.

The general impression given by this research was of a quiet, undeveloped district, where life was tolerable as long as expectations were minimal. The persons interviewed were able to respond intelligently into extreme old age as to their living conditions and had at least some minimal interests outside their main livelihood. Furthermore, the majority had preconceived aspirations as to how they would improve their own life style, given the opportunity. They were able to conceive of a programme in which there could be a community experience for older people, providing them with other options for work and leisure within the traditional environment, but these would be difficult to achieve without some kind of external support.

The Vilcabamba research suggested that the life of a very old person in a developing country need not be one of degradation and destitution even though lacking in major input of social services.

The youngest aged: the Potosi effect

While visiting Potosi in 1983, I carried out a small survey. The diocesan director of Caritas had already reported to Help the Aged, London, that expectation of life in Potosi was believed to be little more than 30, and that there were many cases of miners who died by the age of 30 or were incapacitated by industrial disease at that age. He was unfortunately unable to substantiate his claims with firm statistics, for no survey of the aged or prematurely aged in Potosi had ever been undertaken. He himself was a busy parish priest in addition to being the director of the only significant voluntary social services programme in a vast and poverty-stricken mountain region of Bolivia. He had no resources, financial or human, to allocate to what he saw as the luxury of a survey.[5]

Historically, Potosi was not only one of the main sources of mineral wealth in the Americas, closely connected with the name of the Patiño family. It was also one of the worst areas of native suffering observed by early writers. In 1550, the Dominican priest Domingo de Santo Tomas told the Council of the Indies that Potosi was the 'mouth of hell'. Since the sixteenth century the Indian miners have had to endure extreme altitude (15,000 feet), a terrible climate, excessive labour under the most adverse circumstances, inadequate diet, contagious diseases, accidents, respiratory industrial diseases, toxic dust, and carbon monoxide poisoning in unvented mine shafts.

During a brief visit I decided to undertake a modest survey in the time available and without staff resources.[6] This was based on a random sample obtained by house-to-house visits in a high parish near the infamous hill within which the majority of the silver, tin, and lead mines have been worked. At each door the simple question was asked as to whether there were any people of grandparent status living within. Where such people existed and

---

[5] Padre Gustav Evens, a Belgian war-time Resistance leader who, since the Second World War, has dedicated himself to the service of the indigent peoples of Potosi's poorest areas.

[6] The scarcity of resources will be apparent from the fact that on two days during the visit, 13–14 Aug. 1983, the water shortage was such that the hotel could offer only one cup of coffee daily to each guest, and the only food was a type of hard biscuit–bun that could be purchased in one or two bakeries.

were able to answer questions a simple formula was followed, demanding age, marital status, numbers of dependent and independent children, type of paid labour or other income, caring person if any, and general health condition.

Some 40 persons of grandparent status were located. Their ages were as follows:

Age	No. persons
40–9	4
50–9	11
60–9	12
70–9	9
80–9	4

The first extraordinary finding was the sex of the respondents: the sample included only 9 men as compared with 31 women. In a more normal urban environment one might have expected to have encountered at least 17 or 18 males in a sample of 40. This tended to confirm the Caritas assumption of extreme variation between male and female longevity in the mining areas of Potosí.

The 40 persons resided in 29 households, although a number of the 'households' were only single rooms within a house or a shack in a patio behind a house. Twenty-three of the persons were heads of their 'household', 17 were living in single status. Seven were living 'alone', although one of those classed as 'alone' had two dependent grandchildren living with her but not contributing.

Of the 40, 31 had at some time been part of a conjugal pair (officially married or not), and seven couples were still living together. Only three of the women (one a widow) had never had any children, although eight regarded themselves as single. Only two of the men lived alone, and both were widowed. The total number of children born to the respondents was 178, an average of 4.45 per person. Adjusting this to account for the seven couples living together, who were all fathers and mothers of complete families, the average per marital unit was 5.39 (178 divided by 33). However, of the 178 children born, only 97 survived. Of these 97 survivors, only about 50 were still in contact with the parent(s). This last figure is approximate because, in several cases, it was not clear whether there was any real contact with the children at all; the true figure may have been less. It is also relevant to state that two of the old women were not clear as to exactly how many children they had had, one settling for 16 and the other for 10.

This low rate of survival, taken with the 'out of contact' factor showing only 28% of *born* children still in contact, is a significant demographic figure. World population conferences have acknowledged that the procreation of many children is seen as an insurance against poverty in old age by many people of developing countries. The Potosi figures illustrate the high number of births needed for parents to ensure there would be one or two surviving children still in contact in the parents' old age.

Out of the 33 'conjugal units' (that is, married couples or single people, the latter whether living individually or in multiples), 30 had children at some time, but only 14 responded 'yes' to the question 'Do you get any help from your children?' The insurance factor mentioned in the last paragraph therefore appears an unreliable economic source. Twelve interviewees lived with persons of the next generations, 10 of these being children, 1 a niece, and 1 a grandchild. Again it must be said that some of the data obtained revealed considerable domestic confusion as to who was living with whom, and who was the head of the household or caring person.

Of the 40 interviewed, 16 stated that they had no work—and certainly no pension. Another 15 indicated work of perilous economic prospects, with replies such as 'scraping on the mine tip' (for odd spoilings of metal), 'street cook', 'works sometimes', 'casual', or 'carrying in the markets'. In two of the seven cases where a marriage still existed with dependent children (6 and 2, respectively), the husbands were still of an age when they might have continued working (43 and 50) but were totally incapacitated by lung trouble. In another case, the husband (aged 55) was incapacitated to an extent but was able to do some casual scrabbling on the mine tip on his own account in order to help provide for the four dependent grandchildren living in the home.

Twenty-three of the persons were in a physical state which constituted a very considerable handicap, such as being blind, bed-ridden, unable to work due to industrial disease or stroke, or extremely frail, possibly due to malnutrition.

Rural patterns: the Beni effect

The Beni effect was first described by me in a number of internal HelpAge reports based on visits to the area between 1981 and 1985, and consultations with the local authorities as well as people working with the elderly. Its distinctive features are geographical rather than gerontological. The River Beni is one of the major tributary rivers, like the Mamore and the Madre de Dios, which help to swell the Amazon. It gives its name to the vast department of Bolivia which lies between the Andes Mountains and the Brazilian border. The region is a combination of wild plains and thick jungle. There are no all-weather roads, and communications are either by slow river boat, expensive aeroplanes, or horse- and mule-back. Frequently the rivers swell and flood the plains.

The principal occupations on the plains are related to cattle-ranching of a primitive type—probably similar to the earliest days of ranching in the west of the United States. The occupations of the jungle are nomadic and relate to rubber-collecting (no longer a boom industry), fishing, and hunting. These are all hazardous and energetic pursuits, the province of the younger man. Consequently, in an area the size of England, Wales, and Ireland combined, when a person becomes too old to contend with the savage environment, two options are available: either to remain in utter and hopeless destitution in some primitive cluster of huts, where the macho tradition rejects the person unable to participate fully in the daily task; or to migrate to the central town of Trinidad which, with its 40,000 inhabitants, shops, markets, and plazas, is a metropolis in the eyes of the rural dweller.

The new arrival will probably find some kind of rudimentary shelter in the shanties of Pompeya with some 10,000 other immigrants who are prior contenders on the job market for casual labour in the small 'frontier town'. In 1981 the only recourse for a destitute over-age person was a tiny municipal purse for charity—mainly intended for orphans—the door of some parish priest or nun themselves living on the bread line, or Sister Pacifica's always overoccupied 27-bed old people's home, Hogar Sagrado Corazón. This situation has now changed to some extent due to a programme which will be referred to in

Chapter 7. One small statistic may illustrate the local circumstances in Beni. In 1985, a school teacher's salary was about
US$180 *a year*, and the income of a rural farmer was estimated at
US$110 a year. At the same time I discovered that a beer or a
sandwich in a Trinidad café cost more than twice the cost of a
similar snack in an English pub. In San Ignacio, more than 100
miles out into the plains, two aspirins cost US$3.50—almost
exactly the weekly salary of the school teacher.

Metropolitan factors: the Bogota effect

The Bogotá effect represents the metropolitan milieu and is
significant in the planning of care programmes, as will be
described in Chapter 7. The approach to communal problems
obviously needs to be considerably different between the Beni
and Bogotá, although with the same objective of enhancing the
lives of older people. One quotation from an experienced local
observer will underline the fact that the metropolitan environment of Bogotá is no more hospitable to older migrants than the
primitive environment of Trinidad town, Beni, especially in 'the
case of the aged beggar who sleeps in the street and is in need of
care. Sometimes the police or other organization brings the
person to "Mi Casa" seeking urgent admission. Other times he is
deposited in inhuman condition at the door of one of our
houses.'[7]

Migratory invasions: the Lima effect

In Lima, a Help the Aged survey has been taking place and an
American researcher has investigated the area of origin of an
invasion.[8] The researcher's preliminary observations do not add to
the macro-data of the demographic statistics regarding the
massive immigration from rural districts of Peru into the capital
city of Lima. In the microcosm of the individual cases and
families or small communities investigated, the research does

---

[7] Amaya, Sor Clara, Provincial Superior (Bogota) of Las Hermanitas de los
Ancianos Desamparados (Little Sisters of the Abandoned Elderly).
[8] Loughran 1986.

confirm, at both departure and arrival/settlement points, trends indicated by the more general statistics. Migration is most frequently undertaken by younger people, often unmarried youths with better educational preparation, looking for adventure and a more comfortable mode of life. The tendency is for the older people to stay in the rural villages, often with grandchildren in their care, either supported by one or two daughters or left to their own devices. The effect of emigration is least in the smallest rural villages, as people in the tight, tiny community, often bypassed by education and political awareness, tend to cling together in the known environment. In the larger villages, with benefits of education and a somewhat looser community organization, younger people detach more frequently. In addition, the entire village may get together to plan another *invasion* into Lima. Meanwhile many of the older people found in the Lima shanty towns are ageing survivors of the earliest *invasions*.

Small country problems: the Belize effect

Belize is a small, sovereign country with only some 150,000 resident inhabitants. Having no major industrial complex to form its own socio-economic magnet for migration, the emigration or 'out-migration' flow is directed mainly towards the United States, to which road transport via Mexico or cheap travel on small boats adds to the volume of migration on the still relatively inexpensive air routes. An average young worker in Belize might take an air passage to Miami for about one month's wages; a similar worker from the Beni area would need six months' wages to take an air passage to his own capital city of La Paz.

The Help the Aged/OPEC study on Belize is one of the few fairly comprehensive studies of ageing in a developing country and gives a picture of ageing in Belize which has been accepted as accurate by authorities of that country.[9] An unusual factor in the Belize population, especially as contrasted to, say, Potosi, is that in the total population there is an excess of males compared with females. This is only minimally reversed in the 65–9 years age band and even in the 70+ age band is still only a 52 : 48 ratio of females (a 'sex ratio' of 96).

[9] Tout and Tout 1985.

Another anomaly arising from the sex ratio is that in a review of old people in need of care or medical assistance, it was found that only 24.8% were males while an overwhelming 75.2% were females. With no longitudinal studies available or even likely for years to come, it was necessary to rely on expert local opinion in seeking reasons for this disparity. These reasons included the high rate of male work activity (74% in the 65–9 age band), the effects of excessive child-bearing on the female, the higher rate of widowhood in females (43.8% of females over 70, compared to 15.3% of males over 70), and the social habits of the sexes, whereby the females were more likely to congregate in centres where aid was available or where information on aid was made known.

In total terms, an expert population study had projected that whereas the over-65 population in 1980 had been 6,685, by 2030 it would be between 20,966 and 31,280.

Even within such a small country as Belize, living conditions for the aged varied considerably. The small population notwithstanding, the geographical extent of the country is comparable to the whole of Wales, with an area of 8,866 square miles—vastly bigger than Luxemburg and larger than El Salvador which has a population more than 10 times as large. An average of 59.3% of households in the country are lit by electricity, but this varies from 90.3% in Belize City to only 3.8% (and 87.9% kerosene) in Toledo rural area. For cooking, only 0.7% of the households in Belize City relied on wood, as against 75.9% in Toledo rural area.

The study checked a sample of 121 people over 50 years of age, of whom 109 were over 60 and 81 over 70. Domiciliary arrangements of this sample varied as follows:

Domiciliary arrangement	No.
Living with partner (married or not)	22
Living with other aged person	13
Living with non-aged friend	3
Living with adult children	5
Living with dependent grandchildren	14
Living alone	64
Total	121

Access of members of the sample to care in the community was:

Access to	No.
Children/grandchildren in Belize who care	18
Other caring visitor	8
Sharing home with adult (mutual care)	38
Caring *for* dependents at home	14
Nobody to care	43

Although this was a sample comprised of people who were 'in need of care' to some extent or other, rather than a random sample from the community, the survey does reinforce the Potosi indications that having a considerable number of children as insurance against age problems is a very inefficient method of provision. In several cases there was actually specific mention of the 'disappearance' of children through emigration to the United States and subsequent loss of contact.

Among the sample, the following disabilities were recorded:

Disability	No.
Blind or partially blind	16
Bedridden or permanent housebound	21
Lesser mobility problems	6
Extreme age, mentally ill or other chronic illness	18
Total reporting disability	61
Total not reporting disability	60

The 'non-disability' cases, as indeed all those noted, had come to seek solutions to socio-economic needs rather than medical needs. The illness report was subjective. Some of the 'non-disability' individuals might well have been diagnosed as ill if there had been a medical check.

An interesting sidelight in this study was that, while the 'living alone' factor peaked at 70–9 years, it then fell progressively in higher age bands, suggesting perhaps that the very old attract more spontaneous community care, and also that the carers might be older and more static. Major unfulfilled needs perceived were medical/medicine, 78%; company/social life, 78%; food, 47%; and clothing, 12%.

The economic conditions of the sample were very low; 35%

were classified as 'extremely poor', with only US$1.25 per week income (the level of government social security payments); 35% had less than US$2.50 per week; 30% were aided by relatives or friends. Specific problems mentioned included a blind person living in a wooden house perilously lit by kerosene; a broken hip; arthritis; diabetes; asthma; looking after nine small children whose parents were out of contact in the United States; and the need for spectacles which were too expensive to buy.

Another problem revealed by the Belize study, and which well be more widespread, related to the receipt of cheques and money drafts from relatives in the USA. Most of the recipients had never used a cheque or bank account and did not themselves change the money into local cash. This was usually done by a 'kind neighbour'. As two Belizean dollars equal 1 US dollar, it was not unknown for the 'kind neighbour' to cash the US cheque or draft and then pay the old person the number of dollars indicated on the face of the cheque, but in Belize dollars, thus making a 100% profit on the short walk to and from the bank. In Belize, as in other out-migration rural areas, there is need for advice and assistance to old people receiving unaccustomed sums of money or unfamiliar monetary tokens.

The main lesson of the Belize study appeared to be the ability of an old person to stay alive for a considerable period in apparently impossible financial circumstances, with no variation in the diet or the social round, and with the most meagre of shelter and domestic facilities.

Trends in Africa

There are a number of excellent, if somewhat specialized and localized studies available from certain regions of Asia and Latin America. Others of these will be quoted in later chapters. In African countries such studies are harder to come by, partially because industrialization, and the consequent breakdown of the extended family, is on the whole taking place somewhat later in Africa than in Asia and Latin America. Another version is that African academics have so many other priorities, when establishing an indigenous academic authority and tradition in so many subjects in such a short space of time, and do not perceive ageing as an urgent problem.

In some regions of Africa the only reliable data, apart from basic census material, appears to come from consensus reports of national or international conferences. One or two fairly recent studies, such as those by the Nigerian team of Ekpenyong, Oyeneye, and Peil, and the Ghanaian Nana Apt, merit close scrutiny. Before passing to such a scrutiny it is necessary to clear up one or two misunderstandings about ageing in Africa.

In the first place, Africa, more than other continents, has an extreme diversity of cultures, environments, and ageing processes. There are variations more extreme between the environments and cultures of, say, Tunisia and Lesotho, or Somalia and Zaire, than the variations across some inter-continental divides, such as, say, the differences between Argentina and Italy, or between Algeria and Jordan.

Secondly, there are probably wider economic variations in Africa than in any other comparable continental population mass (about 500 million). The range varies from countries like Libya and Gabon, where GNP per capita is well above the world average, to several countries within the list of 20 with lowest per capita income.

Thirdly, religious traditions include traditional Muslim countries, majority Christian countries, systems of deities, and also animism—much more variation than, say, Latin America. Such variation also extends into the realm of ageing. Whereas the Nigerians researchers mentioned found in one area only about 2% of aged men living with children, and the extended family still well established, in Kenya in 1985 the government's Assistant Commissioner for Social Services referred to the extended family as having suffered breakdown.

Probably most misunderstandings of ageing, as it will affect the future of Africa, are based on a misunderstanding of the rate of modernization, industrialization, and urbanization. Modernization is hard to quantify, and industrialization in itself would not necessarily be a negative factor if it could be so allocated geographically as to leave the natural population distribution fairly intact. It only becomes a negative factor in age care and age opportunity when it concentrates in commercially convenient, socially inappropriate zones and provokes unnatural waves of migration. The urbanization data are therefore most relevant and highly revealing.

There appears to be general awareness of the rate of urbanization in Latin America and of the massed hundreds of millions of inhabitants of India and China in their mega-cities, but it is perhaps not so widely realized that Africa is facing probably the most rapid urbanization rates in the world. Table 4.1 illustrates this rapid urban growth rate, as experienced in some selected countries of eastern and southern Africa.

TABLE 4.1   *Urbanization in Selected African Countries, 1985*

Country	Urban population ('000)	% total	Growth rate p.a. (%)
Botswana	250	25	12.0
Djibouti	229	74	8.3
Ethiopia	4,508	14	5.5
Kenya	2,595	15	7.3
Lesotho	168	12	16.1
Madagascar	1,710	19	5.2
Malawi	610	10	7.0
Mauritius	504	52	3.6
Somalia	1,519	31	5.4
Tanzania	2,220	12	8.6
Zambia	2,640	44	6.5
Zimbabwe	1,824	24	6.3

Source: Diaz (1986).

Traditional cultural influences

Before looking at the actual statistics provided by Nigerians, Ghanaians, Kenyans, and others already referred to, it is of interest to consult an extraordinary study by Leopold Rosenmayr of the University of Vienna, with the close association of Gaoussou Traore of Mali and other African researchers. The study, entitled *More than Wisdom*, looked at old age in a changing African society between 1983 and 1986 and was focused on an area of the Sahel in the Republic of Mali.[10]

[10] Rosenmayr 1986.

Rosenmayr's central finding is that the position of prestige, which the old man in particular holds in traditional African society is not necessarily the *product* of his wisdom and expertise, but rather the reverse. Traditional African society is structured so that chronological and tribal *seniority* is in *itself* prestigious and lends authority to the old man's acquired wisdom and expertise in whatever matters. Rosenmayr admits that when he commenced his study he did not expect to encounter a '*principle* of seniority' as an established essential of traditional culture. But, throughout the 'social architecture' of the basic community, all decisions were referred back to the senior who was, in almost every case, the chronologically oldest born of the blood line.

Whilst Rosenmayr's basic study focused on a village area of the Sahel, he also found in parts of poorer areas of Senegal's capital, Dakar, a 'sort of moderate gerontocracy' still obtaining, so that the old men were the negotiators of improvement projects involving the community. However, he refers to the 'chaotic pluralism' of culture created by urbanization in the 'megalopolis-type' areas such as ' . . . Dakar, Abidjan, Ouagadougou, Nairobi, etc. . . . where *non-African* elements of design, habitat, and symbols may dominate traditional forms of life and value'.

In a society 100% illiterate, 'spoken verbal power is decisive . . . the old do all the talking'. The life-long practice of rhetoric and articulate expression of experience reinforces the prestige which the elders already enjoyed *de jure*. On the negative side the 'fear of the young is stronger that they will be hexed or poisoned by an old woman than by an old man. The curses of an old woman are more powerful.' The first wife of the senior never loses her dominant position.

Rosenmayr and Traore were of the opinion that in modernized cities the 'elaborate mythological legitimation of the principle of seniority' was the first natural African element to perish. School, however primitive, 'evokes individual competition' and challenges the prestige of the senior as being the person who knows and achieves most. The remnants of natural mythology become 'fragments, difficult to understand, they tend to deteriorate into folklore. Witchcraft and fortune telling more easily and more broadly continue . . . ', and the latter pursuits do not enhance the prestige of the elder.

At one point Rosenmayr, the objective academic, is personally

disturbed by individual cases of disintegration which he distinguishes. He uses as a 'paradigm for the desertion of the old in the
African bush' an incident which can suitably be told only in his
own words:

> Before returning to Yaounde I left a few tins with food to the poor
> woman and she knelt down before me, clasped her hands around mine,
> it was one of the most terrible experiences I had. I once tried to send
> some money to her through an intermediary who had relatives in the
> bush in the same region, but never heard from her again.

Rosenmayr and Traore found that 'there are parents with young
children in the city who rather "sacrifice" their old in the bush
instead of letting their children run out to the streets of the city
without offering to them some schooling'. They agreed that the
family cannot be looked upon as the panacea for all the ills
accompanying modernization. The age–class structure tends to
break up even more quickly than the lineage organization, and
the authors cite the atomization and singularization of the Masai
in Tanzanian or Kenyan cities as an example of this process.

They recommend income-generating projects for the old as
being an essential response to the problems, a response which, at
least at the beginning, will have to be supported by finance from
outside. And, in this type of programme, market/technical
knowledge and skills may be as important as finance in leading to
the selling of products and the generating of income.

They also suggest that new social models will have to be
introduced. Otherwise 'the old traditions . . . will be rather
despised than used for the flexible continuity which Africa may
need now, more than any other spiritual and practical value'.

West African variations

The findings of Ekpenyong, Oyeneye, and Peil are more useful in
that, although based mainly on available data and new research
in Nigeria, they also overlap into neighbouring countries as well
as making clear distinctions between regional variations within
Nigeria.[11]

These researchers point out that 'the concept of age is some-

---

[11] Ekpenyong *et al.* 1986. (Ekpenyong and Oyeneye are Nigerians; Margaret Peil is
Scottish.)

what different in West Africa than in industrialized countries. It is more related to social position and physical capacity than to calendar age.' They quote *young men's* clubs with men of 40 as members. Respondents in the study had a high ceiling for the concept of 'old', two-fifths of them not considering any person to be old until over 80.

This, say Ekpenyong and his colleagues 'shows the artificiality of official retirement at 60, except for its function of clearing jobs for the younger generation'. The official retirement age applies mainly to men, as most women lacked the educational qualifications to enter work which carried a pension scheme. In the rural areas women are expected to produce most of the family food and so to continue working, irrespective of age, as long as their health permits. 'Retired' women tend to be teachers who retire from city schools and return to their villages.

In fact, regulations on retirement in West Africa apply mainly to government and higher commercial occupations. In rural areas many elderly do not even know their age. The researchers found several claiming to be, but patently not, 'over 120' years of age.

In The Gambia, Ekpenyong *et al.* found older women working at home and in the fields. This throws up a rather unusual work participation profile for females in The Gambia. In younger years, relatively few women work. The rate drops even lower for the child-bearing years. Then it rises to a peak as husbands die or go to live with another woman, and the children move away. Older women therefore may need to procure their own incomes more frequently than in younger years.

Sierra Leone has more widespread education and female work-force participation than The Gambia, but the proportion is still lower than in Nigeria or Ghana. There is likely to be a sharp drop in female work-force participation in Sierra Leone over the age of 65.

In The Gambia and Sierra Leone, some men who have to retire from wage employment find other work on a casual basis. However, some do leave the work force permanently, creating an economic problem not only for the individual but also for the country, which has to support a large number of dependent children. The researchers consider that these and similar countries are under considerable economic threat from the combined problems of a child population forming 40% of the total, plus a growing number of elderly outside the work-force.

Even so, the researchers point out that in all West African countries 'any official retirement age affects only a small proportion of the population'. The average individual is likely to be less healthy than in industrialized countries, but he or she will have to continue doing some kind of work from sheer economic necessity in order to purchase daily food and essential manufactured goods. The researchers agree with Rosenmayr that there are authority roles which give status, but these do not normally exclude the office-bearer from the need to work in some gainful occupation.

Ekpenyong *et al.* discovered some significant facts on migration and its impact on the extended family. In a survey of Southern Nigeria they calculated that about 45% of villagers had never migrated, and that few of those who had migrated had ever gone beyond their own known district. Many of the 'migrants' were young rural women moving a short distance to join their husbands on marriage. On the other hand only a quarter of urban dwellers surveyed in Port Harcourt had *never* migrated. Over 44% of urban dwellers interviewed were living outside the area where they were born, and were likely to spend their older years in the urban setting. This compared with 11% of rural men and 20% of rural women who were resident in some place other than where they were born. This reflects the urban life-style of much of Southern Nigeria.

Less than 3% of urban elderly and 7% of village elderly received no financial or material support from family or kin, and this appeared to indicate that the extended family system was reasonably intact and providing well. Also, abandoned villagers appeared to be able to obtain community help more easily than similar people in urban settings. Only 2% of older men and 9% of older women overall had no living children, the figure being higher in rural than in urban areas.

In spite of these apparently reassuring figures, the researchers believed that 'as urban birth and long-distance migration increase in Africa, ties to an ancestral home place are weakening and urban governments will have to acknowledge the needs of elderly people who have lost such ties'.

Where living children were in contact with elderly parents, not all were 'able or willing to help their parents'. Some of the children, indeed, were still minors themselves requiring everyday support; some of the working children were themselves just surviving on the poverty line with nothing to spare for their old parents, and some had totally lost contact. Again the researchers point out that 'attention should be given to the isolated, poverty-stricken elderly in rural areas'.

The problem of support appears to be more acute for women than for men in old age. A quarter of urban men in Nigeria and two-fifths of rural men have more than one wife. The majority of older men live in a nuclear household with one or more wives and with dependent children. Very few old men are left to themselves without younger female support. Widowers generally remarry and continue to have children. Only young widows remarry, and all of a woman's children are grown up by the time she is 65. This is all to the good if the ties with children continue. But in some cases, the researchers found, 'the result may be living alone'. This is more likely for women in Eastern Nigeria than in Western Nigeria. This variation within a country is frequently encountered. Men in Eastern Nigeria were more likely than men in Western Nigeria to retire early.

People in Nigeria were generally of the opinion that less care was available to the old from the family than in the past. This was a subjective view, and the researchers felt that older people tended to romanticize about the past, for which there are few precise data. Reasons given for lesser care included migration of children and inflation.

Ekpenyong, Oyeneye, and Peil interviewed 1,000 older people in depth and found that declining strength is the major reason for giving up work, especially in the farming communities. Economic necessity drives the farmer to work until health makes it impossible. Weakness, poor vision, problems in bending, and arthritis were the main health problems (see Table 4.2). The researchers reported that at 65 years of age, declining strength was affecting 42% of rural men and 56% of rural women. The figures in rural areas were twice those of urban areas.

Few complaints were made about deficient diet or about problems with chewing as a result of losing teeth. Neither was dysentery reported as often as it was probably experienced. The onset of various weakening physical conditions underlined the

TABLE 4.2   *Nigeria: Health Problems of Over-60s in Urban and Rural Areas, 1986 (%)*

Disorder	Urban		Rural	
	Male	Female	Male	Female
General weakness	29	40	54	69
Poor vision	25	20	39	44
Bending problems	14	16	42	46
Arthritis	11	23	34	46
Poor digestion/teeth	6	5	21	24
Other	10	6	21	12
No problems	24	21	13	11

Source: Ekpenyong *et al.* (1986).
Note: Based on sample survey interviews.

general need for alternative, less physical, means of livelihood in rural areas.

Many of the findings of the Nigerians are confirmed by Nana Apt of the University of Ghana.[12] Ghana is passing through a period when half its population is under 18 years of age and the median age of its inhabitants is 11 years. A retirement age exists, but, as only 5% of the population is in organized employment, the vast majority of the elderly population has no social security entitlement and depend on the extended family or local community.

Traditionally, the aged enjoyed status as a principle, as reported by Rosenmayr, and were regarded as a symbol of diety. An affront to an old person was an affront to the gods, and required 'costly expiation'. The relationship with deity and ancestors was so pronounced that the extended family in Ghana included all the descendants of 'the remotest known ancestors'.

Nana Apt considers that the rapid processes of modernization in Ghana has taken only two decades, and that 'getting ahead is almost synonymous with living in the city'. Amenities in urban areas are very attractive compared with those in rural areas.

[12] Apt 1981, confirmed in subsequent presentations to international conferences, such as World Assembly on Aging 1982 and Congress of International Association on Gerontology 1985.

Educated youngsters have no chance of a professional future in their own villages. So 'there is a permanent flow and drain of young and *able-bodied* people from the rural areas to urban centres, leaving the aged behind to tend the farm without much help'.

In one survey by Apt in Ghana, as far back as 1962, 18% of rural households had virtually 'lost contact with their educated children who migrated to the towns'. Of all children ever born to those interviewed, 'only 35% had become what their parents regarded as good providers'. In a ninth of all rural families and a sixth of all urban families studied, no help at all had been given to the old parents.

Apt states that Ghanaian hospital reports since 1966 consistently express concern at the numbers of over-60s who have problems on discharge from hospital treatment because of relatives' reluctance to care for an elderly, bed-ridden person. Hospitals also reported old persons being 'dumped' in their wards by relatives no longer wishing to care for them.

Nana Apt's studies have led her to conclude that the priority concerns for old people in African urban areas are (in order of gravity) housing, loss of status, income, and recreation. In rural areas the main concerns are medical care, nutrition, income, and loss of status.

The trend towards family breakdown is as yet minimal statistically. Most Ghanaians still willingly take responsibility for aged parents. Young people frequently complain of their own financial inability to care as much as they would wish for aged relatives. The overall effect of modernization is pressure on the nuclear family of the younger wage earners to provide for themselves, with little available for aged parents who may be at a distance and inaccessible to personal care. Although Nana Apt hopes for a continued system of family care, the indicators suggest to her that, in comparison with the present generation of people over 60, new generations of elderly are likely to have less help and less security from fewer children. The problem is that not only will people have fewer children, but that because of migration the children will simply be available less to support their aged parents, and frequently less able to contribute material assistance.

An interesting sidelight on the continued dominance of the

older person in rural Africa occurs in a study of Nigerian peasant co-operatives by Chris Beer.[13] In a survey of co-operative committee members, 26.9% were over 65 (in a population where over-65s accounted for less than 4% of the total), 50.5% were aged between 50 and 65. *None* was under 36 years.

Kenyan commentary

It was in a conference organized by HelpAge Kenya in Nairobi that, as mentioned earlier, a Kenyan government official referred to the breakdown of the traditional extended family as having 'completely died off and some traces of it can only be found in particular rural areas'.[14]

In the same conference the Minister for Health referred to the loss of prestige of the elderly whose role had been 'the people who give the answers to all family problems. Regrettably, many factors are now rendering that role obsolete . . . the younger generation, because of formal education, think that they have nothing much to learn from old people.'

Another presentation to the same conference listed the five economic groups into which the elderly were divided:

(i) those retired from government service, with pension;
(ii) those retired from the private sector who might have some benefits put aside for them;
(iii) those retired from self-employment who could have assets such as houses for rent;
(iv) those, none of the above and living in towns, 'could be considered as poor and destitute';
(v) those, none of the above and living on a family farm, might have a share of the farm's income.

A further participant identified the major causes of old people in Kenya being found without support, and claimed that migration was often the root cause:

Most . . . come from other regions of Kenya or from neighbouring countries . . . the majority have little or no family. Some have left their villages so long ago that they have lost contact or are the only surviving members of the family. Others are childless. A few have a family who

---

[13] Beer 1976.
[14] HelpAge Kenya, *Seminar on the Aged*, Nairobi, Aug. 1985.

cannot care for an elderly parent because of unemployment, acute housing conditions, an ailing husband or wife. These families cannot be accused of indifference . . .

Old people in Kenya, as in Zimbabwe, also suffer from the effects of the era of white settlers, which reduced access by elderly Africans to traditional land holdings and rendered both the aged person and the extended family more vulnerable.

Southern Africa

A study in Zimbabwe by Joe Hampson discovered similar trends.[15] Only a year before Hampson's study Zimbabwe gained its independence, and the new government inherited one of the most economically divided nations in the world with great extremes between rich and poor. A pre-Independence survey of the urban African aged found 'half of them living alone, with no regular income, and it was not uncommon to find them having gone without food for one or two days'.

Such conditions are not easily remedied, and Hampson's survey found that

too many lacked even the resources to buy food . . . many elderly in the sample had worked all their lives for subsistence wages and had not been able to save anything for security in retirement . . . The survey demonstrated the existence of gross overcrowding, lack of food and health care, and in general a life of poverty, sometimes of abject destitution.

The elderly who were able-bodied tried to eke out an existence in the twilight zone of informal . . . activities, worrying all the time that the onset of senility or illness would make them even poorer than they were. Those who were disabled or incapable of working had to rely on the extremely meagre resources of family or friends.

As in Rosenmayr's study, in Southern Africa the elder traditionally has absolute authority and, in some cases, an almost superhuman prestige. Shona society refers to the very old person by a word also used for ancestral spirit, indicating a respect towards the old person as 'the living plenipotentiary of the ancestral spirits even before he has died'. Among the Ndebele Sithole the elder was closer to the spirits than younger people. If

[15] Hampson 1982.

the elder died discontented with the behaviour of a younger family member he could carry that discontent over into a spirit world where he could exercise a malign influence on the misbehaver. The destitution often imposed on older people by an industrialized, mobile, and racially divided society is therefore a far cry from the natural African respect for the elder.

In the matter of accommodation, 43% of the sample were paying rent for their mainly two- or three-room dwellings, while 40% were looked after by sons or married daughters. Some four individuals were dependent on friends, six on siblings, and six on grandchildren. Only two were dependent directly on young in-laws, for it is not the custom for older people to live with in-laws in a situation where the natural child is not present.

Of the people interviewed, 40% wre economically engaged in the informal sector 'to ease their condition of near or complete destitution'. In this urban-based society many of the elderly retained their rural plots of land of between 5 and 10 acres. These plots were either tended on a kind of commuter basis so as to supplement food availability, or were left in charge of a relative on a crop-sharing basis. Although the value of such income could not be quantified it is evident that the cash outlay required to travel to the plot would seriously deplete it. In the owner's absence, the crops were frequently distributed among relatives and friends living in the rural location.

Another identified problem which will concern governments in future planning is the extent of international migration, much of it a normal manifestation of work-seeking and not necessarily of the refugee category. In 1967, 14.6% of all aged Africans in the then Rhodesia were from other countries. This proportion has been reduced but non-Zimbabweans were frequently encountered during the Hampson survey of older people. Of a sample of 117 old people, 13 were from Mozambique, 20 from Malawi, and 5 from other countries.

Of all the elderly people surveyed, none had *never* been married and only one had never had children. Almost half had had 7 or more children, with 25 as the record claim by one father. However, very many of the children born had soon died. Of 38 respondents who mentioned deaths of children, 29 had seen 2 or more of their children die. One woman reported 10 of her 11 children dying young. This again underlines the problem of begetting enough children for survival as old-age insurance, as noted in the Potosi study.

As in many areas, the survey encountered difficulties in trying to produce clear statistics for the upper age bands. Few people were able to prove their age if in the upper age brackets. Some claimed to be 'over a 100'. Some referred to their birth dates in vague terms like 'before the white man came to Malawi' or 'before the First World War'.

Much of Hampson's survey was concerned with details about individuals and some of this detail will be referred to in the next chapter.

Dakar Conference résumé

Another conference giving insights into recent developments in ageing in Africa was that organized by the International Center of Social Gerontology in Dakar in December 1984. This brought together representatives from 29 African countries. General consensus was reached on the trends in ageing problems which Africa will have to face over the next decades, and also the root causes of those problems. These have rarely been expressed so adequately and succinctly as by the two African rapporteurs, Professors Nana Apt and Ag Rhaly; who pointed out that

immediately following political independence, African societies abandoned agriculture in favour of industrialization which seemed to them the only way to achieve economic autonomy and assure their development. Urbanization which resulted from this choice deprived the countryside of its most dynamic and innovative manpower. The technological choices made, moreover, have contributed to the marginalization of aged persons whose wisdom is wasted.

It was also pointed out that 'inadequate educational programmes in rural areas have been a determinant factor in rural out-migration and have contributed to the marginalization of older persons'. These problems have been further exacerbated by the encroachment of desert and by extraordinary drought conditions. The conference also stressed the 'scarcity of information in the different fields of ageing in Africa and the clear inadequacy and lack of dissemination of existing information', and the need to adapt the methodology of research to forms appropriate to African culture and concrete realities.

The conference made a considerable contribution towards highlighting the differences between European and African pathologies, citing specifically atherosclerosis which presents distinct biological and clinical aspects as between inhabitants of the two continents. The need arises to avoid risks inherent in borrowing European genetic and health models for African consumption. Outstanding extrinsic factors in African pathology were reported to include nutritional problems, severe tropical endemic diseases, chronic digestive infection, and eye diseases which cause blindness or poor vision, or communicable cosmopolitan diseases (poliomyelitis, hepatitis, etc.)

All these diseases are determinants of the longevity of African peoples as also is the quality of life enjoyed by the aged African. Water and food are seen as particular factors in Africa which can 'from infancy on be a prelude to abnormal ageing'. Housing conditions also contribute to early ageing. In addition to endemic health risks, African society is also under siege from 'modern' psycho-social factors such as mental disorders, alcoholism, tobacco and drug addiction, especially in those countries where tobacco manufacture and brewing are the only flourishing industries. These trends are clear to the eyes of the observer but have not yet been adequately researched in a scientific way.

Asian Trends

Migration in India

Many gerontologists believe that the breakdown of the traditional, extended family is one of the main reasons, if not the prime reason, for most problems of ageing individuals in developing countries. And migration, linked to industrialization, modernization, and urbanization, is seen as probably the major factor in the breakdown of the extended family. It is therefore appropriate that the first study to be cited in this section should be related to migration in a developing country.

In 1983 an Indian case-study was prepared for the International Labour Office by Oberai and Singh.[16] Its title was *Causes and Consequences of Internal Migration*, and it was based on surveys in

[16] A. S. Oberai and H. K. Manmohan Singh, the former a senior economist in the ILO, the latter professor of economics at the Punjabi University, Patiala.

the Punjab. Whilst the gerontologist may be inclined to view migration as a negative factor, the authors point out that 'migration may, indeed, yield substantial benefits to individual migrants and their families and, at the same time, have a positive and significant impact on economic development'.

Among the findings of the survey, which covered about 4,700 households, was that migration is still on the increase, and that out-migration from rural areas was the most forceful movement. It also revealed that districts in which there is agricultural development may well be a focus of migration into that district from other, less progressive agricultural areas.

The majority of migrants are young adults (15–29 years) and they tend to be better educated than their peers who do not migrate. This therefore signifies a qualitative loss in rural populations as well as a quantitative loss. While in some regions it is assumed that migration owes much to the small size of holdings and the constant division of inheritances, the Punjab study found migration to be low where holdings were under 5 acres. Education and economic reasons were found to be more important incentives to migration than the improved amenities of the city. Relatively educated young people from rural areas moved into cities in search of jobs commensurate with their level of education, while other young people migrated in order to gain access to better educational and training facilities.

Educational levels appear to have little bearing upon whether a migrant sends remittances to those who remain at home. And, surprisingly, the new level of income in the city also has little general effect on whether the migrant remits or not. There is a tendency for migrants from 'cultivating households' to remit less frequently, perhaps because they consider the home family has a supply of life's necessities from the land.

Migrants who leave their own country tend to remit larger sums of money than those who emigrate within the country. On the other hand, migrants to other agricultural regions are as generous with their remittances as migrants to urban areas. The size of the remittances tends to vary according to the family's own basic financial circumstances; poor families do not receive more than rich families. However, in many cases, the remittance to the less-well off although intrinsically low, may constitute the entire income of the home-based group.

Possibly the most significant factor, as far as the elderly are concerned, is that the greatest variations in remittances relate to the relationship between the migrant and the persons at the home base. About 50% of migrants do not remit. The most likely to remit are the parent or parents of younger family remaining at home. Those least likely to remit (as few as 26% of those migrating to urban areas) are migrants leaving older relatives at home. The survey of urban households also revealed that immigrants living in the city tend to decrease their remittances home to rural areas after a period of time.

Another related factor is the impact which migration appears to have on fertility. Migrants into urban areas tend to have lower fertility, partly because of modernized ideas and partly because of the economic and accommodation constraints of city life, as also the alternatives for leisure. Home-based families in the rural areas tend to have a lower fertility rate because of separation of spouses and also the import of more modernized concepts. Overall, migration has the effect of delaying marriages generally and thus further reducing fertility. As already observed, the reduction of the fertility rate accelerates the ageing rate of the population as a whole and also reduces the number of children upon whom ageing parents can rely for support as they themselves become less able to work.

Bombay studies

Reference has been made earlier in this chapter to the incidence of socio-economic effects of migration in India having particular impact on the rural aged.

In Bombay, Dr J. D. Pathak has for many years been carrying out surveys which give both general and specific medical information on life for the urban Indian of older years.[17] Like so many observers in other countries, he sees the culture of his own country breaking down in the wake of industrialization. He regards the younger generation of Indians as 'apparently more tolerant than their counterparts in the West and 70% of our old in the towns are accommodated with their families. Only 5% live alone (compared to 30% in Britain in a contemporary study) and

[17] Pathak 1975, 1978, 1985.

10% with their spouse. The rest have varying types of arrangements though not satisfactory.'

Over a period of decades, life expectancy has increased dramatically in India and is projected to continue increasing at an even more rapid rate, as in Table 4.3. In order to acquire reliable data, Pathak carried out one survey with only educated old people able to respond accurately to questions. Of these, 81.3% lived with their families, 13.4% with their spouse, and 3.3% lived alone. The average size of family was 5.26 persons. This sample was obviously biased towards middle-class and educated working-class people. Even so, 72% of them said their uppermost problems were financial; 29% complained mainly of health; 19% of adjustment to the family; 13% of lack of proper accommodation.

TABLE 4.3   *India: Life Expectancy at Birth, 1901–2020*

Year	Males		Females
1901	22.6		23.3
1921	30.0		26.6
1941	32.5		31.7
1961	47.0		45.6
1981	(all)	52.5	
2000		60.7	
2020		67.9	

Source: Pathak (1985).

In another survey, older men were found to consume about 1,600 calories daily and women 1,250 calories. Not surprisingly, most 'showed grey hair, wrinkles and obvious signs of ageing before they were 60'. Pathak's detailed nutritional study provides Tables 4.4 and 4.5. In respect of psychological factors Pathak found only 8.5% of older men and 11.5% of women depressed, whilst 24.1% men and 20.6% women were positively interested in life.

Visual reaction time for the elderly, covering a sample of men of average age 67.0 years and women of 62.7 years, was found to be delayed by 50% compared with persons in their 20s: 86% of subjects needed plus glasses and 8%, being myopic, needed

TABLE 4.4   *Bombay: Per Capita Food Intake of the Elderly, by Sex, 1985*
(g/day)

Food	Men	Women
Wheat	135.1	111.3
Rice	53.3	46.6
Pulses	39.4	27.4
Vegetables	174.9	125.2
Fruits	147.2	126.8
Fats–oils	18.1	13.9
Sugar	29.1	25.9
Milk	315.9	206.8
Buttermilk	156.5	112.1
Curd	83.6	64.6
Eggs	57.1	52.9

Source: Pathak (1985).
Note: Based on sample of 240 men and 60 women.

TABLE 4.5   *Nutritional Value of Food Consumed by the Elderly in Bombay, by Sex, 1985*

	Males	Females
Calories/day	1,590 + 493.8	1,241 + 361.5
Calories/kg	26.65	21.66
Protein (g/day)	52.0 + 24.2	42.0 + 15.5
Animal protein (g)	15.5	10.8
Protein/kg	0.87	0.73
Fat (g/day)	40.0 + 16.5	30.0 + 17.2
Carbohydrate (g)	254.0 + 161.9	200.0 + 70.7
Minerals		
Ca, (g)	1.0 + 0.47	0.6 + 0.27
PO^4, (g)	1.0 + 0.42	1.0 + 0.34
Fe, (mg, %)	20.0 + 6.9	15.25 + 5.5
Vitamins		
A IU	5,750 + 324.5	4,053 + 1,757.2
B_1 (mg)	0.7 + 0.31	0.6 + 0.62
B_2 (mg)	1.0 + 0.52	0.9 + 0.4
B_7 (mg)	5.0 + 3.3	4.1 + 2.8
C (mg)	44.0 + 20.0	51 + 25.3

Source: Pathak (1985).

minus glasses. At 60 years of age, 2.5% of men and 7% of women had already been operated for cataract; 72% showed incipient cataract at various stages. Pathak observed that not only was the incidence of cataract higher in the tropics, its onset was also earlier. He presumes reasons for ophthalmic problems to include exposure to bright light, faulty reading habits, working conditions, nutritional deficiencies, etc. He also thinks that 'a genetic factor cannot be ruled out . . . Indians acquire opacities earlier and oftener'. Hence the importance of ophthalmic programmes, especially those making treatment available at low cost, as described in Chapter 7.

Pathak analysed his 1970 case papers to calculate incidence of multipathology and discovered an average of 2.5 multiple troubles per head. Repeating the process in 1980 he calculated 2.1 per head. He points out that this is low compared with some European statistics showing 4 or 5 serious disorders per head, but elsewhere indicates that Indians are less likely to complain or identify symptoms spontaneously. This would suggest a need for more screening programmes for the elderly.

He makes an interesting case for expanding geriatrics as a medical discipline in developing countries. Table 4.6 indicates the local incidence of illness in children up to 12 years of age and

TABLE 4.6   *Bombay: Incidence of Illness in Children and the Elderly in Two Hospitals (Percentage of patients of the age group suffering from a particular disease for more than one year)*

Disease	Children	Old people
Lymph and blood	5.49	2.09
Cardiovascular	2.55	23.90
Respiratory	11.77	8.64
Gastro-intestinal	20.83	11.68
Urogenital	6.26	17.87
Nervous	13.76	9.82
Eyes, ears	2.08	7.45
Orthopaedic	4.85	9.82
Others[a]	32.24	8.64

Source: Pathak (1978).
   [a] Fevers etc. in children, diabetes and cancer in old people.

old people over 60 years. Analysing this he underlines the fact that children suffer from *acute* infections, quickly cured or fatal. The elderly are prone to *chronic* diseases uncommon in younger years. He says 'this fact alone is sufficient argument to introduce geriatrics, like pediatrics, as a separate medical discipline, academically and practically in India', and presumably in other similar developing countries.

Older women appear to be affected by certain local conditions. Pathak believes that earlier ageing in women in India is related to the earlier termination of menstruation in tropical countries. Frequent child-bearing may also have several negative effects. He found that 58% of older women had had a hysterectomy, and that 43% of cancers occurring in older women were sited in the genital organs.

As a medical researcher looking at all aspects of ageing, Pathak observed that older people regarded themselves as satisfactorily healthy although in fact they suffered from osteoporosis, kyphosis, stooping posture, cloudy vision, cataract, giddiness, atherosclerosis, inefficient heart, laboured breathing, poor appetite, malnutrition, wasting, weakness and similar handicaps. He commented that psychologically their activities were nominal, their mental outlook morose, frustrated, and unworthy, as they await their inevitable finale. He tempers this pessimistic assessment by subscribing to the WHO commitment of 'health for all' by the year 2000, and puts forward the view that 'a correct symbol of civilisation of any society is how it arranges for the evening of life of its members'.

Ageing in the Western Pacific

In the Western Pacific study already referred to, the countries studied were Fiji, South Korea, Malaysia, and the Philippines.[18] The first significant factor to emerge was the difference in marital status according to sex. The greatest variation was noted in urban areas of Fiji, where 82% of elderly men were still married

[18] G. R. Andrews, A. J. Esterman, A. J. Braunack-Mayer, and C. M. Rungie, all Australians. Gary Andrews has carried out a number of projects with the WHO and is now Chairman of the Department of Primary Health at Flinders University, South Australia.

but 52% of elderly women were widows. A similar disparity was reflected in all four countries for both urban and rural areas. Among the over-80s in the Philippines more than 80% of men were still married compared with about 20% of women. Among the over-80s in Korea more than 80% of women were widows, whereas only about 40% of men were widowed.

As regards education, there was a large group in both urban and rural areas who had no formal education at all. This ranged from 27% of all elderly people in Fiji to 91% of elderly females in rural areas of Korea. There was a tendency throughout the four countries for 'older aged' to have had less formal education than 'younger aged', although this pattern was not universal. The least educated cohorts of females in Fiji were ages 70–4 and 65–9, but generally, people over 80 had less formal education than people aged 60–4.

When asked for a subjective reaction on the question of health, more than half of all those studied in all four countries considered themselves healthy. On the other hand, when asked about some problem which 'impinged on functional ability', 59% of older people in Fiji reported some such problem, the percentages ranging from 52% of women aged 60–4 up to 71% of women aged 80 or more. (This still left 29% of over-80s reporting no problems at all.) In the Philippines the problems were higher, and in Korea and Malaysia lower. Conditions identified included hypertension, tuberculosis, peptic ulcers, heart disease, asthma, and unspecified abdominal pains.

A considerable proportion of the sample found difficulty in chewing (60%, 57%, 48%, and 33% for the various countries surveyed), and this difficulty could have had adverse effects on their choice of diet and their level of nutrition. Visual impairment was an even more serious affliction. Those reporting impaired vision in at least one eye reached 81% in the Philippines, 75% in Fiji, and 68% in Malaysia. It has to be remembered, too, that in some places ophthalmological services may be inaccessible or inadequate, and that availability of spectacles at convenient prices is not universal. While problems of walking (300 metres) appeared lesser in comparison, with 42% in Fiji, 29% in Philippines, and 15% in both Korea and Malaysia, the ability to walk distances is essential where the elder has to continue to work, often in competition with younger workers, or in order to purchase the staples of life in conditions of physical hardship.

Most old people surveyed were able to care for themselves in the normal tasks of daily living, such as getting in and out of bed or eating and dressing. A significant number of over-80s had problems with management of money (29% of women in Fiji), with travelling beyond walking distance, and, especially in rural areas, with incontinence. While the survey warns against too rigid a judgement on such issues as management of money, usually handled by younger people in Asian society, these problems do assume supreme importance if the family link has broken down.

The survey took note of the important question of mental health and found frequent incidence of early depressive and paranoic states. As noted earlier, the problems were much less frequently found in the Philippines than in other countries (4% depressed as against 14%, 26% and 34.5% in the other countries; and 19% who reported having 'lost interest' as against 31%, 39%, and 65% in the other countries). This could be related to the comparative stability of the Philippines population. It was noted that throughout the four countries, those who believed they did not have sufficient financial resources to cope were more likely to have a lower cognitive score and a higher incidence of mental problems.

The study compared loneliness in developed countries (1% of elderly Danes, 7% of elderly British, and 9% of elderly Americans reported as lonely in a corresponding study) with the countries surveyed. Except for the Philippines these countries reported a higher incidence of loneliness: 10% in Malaysia, 22% in Korea, and 24% in Fiji. The most contributory factor in loneliness appeared to be separation from the family, followed by widowhood, insufficient income, and unemployment. Although to the visitor sanitation and housing appeared poor, this did not coincide with the perception of the local elderly themselves. Relatively few of the sample had complaints about the accessibility of basic services such as water and toilet, and reports of poor housing were equally few, ranging from less than 1% in urban Philippines to 12% in urban Korea.

In two countries, most of those surveyed did not see family or friends often enough (Fiji 60%, Korea 58%). In Malaysia and the Philippines a majority did report seeing family and friends with sufficient frequency, a still substantial minority appeared to be out of contact (17% in Malaysia and 29% in the Philippines). The extent to which elders helped care for their grandchildren varied from 41% to 71%, but the implication that between 29% and 59% did not seems to indicate some hiatus in the close, extended family system of more primitive societies.

A further revealing statistic relates to the sources of income as set out in Table 4.7. This is supplemented by Table 4.8, which comments on the inadequacy of that income. Unfortunately, the survey was not able to test the adequacy or quality of the family support on which so many depended.

TABLE 4.7   *Sources of Income for Over-60s, Four Western Pacific Countries, 1986 (%)*

	Males	Females
Fiji		
Work	16	11
Family	28	40
Pension/welfare	14	12
Other	42	37
Korea		
Work	28	19
Family	60	67
Pension/welfare	5	6
Other	7	8
Malaysia		
Work	30	19
Family	42	62
Pension/welfare	23	14
Other	5	5
Philippines		
Work	32	22
Family	39	54
Pension/welfare	18	13
Other	13	11

Source: Andrews et al. (1986).

TABLE 4.8   *Adequacy of Income for Over-60s, Four Western Pacific Countries,* *1986*

Country	Males	Females
Fiji	56	53
Korea	31	30
Malaysia	8	8
Philippines	42	44

Source: Andrews *et al.* (1986).
Note: Figures indiçate percentage who consider they do *not* have enough money for basic needs.

Bangladesh survey

A survey carried out in Bangladesh in June 1985 found that 85% of the country's population still resides in rural areas, but also noted the rural–urban migration of the young and able bodied.[19] However, landlessness increased in rural areas from 20% of the population to over 50% in the course of three decades. Although landlordism of the old type has been legally abolished, 'the old feudal lords were replaced by a new class of exploitative surplus farmers combining the roles of farmer-cum-trader-cum-money-lender'.

In Bangladesh, 70% of households are nuclear, comprising parents and unmarried children. The traditional rural extended family is composed of several *khanas* (nuclear households) bound by kinship derived from paternal and maternal lineages and living in a compound within a village or beyond the village. The elderly are the *murubbi* or guardians of the immediate family and extended family as well as of the community as a whole. There is therefore no normal reason for alienation of the grandparents.

One striking fact in the Ibrahim study is the disparity between males and females over 60 in respect to marital circumstances, as indicated in Table 4.9. Remarriage of widows is 'culturally restricted'. Female dependence is normal throughout the stages of life, and accentuated by the frequency of widowhood in old age, when the dependency of the woman is upon the sons rather than upon the spouse. At the same time the older man has the

[19] Ibrahim 1985.

TABLE 4.9 *Bangladesh: Marital Patterns* (%)

	Never married	Currently married	Widowed	Divorced
Male over 60	0.7	90.7	8.6	–
Female over 60	0.5	32.9	66.5	0.2

Percentage married twice or more

	15–19	25–29	35–39	45–49	55–59	60–64	65–69	70+
Males	4.8	9.6	15.1	22.3	29.4	30.2	33.3	34.1
Females	3.9	7.5	10.6	11.2	10.6	9.7	9.4	9.5

Source: Ibrahim (1985).

services of younger consecutive wives to benefit him, without the same stigma of dependency.

Ninety per cent of elderly males in Bangladesh are heads of households; female heads of households are rare, but their number is growing because women increasingly have 'no grown-up sons or no son at all'. Some of the elderly females are found to rely on the married daughter and the son-in-law to manage family property, especially land. However, most households headed by females over 60 are either destitute or beg for their livelihood. Of the old people surveyed, 70% received some form of financial help, 55% of them from their children. Support from children was lowest in the city and highest in rural areas.

The attitudes of the younger people towards them were considered satisfactory by 82% of old men and 95% of old women; 29% thought that old age had brought them more respect, but 26% thought that respect for them had decreased because of age. Only 5% thought themselves to be in good health; 84% had some complaint about health and 11% felt themselves to be in bad health. Among younger people, 55.6% had a good opinion of older men and 71.1% had a good opinion of older women. The younger people's observations as to the health of their elders coincided very closely with the older people's own opinions. Younger people thought their elders had suffered total mental loss in 5.3% of cases, and partial loss in 21.1%. Surprisingly, in 28.9% of cases young people thought their elders were better mentally as they aged.

One stark economic fact which emerged was that income was inversely related to dependency. Where old people existed with most dependency on younger people, those younger people had least economic resources available to meet the needs of the elders.

Ageing in China

Any study of ageing in developing countries which ignores China is, of course, ignoring a significant part of the world's population. China has been cut off from Western society for many years, and it has often been ignored in international studies because of lack of information. However, demographers and policy-makers in

China are well aware of the problems of their increasing numbers of aged.

Some of the research findings have been analysed by two American sociologists who spent time in China during 1983 and have ready access to scholars and officials there.[20] Alice and Sidney Goldstein point out that the problems of the ageing of China's population are made unique not only by the immense numbers involved but also by the long-term implications of China's one-child family policy. The 1982 census in China recorded 49.3 million persons aged 65 years and over. At that time only one African country (Nigeria) had a *total* population of all ages larger than China's aged total. And only two Latin American countries and four other Asian countries had *total* populations larger than China's aged population.

The Chinese demographer Tian estimates a rise in the proportion of aged people from 4.9% of the total population in 1978 to 20.3% in 2040, with an increase in total number of persons over 65 to 232 million. By 2040, China could have 23% *more* persons over 65 than children under 15. Even by the year 2000 Tian would anticipate a total of 90 million persons over 65. Other projections by Chinese and non-Chinese demographers tend to agree generally with the trends projected by Tian.

Traditionally in China the elder held high status, for in a generally illiterate society experience was the main source of knowledge. As in some African societies the very old were regarded as being close to the prestige of ancestors. Although the international image of China still portrays a tendency to gerontocracy in the very highest political positions, the Communist revolution since 1949 has given the youth a very conspicuous role at various levels of power and influence. The emphasis on productivity has also enabled the young worker to claim recognition on a par with the elder.

Perhaps more seriously in its impact on a traditional social structure, the global use of the work unit within the commune structure 'de-emphasized the family as the basic unit of production and thereby weakened the position of its oldest members'. The young also took most advantage of the new educational opportunities. Respect is still insisted on and inter-generational co-operation has been encouraged.

[20] Goldstein and Goldstein 1986.

The 1982 Constitution required that 'children who have come of age have the duty to support and assist their parents'. Under the 1980 Marriage Law, parents who have lost the ability to earn have the right to demand that children pay for their support. If the immediate children have died, the legal duty devolves upon grandchildren who are of age to work. The Criminal Code of 1981 imposes a sanction of up to five years imprisonment for flagrant failure to comply.

In this insistence on the duty of the children, China has run into a problem of contradiction in that the one-child family policy 'not only subverts the traditional values favouring large families, but especially jeopardizes the system of social security that depends on children's support of elderly parents'. The patrilocal system means that where a couple's one child happens to be a daughter, she will, on marriage, move away to the husband's home, leaving her parents bereft of both child and possible grandchildren. Where the removal is to a distant region this produces a conflict between the intention of the law and the realities of life.

At the same time the dearth of children is removing one of the traditional duties of grandparents, that of caring for the multiple grandchildren while the parents are working in the fields. In many cases, one grandchild may have to be shared among four grandparents.

The official system of job allocation requires that, on graduation, students must accept assignments to whatever part of China requires their skills. Many inevitably find locations far removed from their parents in a vast country where communications may not always be of the easiest. Where rural youths obtain urban work assignments, the housing regulations aimed at containing urban growth may make it impossible for other members of the family to join them.

At the same time, the Chinese system encourages the development of smallholdings from which produce can be sold in free markets. As this type of work is traditional for older people, it offers one means of income maintenance. Numbers of older people have also become vendors in the free markets.

In non-agricultural work, it is customary in China for the child to inherit the job of the father. As some 4 million youngsters enter the labour market annually, there is frequently pressure from the school-leaver upon the parent to 'retire' so that the child can then inherit the job, no other being available in the open market.

Many older people are used as volunteers, sometimes with a minimal reward, as inspectors maintaining regulations in free markets or as trainers continuing to use their technical skills in factories on a part-time basis after retirement. Many more have no resources and, as one Chinese social researcher interested in the problems of his nation's aged commented, 'many are just waiting to die'.

The Goldsteins comment that on the whole China's elderly 'are probably better off today than they were in the past'. The major problem lies in the enormous additional numbers of aged who will have to be absorbed into the nation's economy and social life, and their relative increase in relation to younger age groups. The index of ageing (taking over-65s as a ratio of the total population under 15) may rise from 13.7 to 33.5 by the year 2000. It could even rise, according to Tian's *middle* projection, to 123. If the ratio is related to the aged as a proportion of those of 'working age', the rise could be from 9.2 at present to 32.3 in 2040. This has grave implications in a country where the traditional age insurance of depending upon one's children requires an index of ageing no higher than at present.

Maltese Research

Turning to the Mediterranean region, an unusually exhaustive study was carried out in Malta in 1982 by the Centre for Social Research, with well over a hundred persons collaborating as researchers, interviewers, and in other capacities.[21] The report clearly indicated that

old age is more a continuing process of change rather than a process of loss and decline, and includes adaption and compensation to such changes psychologically and socially. Genetically determined character-istics . . . are modified by a number of environmental factors such as diet, exercise, whether or not the individual smokes, etc.

The report isolated two statistical factors which may be of use to students trying to correct forecasts from regions where base data

---

[21] Malta, Centre for Social Research 1982.

is neither so accessible nor so accurate as in Malta. The Central Office of Statistics figure for people over 60 years of age, based on the electoral register, was found for various reasons to be 4.4% less than the true figure as discovered by the survey. One reason for this was doubts about accuracy of persons' ages, doubts which sometimes cannot be fully resolved.

The Central Office projections for 2000 and beyond were based on zero migration, assuming that the number of out-migrants from Malta during the period would be cancelled out by the number of return migrants, a reasonable assumption on the basis of recent trends. However, if applied across the age bands, this would be misleading. Out-migrants from Malta tend to belong to age groups up to 30 years. Return migrants belong mainly to the 35 to 50 age group. This bias will therefore weigh the population towards an older profile than the average projection for the nation.

Trends of ageing in Malta correspond to trends for the developing world as a whole. The median age has risen from 26.8 years in 1948 through 31.4 in 1977 towards a projected 36.3 in 2010. Expectation of life has increased from 41.35 years at birth in 1930 to 68.49 years in 1980.

However, within these general trends, unexpected subtrends can be discovered by exhaustive investigation. For instance, life expectancy for Maltese men up to 45 years of age has shown a consistent gain from 1948 to 1980. But life expectancy for men aged 55 and over has actually *declined* during that period. The decline between 1948 and 1980 has been by 10 months for men aged 55, 25 months for men aged 65, and 33 months for men aged 75. The same decline is noticed for women. So, as the report says 'More men and women are living longer than 60 years today than they used to in 1948, but the probability is that they will, on average, live a shorter life than those who survived the 60 year mark thirty years ago!' So increase in the mere life expectancy at birth indicator does not necessarily mean longer lives for most people.

Another illuminating discovery, illustrating the differences that can occur within small regions, is the difference in longevity between Malta and Gozo, two small neighbouring islands of the same nation. On Gozo, one person in five is aged 60 or more, on Malta, only one in nine is 60 or more. The projected level of people over 60 in Malta as a percentage of the total population in the year 2010 is 16.5%. Yet in Gozo it is already 21%.

A further difference between the two islands is that on Malta 62.3% of people aged over 60 are concentrated in the 60–9 bracket. On Gozo only 52.3% of over 60s are in the 60–9 band, with the rest exceeding 70 years.

People over 60 who live alone constitute 19.8% of the elderly population who are not residing in homes for the elderly. More than 64% of the 'loners' are females. The disparity between sexes in marital circumstances, noted in other countries, is again true: 71% of men were still married compared with 40.9% of women. Only 13.7% of men were widowed compared to 39.9% of women.

To 752 respondents who were married at some time, 3,984 children had been born. The average number of children born per family was 5.3 of whom 4.3 lived beyond childhood. Some 33% of the respondents had never attended school or had less than primary education; only 3% had proceeded beyond secondary education, and 1% had technical training. Females were disadvantaged in respect of secondary and tertiary education compared with males.

All old people in Malta have some pension or benefit income: on examination of home circumstances only 2.3% of over-60s were described as 'poor', while the situation of 44.5% was considered 'modest', and 9.5% were even observed to be 'well off'. The considerable figure of 50% owned their own house, but, perhaps surprisingly, the lower level of formal education the *more* likely an old person was to own a house. This is probably related to the fact that the majority of the less educated engaged in agricultural pursuits and owned land.

For people over 60, education directly affected the level of income. Those without education had an income of 1,035 Maltese pounds (Lm), those with primary education had Lm 1,121, those with secondary education Lm 1,484, and those with tertiary education Lm 2,090. Of those with an income in excess of Lm 2,000, only 2.8% had been involved in agriculture and only 1% in industry: 20.5% came from commerce, 26% were professionals, and 22% clerical workers. Of all over 60s, 77% considered that their income was sufficient. Only 9% received financial aid from their families.

The problems of daily living posed no problems to 80% of those surveyed, 15% needed help, and 5% needed 'custodial care'. Loneliness was felt by 19% but only 11% felt 'useless'. Loneliness was generally the characteristic of people with low incomes, those who only sleep for a couple of hours at night, and those who have no hobbies within the home. Widowhood, living alone, and confinement to bed showed significant relationship with the feeling of loneliness. The level of education was also a major factor with a significant majority of the lonely having had very little education. The 'guilt' feeling of being a burden on the family was also a factor.

The Caribbean

Jamaica

Mention was made earlier of a study on Belize, a country which, although located on the mainland of Central America, has many cultural characteristics of the Caribbean communities. Many of the ageing factors evident in Belize are reflected through the Caribbean.

One of the most eminent age-care practitioners of the Caribbean, Sybil Francis, says:

It is somewhat of a paradox that, while the gift of long life for the many is a direct consequence of twentieth century development, other aspects of that development seriously threaten the ability of the elderly to maintain meaningful roles, or to enjoy the extra years in conditions of dignity, security and happiness. In the Caribbean, as elsewhere, the increasing numbers of elderly in times of rapid social and economic change present numerous challenges both to the elderly themselves and to the society at large.

Like Belize, Sybil Francis's own country, Jamaica, is affected by out-migration to Europe and North America. Jamaica is also large enough to have its own internal migration patterns, so that the major factor causing breakdown of the extended family has two different manifestations as contrasted to Belize.[22] This produces variations in levels of family support or abandonment,

[22] Francis 1987.

whereas in Belize, or the Peruvian Andes, abandonment of an elderly individual is frequently total.

Another Caribbean authority, Dr Henry Frazer, is quoted as saying:

In the Caribbean, mass emigration of young adults in the nineteen fifties and sixties, followed in most cases by their children, has compounded the problem (of the elderly) by removing from the society many of the sons and daughters of the present over-sixty-fives, the present 'middle-aged' or 'caring' age group.

This absence of the middle of the three predominant generations is most remarkable in Barbados, where the percentage of over-65s in the population is only 9.4%. It has the lowest ratio of middle-aged persons, with only 2.4 'working-age' persons for each elderly person. The ratio in Jamaica is 3 : 1, and neighbouring Trinidad and Tobago has a 6 : 1 ratio. And even these stark statistics are far from illustrating the whole truth, for in a ratio of 2.4 : 1 or 3 : 1 it cannot be assumed that every one of the 2.4 or 3 middle-aged persons is directly related to one elderly person. Many middle-aged persons are orphaned or remote from the grandparents. In other families the one grandparent is still surrounded by many grandchildren. And, of course, many of the grandparents are married and share grandchildren. So the bare statistical ratios quoted for Jamaica and Barbados imply a very considerable number of grandparents without middle-age links.

Francis also points out the inter-generational importance of grandparents in Caribbean society. In Jamaica, with a total of no more than 208,911 persons over the age of 60 in 1982, it was estimated that as many as 100,000 mothers (working locally or migrant) leave their children in the care of grandparents, and that the children so cared for number at least 125,000. One person cited in the study was a great-great-grandmother who at the age of 78 'was still caring full-time for several of her great-great-grandchildren. She had lost track of the number of grandchildren who had passed through her care.'

Jamaica's birth rate declined from 42.5 per 1,000 in 1960 to 25.2 in 1984. The death rate declined from 8.9 per 1,000 in 1960 to 5.9 in 1984. Infant mortality rates also declined from 32.2 in 1970 to 13.2 in 1984. Statistics confirm that 'more women than men survive into old age. The differential increases with age, and from age 85 years there were, in 1982, more than twice as many women as men.'

In a survey, almost 50% of the rural elderly in Jamaica were found to be living on their own. Of those living with younger people, 36% had left their previous dwelling to do so. In 16% of the cases, younger relatives had come to live with the elders. In the remaining very few cases the young and old had always lived together in the same house. Reasons for sharing accommodation included retracted family size due to migration, economic security, illness, and physical security (5% of the old people studied had been victims of crime). Of those who lived with younger people, 25% felt younger for doing so, 21% felt safer, 16% had a 'sense of belonging' and 10% recorded feeling more useful and in better health.

The types of illness recorded were: cardiac diseases, 5%; loss of hearing, 14%; blindness, 20%; arthritis, 25%; multiple pathologies, 36%. A significant statistic refers to deaths in an infirmary (chronic nursing home): of the 68 deaths recorded over a period, 37 old persons died within the first six months of residence. In the entire sample, between 14% and 15% were recorded as non-coherent. These infirmary statistics illustrate the effects of institutionalization, a syndrome which is considered further in Chapter 6.

As regards marital circumstances, 15% declared concubinage; 27% had formerly been married, of whom 5% were separated and 2% divorced. In 12% of cases the partner had died or the remaining spouse was unaware of the partner's whereabouts. Almost half (48%—30% were male and 18% female) had never formed a stable marital relationship.

Various studies have pointed out the importance of the elder for the survival and transmission of Caribbean culture, which is largely an adaptation of West African cultures flourishing in an alien environment and tinged by contacts with many diverse societies.

The elderly in Jamaica are being encouraged to recall this 'patrimony' which is thought, in some cases, to be more than a social message. Music, singing, and particularly drumming has been used traditionally in Jamaica as a kind of psychiatric resource. It is used to get rid of jealousy, hatred, anger, resentment. Singing it out, dancing it out, crying it out, and drumming it out were proven means of psychological relief from the sorrows and the burden of guilt or ill-feeling. Certain types of music could even 'put the *bosy* (evil influence) out of the way' and induce a state of trance.

Barbados

One of the most intensive studies of ageing in a developing country was carried out by Farley Braithwaite in Barbados and published in 1986.[23] This gives a total view of the life of an elderly person in Barbados, ranging from obvious factors such as economic conditions to less apparent factors such as attitudes to death and dying. As elsewhere, the statistics show a steady increase in both the gross and percentage numbers of elderly in Barbados, except for the years immediately following the Second World War (see Table 4.10).

TABLE 4.10   *Barbados: Total Population and Over-60s, 1871–1980*

Year	Total Population	Over-60s	% Over-60s	% Increase
1871	162,042	6,942	4.3	—
1881	173,860	8,716	5.0	+0.7
1891	182,867	10,354	5.7	+0.7
1911	172,337	12,083	7.0	+1.3
1921	156,774	13,299	8.4	+1.4
1946	190,800	16,851	8.8	+0.4
1960	232,327	14,867	6.4	−2.4
1970	235,229	19,499	8.3	+1.9
1980	244,228	25,501	10.5	+2.2

Source: Braithwaite (1986).

Another set of statistics adapted by Braithwaite might possibly point to a racial factor in survivability. While some of the samples may not be large enough to be statistically significant, there is in Table 4.11 some hint of a tendency for 'whites' and 'Portuguese' to have a good survival rate, their percentage in the population actually increasing with the ageing process. On the

---

[23] See Braithwaite (ed.) 1986.

TABLE 4.11   *Barbados: Racial Distribution, Total Population and Over-60s, 1980*

Race	Total population		Over-60s	
	No.	%	No.	%
Black	224,565	91.9	23,050	90.4
East Indian	1,257	0.5	43	0.16
Chinese	66	0.03	4	0.02
Amerindian	39	0.02	2	0.01
Portuguese	101	0.04	18	0.07
Syrian/Lebanese	90	0.04	3	0.01
White	7,593	3.1	1,337	5.2
Mixed	6,362	2.6	776	3.04
Other	134	0.05	8	0.03
n.a.	3,661	1.5	260	1.0
TOTAL	244,228	100.0	25,501	100.00

Source: Braithwaite (1986).

other hand, a decline is evident among the majority 'blacks', and a very severe decline among 'East Indians' (people originating from India, probably some generations ago). This may not reflect a genetic potential for survival but it may be the reflection of economic capacity to obtain adequate nutrition and other living conditions throughout the life span; however, it could also reflect out-migration on the part of the 'black' and 'East Indian' populations.

When asked about their economic conditions by Braithwaite's team of researchers, 31.9% of the elderly felt that they had serious economic problems, and only 42.9% stated that they had no financial problems at all. The deterioration in finances suffered by the elderly was highlighted in that those receiving less than 50 Barbados dollars a week comprised 75% of all elderly while only 25% of the non-elderly population came within that income bracket. Of the sample, 15.2% were still in formal employment, but 18.8% found it necessary to engage in informal employment. Some of this economic activity was very sporadic and low-key, such as selling sweets and nuts.

An important point elicited by Braithwaite was that

whereas the findings here . . . bear out the findings . . . about Third World societies that kinship network support is widespread, they *do not bear out the conventional view* that the elderly are the recipients of widespread financial support from their relatives because *only a third* said that they received such support.

On the subject of intake of food, 60% reported 'good', 30% said 'so so', and 10% 'bad'. When further investigated, 8.5% had eaten no meal in the past twenty-four hours, while 10% had eaten only one meal. This 18.5% represented mainly low-income households. However, those living alone ate *better* than those not living alone. Males ate less frequently than females. A majority had an intake of protein-rich food (meat, fish, dairy products), and also energy-rich food (cereals, starch, sugar, fats, oils). The significant deficiency was in protective foods such as vegetables and fruits. This last factor may reveal a lack of nutritional knowledge, for it might be assumed that fruits and vegetables would be available in Barbados.

Housing was considered by 81.5% to be satisfactory, with 82% of the sample owning their own house; 68.7% had water piped into the house and 47.2% had water closet latrines. Most of the remainder (50.6%) used pit latrines. Some 81% had electric lighting but 37% depended on wood or kerosene for cooking.

Table 4.12 clearly indicates the decrease in household sizes with age, although the variation in size of house itself is minimal, suggesting that many old people continue to live in the family's traditional house (see also Table 4.13).

When asked about their worst perceived problems, 47.8% of the Braithwaite sample identified financial problems, and 16.5% were most worried about health, and 9.6% cited loneliness. Those concerned about loneliness included those living alone, persons aged over 75 years, and those who had never married. Also unexpectedly included in the list of the lonely were many former white collar workers and those having had post-primary education. The working years' advantages of salary and qualification do not compensate for retirement losses of contact in developing, as in developed, countries.

When asked about their major fears as opposed to actual

TABLE 4.12   *Barbados: Size of Households Headed by Over-60s and among the Total Population, 1980*

Size of household	Total population		Over-60s	
	No.	%	No.	%
1	11,501	19.6	4,208	31.8
2	10,438	17.8	3,597	27.2
3	8,153	13.9	1,847	14.0
4	7,116	12.1	1,115	8.4
5	5,772	9.9	789	6.0
6	4,670	8.0	579	4.4
7	3,992	6.8	393	3.0
8	2,488	4.2	226	2.0
9	1,679	2.9	139	1.1
10	1,100	1.9	118	0.9
11	679	1.2	59	0.4
12	410	0.7	45	0.3
13+	600	1.0	72	0.5
TOTAL	58,598	100.0	13,227	100.0

Source: Braithwaite (1986).

TABLE 4.13   *Barbados: Number of Rooms Occupied by Households Headed by Over-60s, and among the Total Population, 1980*

No. of rooms	Total population		Over-60s	
	No.	%	No.	%
1	1,433	2.4	396	3.0
2	8,678	14.8	2,349	17.8
3	11,144	19.0	2,675	20.2
4	22,068	37.7	4,656	35.2
5	9,242	15.8	1,938	14.7
6	2,551	4.4	518	3.9
7+	1,292	2.2	255	1.9
n.a.	2,190	3.7	440	3.3
TOTAL	58,598	100.0	13,227	100.0

Source: Braithwaite (1986).

problems, 27.4% feared crime, 19.1% feared an increase in the cost of living, and only 2% feared having to live alone.

In the opinion of 51%, life for the elderly is better now than ever before. What did they most think about when alone? God was the majority subject of thought, with 32.9% followed by the cost of living for 21.5%. Only 7.1% regularly thought about past life and 5.7% about death. Checks on time orientation of the sample confirmed that only 10.9% were past-orientated, with 62.4% mainly concerned with the present and 26.7% with the future. This appears to deny the picture of the weary, elderly person sitting patiently waiting for death and brooding about the good old days.

Of the sample, 75.3% had children living and 31.8% had five or more children still alive. However, 20.7% of those with living children had no contact with them and 24.8% received no help of any kind, only about a third receiving actual financial support.

Summing up his findings, Braithwaite concludes that 'the proposition of role theory, that those among the elderly who lose roles and status in their old age are more likely than their peers to experience adjustment problems, is borne out'. Social breakdown came in the forms of 'economic deprivation, psychological difficulties, social isolation, health problems, unsuccessful retirement, and lack of policy programme awareness and usage', and this kind of breakdown was most likely to be found among 'low income groups, the old, the retired, those from lower occupational backgrounds, the highly socially isolated, those in bad health and those with lower levels of education than their counterparts'.

The selection of studies cited above will be supplemented in the next chapter by a closer look .at some specific studies and a number of personal cases which may help to make the welter of statistics more realistic. If, however, the above studies are taken to cover all the significant circumstances and problems of ageing in the developing world today, there is one serious omission which must be referred to as a global menace and which will be dealt with more specifically in Chapter 10: the killer disease AIDS.

AIDS is already beginning to have an impact on certain communities, mainly in Africa and Latin America. It might be thought that since epidemiologically it is an affliction of the sexually active age groups, it is not likely to have a major impact on the elderly. However, in some Third World communities the new disease is seen to be adversely affecting the lives of older people, especially grandmothers, as people of parent age, both mothers and fathers, die of the disease. Thus, to the problems already detailed, there is added the responsibility of nursing the dying and then making provision for the surviving infants.

The visible and horrific nature of AIDS may help to draw attention to the statistically greater but less visible and shocking problem of a greying population. The latter is a more insidious phenomenon, yet no adequate provision has so far been made.

5

SELECTED STUDIES OF AGEING

THE aim of this chapter is to reduce the global statistics to individual cases and specific themes. Thus, the overall trends may be illustrated by the experience of the individual person in a variety of environments and cultures. Most of the individual cases cited are taken from the confidential files of programme reports. They often portray harrowing sufferings and therefore, to protect the individual's identity, no indication is given as to name or location. From the experience of many people working in this field, however, it can be stated that the circumstances of individual old people reveal certain similarities across cultural boundaries.

The previous chapter indicated that for many old people in developing countries, life is seen as tolerable. The extended family still exists to a greater or lesser extent, and, where it has broken down, communities often step in to relieve the elderly individual of the worst problems. The effects of industrialization and migration are very irregular and varied. Some elderly people are able to adapt extremely well to their new conditions. In some places the elder is still accorded certain prestige and respect. The majority of the elderly are, by force or by choice, still very much involved in the everyday life of a family or a community.

The concern of the present study is not so much with those elderly who are able to continue within a traditional structure or to adapt to a new environment. It is concerned, rather, with those individuals who do not make the transition or who are totally abandoned because of a coincidence of unfavourable factors. It is also trying to point to a possible rapid increase in the numbers of those who do not adapt and to an exponential rise in the frequency and force of unfavourable factors which will be affecting tomorrow's elderly.

Plight of the Individual

The following brief descriptions of individual cases will therefore serve to illustrate problems in need of urgent solution and warn of the likely severity of future problems if adequate planning and research is not undertaken without further delay. Among individual cases encountered by me or by my close colleagues, the following reveal typical circumstances of ageing in a developing country.[1]

Mr A., aged 83 years. Marital status: single. Family: nil. He is a very frail man who does not have any relatives in the country to assist him. He migrated from India 25 years previously. He was living with a friend before being admitted to hospital for treatment. His friend is now returning to India to settle but there is no way Mr A. can make the journey. He is somewhat senile and will now have nowhere to live when he leaves hospital.

Mr B., aged 77 years. Marital status: widower. Family: a son aged 36 and two stepsons. Mr B. was living with his son in a rural village. The son's family was existing on a hand-to-mouth basis, and when the family could not provide food for the father he was taken to live with a stepson. He is suffering from chronic cancer and needs a lot of attention. The hospital cannot keep him as a chronic case due to shortage of beds. The common-law wife of the stepson is now objecting to having to care for Mr B. and wants him moved. Mr B. has no income and no possessions except the clothing he is wearing.

Mr C., aged 80 years. Marital status: single. Family: widowed son and granddaughter. There is no room in the son's tiny room for Mr C. so he lives on his own and the granddaughter takes him meals from time to time. He lives in a very small and dilapidated shack with no windows, one door and a leaking roof. The bed takes up all the space. The bed itself is a piece of thick cardboard. The neighbours are now complaining because Mr C. is 'in the habit of emptying his stools from pans and burying them in holes dug in the yard'. The bed linen is covered with faeces. He has a very bad and persistent cough. He is not under treatment.

Mrs D., aged 79. Marital status: widow. Family: two sons and

[1] As already stated, in the interests of confidentiality no identifying notes will be given for these individual cases.

one daughter. Mrs D. owns the tiny shack in which she lives with her daughter and nine grandchildren. The daughter is mentally defective and unable to help beyond the basic household chores. The two sons have migrated to the United States and are no longer in contact with their homeland. Mrs D. has an income from Social Security of US$1.25 per week, the maximum payment. With this she can purchase two kilos of rice or equivalent, which then constitutes the entire diet for the week for 11 persons. Mrs D. is hampered by severe arthritis but occasionally she is able to obtain a little cleaning work or other casual labour. For the most part she relies on the aid of charitable organizations to help her feed and clothe the dependent grandchildren. It was not clear from repeated questions whether Mrs D. is widowed, separated, or single. There is no peer male in evidence.

General E. and Corporal F. The general is a widower and the corporal never married. Both are in their late 70s. General E. retired on an adequate pension 20 years ago. His pension was not inflation-linked and the national currency has been inflated by more than 2,000% since his retirement. His formerly generous pension and savings are now therefore almost worthless. Corporal F. was his servant and retired to serve the general after their army careers. Now they share one tiny room and live on the most meagre of diets but are unwilling to accept charity or even to make their needs known. Because of the deterioration of the corporal's health, the general now acts as the cleaner, caterer, and nurse in this pathetic little household.

Sra. G., aged 75+. Marital status: widow. Family: no husband, two sons killed in civil war. Due to lack of hospital beds after severe civil war bombing of hospitals, this woman and many like her are cared for by nuns in what is nominally an old people's home. More than 80 nursing cases lie on mattresses laid on the floor so close together that there is no room for a chair between patients. They lie in three rows along a narrow room that was formerly the nun's refectory. Sra. G. is passing through a cycle of amputations due to untreated diabetes mellitus. Since 1920 this illness has normally been treated successfully either by diet or by insulin or a combination of both, but in this area since the civil war people have had to eat what they can get when they can get it, and have no control over their diet. There have been no supplies of insulin locally for some years. Sra. G. therefore lost the circulation of one leg. Gangrene set in. The doctors had no option but to amputate the leg. The same symptoms then developed in the other leg, which was then amputated. The symptoms spread to the right arm and that had to be amputated. The prognosis is amputation of the remaining limb.

Sra. H., aged over 90. Marital status: widow. Family: a daughter with whom Sra. H. lives and one son, also living locally. The home is a thatched hut in thin jungle with wattle-type walls. When seen, Sra. H. was lying on an uncured animal skin on the mud floor. Suffering from a high fever she was delirious but intermittently aware of her surroundings. The daughter was doing all possible to help. Question: Have you sent for the doctor? Answer: The doctor will not come because he knows we cannot pay him. Question: If we pay for the doctor to come . . . ? Answer: He will only prescribe pills. Question: Then why not have the pills prescribed and see if they will help? Answer: We know there are no pills in the dispensary. There are no medicines at all in the dispensary even for those who can afford to pay. (Subsequent investigation at the dispensary attached to the local medical clinic proved that the statements were true. There were virtually no medicines, bandages, or other supplies available. The reasons were given as lack of official concern, floods disrupting supplies, and nurses selling off the supplies for their own profit.)

Sra. I. Srta. J., aged in their 80s. Status: sisters, one widowed, one single. No other family. Admitted to an old people's home where the owner collected the sisters' Social Security payments and was responsible for their total care. Visitors' report stated 'The stairs ended into a broad, long, and very damp corridor. All that floor, in addition to being dirty and very damp, was also dark . . . The aged lady was found begging pitifully to be removed from the cubicle where she was lodged. In that cubicle, lined entirely with ceramic tiles, with a single bed, was the other lady. They were inside, shut in by a low, padlocked door. One could tell it was a makeshift affair. We were told that they were sclerosed women: 'They are sclerosed and dirty everything. Urinating and discharging their bowels in their trousers', the owner's sons told us. Along that corridor there was a bench with several ladies sitting, one of them wearing an apron that exposed her bare buttocks. Beside her, a very thin lady was tied by a piece of cloth to the bench.'

Mr K., aged 118 (age verified by baptismal certificate). Marital status: widower. Family: no surviving sons, but several nephews and grandchildren. When seen, appeared fit and sprightly for age. Neatly dressed in clean if ragged shirt, cotton trousers, sandals, and straw panama hat. Using a single walking stick. Attended the town meeting on problems of the aged and spoke coherently. His only means of livelihood was to till a corn patch which he owned more than 1,000 feet up on a very steep mountain slope. Because of his age he now sometimes stumbled and fell on his daily 6-kilometre walk to and from the corn patch. Recently he had struck his skull falling and lay unconscious for several hours because nobody else passes that way. His sole request was for an opportunity to work in some kind of agricultural task on flatter ground nearer his hut. He was selected to take part in the new Help the Aged programme. Before the programme could commence, and having passed his 119th birthday, he caught what was assumed to be pneumonia. In spite of the excellent health care a few miles away, the relatives used their customary discretion to decide that nothing could be done for him. They left him some food, nailed up the door from outside and went away. Three weeks later they broke down the door and buried his body.

Mr L., aged 90. Until age 77 had worked as a self-employed tailor and had some savings still. Widowed 23 years ago. Has no children, no surviving brothers and sisters and no contact with any other family member. Neighbours are kind and supply meals. The house is in considerable disrepair and infested with termites. There is no running water, no electricity, and because of physical frailty he has to rely on neighbours to bring water. His greatest problems were 'loneliness and the way young people treat you . . . they call you all kinds of names'. He does not feel he has any prestige except that a few of his neighbours respect his great age. The religious minister visits weekly and Mr L. says that he is now looking forward to death. He does not talk about death because 'there is no one to talk to'. He describes himself as 'a lonely and sad person'.

Mrs M., age uncertain. Separated from her husband for 15 years. Has worked all her life as a street saleswoman. Is living with her daughter and two grandchildren. One son is out of contact, having migrated. Another son sometimes gives her money for medicines. The daughter pays the rent and buys the food. 'I feel like a beggar', says Mrs M. She suffers from hypertension, a heart condition, and a cataract. She was forced to give up her selling job because of poor sight but feels safer indoors because of young men 'looking to rob people' in the streets. She has no contact with her brothers and sisters after a family squabble about a piece of land left by the father in which she had no share. She has 11 grandchildren but 'they don't help . . . they are rude . . . their parents don't correct them'.

Mrs N., aged 60 plus. Lives with 10-year old grandchild in isolated hut made out of 'rawly chopped wood, twigs and leaves'. Husband deserted her 10 years ago. Daughter died when child was two. Son-in-law went away and has never been seen since. She has very little food for the boy, who has grown wild and runs away often into the forest. Other children will not mix with the boy because they say he is a devil. The village chief says that everybody is poor so that they cannot help the woman. He thinks they have nothing but forest leaves to eat.

Mrs O., aged 67, said 'I lost a daughter and a son one day. The son was sick. He had been sick for some time and was in the hospital. My daughter was married and lived elsewhere. One day on my way to the hospital I passed through my daughter's village to summon her. The person I sent came back to tell me that my daughter had also been carried to the hospital because she was given poison by her husband's girl friend. Both my children died the same night. The daughter left five children and I now look after them here.'

Mrs P., aged 69, widow of a polygamous husband, said 'My husband's death was not so bad, he was old; but what happened later is what I cannot forget. The attitudes of the other wives worsened and I was always lonely. They said I was our husband's favourite and they wanted me to die with him. At one time they put poison in my food. Luckily a child was present when they did this. After that I developed the habit of drinking. I felt so lonely but when I drink I feel a lot better. But here in the town this is expensive and a big burden on my daughter.'

Mrs Q., age not stated, no legal documentation of marriage. 'I have a cousin who was a policeman. I asked for his marriage certificate to get a house [rent accommodation was only supplied to couples who could supply a marriage certificate]. When I got the house and was living in it my cousin came and said he wanted to move some of his things into the house . . . I refused because we were paying rent for a small house and had no extra room. This cousin took the matter to court and I lost the case, but I also lost money. . . . I was stranded.'

Mr R., an immigrant with no legal right to accommodation. 'The firm I was working for was going bankrupt. I was one of the unfortunate people who had to leave. I was told I was going to be re-employed, but I never heard from them again. I went out searching but could not get a job anywhere. The treatment I got from whites discouraged me from looking. I felt so disappointed. I just gave up.'

Mrs S., very old. 'When I was at home I had a field and managed to do all I wanted, but here in town I am hardly able to take a walk. I cannot walk because I am old and, besides, in town there is a danger of cars. I always tell my son that I want to go home to live the life I am used to. I am, however, too old and sick and no one is prepared to come with me. I have no future but to wait for death.'

Mr T., aged 73, on-coming blindness but still the build of the heavyweight boxer he once was. Lives in a one-room shack, an old settee and a cupboard his only furniture. An immigrant many years ago, he has no local rights of residence or benefits and is too old to return to his old country, where, in any case, he knows no one. Is visited regularly by a group of friends from an embassy who bring him supplies. He asks, 'You white people don't eat the heads of fish, do you? Would you save your fish heads for me?'

Miss U., aged 85, single, a former school teacher. When she retired she had ample savings, according to her calculations. Due to her own longevity and national inflation her savings have now run out. She has been admitted to an old people's home because she was living on the streets, picking food from dustbins or gutters. She has just had some teeth extracted in the treatment room of the home. The nuns had to extract the teeth without anaesthetic because there was neither anaesthetic nor pain-killing tablets in the little pharmacy and no money to buy them.

Mr V., aged 89, a widower. During the First World War he served as a soldier and saw fighting in East Africa. Later he emigrated from his own Third World country to another in search of work. Still holding himself like a soldier and very smart, his only income is when he can get a job at waiting in restaurants for large banquets. Normally younger men are preferred. He had one suit which he keeps for waiting jobs. Lives in one room up a flight of stairs which is too precarious to bear two people at once.

W., a woman thought to be in her 80s. Cannot remember whether she has ever had any children or been married. Her friends say that she has existed for years by begging odd articles to sell sitting on the street pavements. Does not like to beg food. Is brought in by religious brothers to a feeding station once or twice a week for her only real food. Sleeps on the streets or, during the monsoon season, huddled under bridges with others in a similar state. No possessions other than her clothes.

Mr X., aged 80 or more. No known family. Was once in the civil service but committed a crime (embezzlement) for which he served a prison sentence. Never able to regain a place in society although he left prison probably 30 years ago. Some time ago was robbed of all his belongings, including identity papers. Too weak and depressed to bother about replacement. Lives on the streets. Because he is rather an attractive old man with flowing, white hair he is given little gifts but is too proud to ask directly for help. Attends a feeding centre twice a week if he remembers the days when his district is served.

Mrs Y., age not known. A great-grandmother. Most of her family killed or lost in racial warfare some years ago. Had been living on the streets with a granddaughter who had three children. Recently the granddaughter died and the father of the three children had ceased to make contact. Mrs Y. now spends most of her time sitting under a cardboard sun shelter while the eldest child begs at the pavement edge. In effect this child, thought to be about seven or eight, maintains the group.

Mrs Z., aged probably about 80. Her only daughter has three children. The daughter used to go out to work and left the three children with the grandmother. As the daughter's income derived from casual market jobs and was insufficient, the grandmother and three children spent the days begging on the streets. Eventually the grandmother felt the task of looking after the three children was too much. Local people contacted the state department for the protection of children. Social workers took the children and boarded them in a home. The daughter went away and had no more contact with the mother. Now Mrs Z. lives in an old shack of cardboard and battered pieces of tin, a shack which was abandoned by another shanty town family as being obsolete. She lives by picking food and oddments from the rubbish tip. She wants to go and live in an asylum. She is due to a pension but does not know how to claim it.

Perhaps it should be observed that once the above cases were brought to the attention of voluntary workers, action was taken to remedy the individual situation as far as possible. Even so this alphabet of suffering represents many, many more who have not yet become known to welfare agencies or for whom the resources of welfare agencies have proved inadequate.

The individual cases quoted can be supplemented by comments and reflections culled from a number of sources. Researching in 42 developing communities, Glascock and Feiman identified 16 cases of abandonment of aged people and 26 cases where old persons were killed.[2] Maxwell and Silverman found similar instances in 20 of the 95 communities which they surveyed across many countries.[3] Colson and Scudder speak of old people whose feet will not carry them beyond the household.[4] 'Sleeping alone without adequate covering, they shiver at night throughout the cold season (even in Africa). . . . restricted in movement they must endure the dust that sweeps through barren villages during the height of the dry season'. In Afghanistan, Shahrani found those who were 'left without any natural or adopted children in their old age, and they suffered from lack of proper care and could not enjoy the presumed rewards of old age'.[5] Foner sums it up in saying 'as long as children and other kin in nonindustrial societies must shoulder the caretaking burden, so long will relationships with the incapacitated elderly remain as they are: a complex and tangled web of attachments, reciprocities, tensions, and antagonisms'.[6] This is a long way from the pretty, simplistic picture often painted of the traditional, extended family but is no doubt justified in many instances.

[2] Glascock and Feiman 1981.   [3] Maxwell and Silverman 1981.
[4] Colson and Scudder 1981.   [5] Shahrani 1981.
[6] Foner 1985.

Perhaps nowhere are the poignant ponderings of aged people more pointedly portrayed than in some of the brief quotations given by Hampson from his Zimbabwe interviews with aged people:[7] 'I am too old . . . at this stage I am just like a child.' 'I am waiting to die. I say this because I have no one to care for me.'

'My future life is very bleak and hard. I am useless and I think it would be much better if I died. My past life was exciting because I used to do everything for myself.'

'In our African custom relations are supposed to look after one another but if the relations think one is too old, then life can be very lonely.'

'I have nothing of my own. I left my home to others and I have to squeeze myself into this tiny room.'

'Today people no longer greet the elders; they even ambush and beat us old people.'

Psychiatric Problems

Passing from the study of specific persons to that of specific subjects, it has been said that 'no aged person is similar to any other aged person', but their symptoms may be similar. A Nigerian researcher, T. A. Lambo, has worked on the problem of psychiatric disorders of the elderly in developing countries. He states that until recently psychiatric disorders in the elderly of developing countries were relatively rare, partly because of the low life span which precluded dementias more common to age. Moreover, where disorders were suffered by an older person they were generally dealt with in the home and were not noticed in the general community. There is also a high tolerance level on the behalf of the community for people with mental disorders.[8]

Compared with the industrialized countries, Lambo finds the proportion of psychiatric patients in developing countries to be relatively low, with a majority of those treated being female. Part of the reason for this sex difference is, of course, that females generally have a longer expectation of life in tropical countries. A majority of females over 55 were found to be suffering from paranoid psychosis. Organic psychoses such as senile dementia

[7] J. Hampson 1982.   [8] Lambo 1981, p. 74.

are more frequent with advancing age. Men over 60 suffer more than women of the same age from depressive disorders.

Reactive depression was more frequent in relation to urbanization and educational status according to Lambo's studies. However, in the villages younger age groups had greater tendencies towards mental ill-health, which Lambo attributes to their being more exposed to cultural change. Alcoholic psychosis and narcotic infections are comparatively rare in Africa, although on the increase in parts of Latin America and Asia.

Endemic tropical diseases can trigger psychiatric disorders in later life. Lambo also regards the effects of migration as proven to be 'the genesis of psychological disturbances of the aged'. He says elderly patients with 'profound psychological disturbances or crippling psychiatric symptoms, had developed their conditions within varying periods of a few weeks to a few months of moving to urban areas to live with their married sons and daughters'. Over the last decade, suicides among the aged have risen significantly in more developed countries such as Hong Kong, mainland China, and Brazil.

Health Problems

It may also be of interest to look briefly at the findings of a Cambridge University medical team which examined more than a thousand patients in a remote area of Ecuador and made comparisons between physiological conditions of people in that area compared with the equivalent in an industrialized country. The first discovery was the preponderance of housewives presenting themselves for examination, which suggested that those who were paid for work could not afford to attend the hospital.[9]

Out of the sample, more than half the patients and a third of the conditions diagnosed concerned the gastro-intestinal tract. Half of these were of parasitic origin. The most common cause was ingestion in water or uncooked food contaminated by human faeces, sometimes used as a fertilizer. The local water supply was contaminated and the faeco-finger-oral route was common

[9] Owen et al. 1985.

within family groups. There were many multiple (more than one parasite) and repeated infections of a particular individual. These infections were often discovered in a patient reporting for consultation for some other reason.

Influenza was common, as in Britain, but in almost every case it led to infection of the lower respiratory tract, possibly due to poor housing and a damp environment. The rate of tuberculosis discovered was suspiciously low; the local explanation was that the majority of tuberculosis sufferers never reach hospital and in older people the symptoms are regarded as typical of normal ageing.

Stomach cancer accounted for a third of all malignancies, the high rate being in accord with theories in industrialized countries that it tends to affect lower socio-economic groups in general and unskilled labouring groups in particular. Only one case of colorectal carcinoma was encountered, as contrasted with countries of low fibre, high protein, and high fat diets. No case of breast cancer was found. The possible relevant factor in this respect noted locally was the early date of first lactation of most mothers. Very few women had children later in life. Lung cancer was also low and was considered to be avoided by reason of lack of air pollution and the few cigarettes smoked, although most people did smoke.

Musculoskeletal disorders were frequent. Arthritis was widely underdiagnosed and was regarded as a normal ageing development, not to be reported. Traumas were frequent, especially neck fractures related to falls. One accident causing multiple fractures involved a tractor driven by a 100-year-old worker!

Systolic blood pressure was significantly lower than in Britain. Pulse pressure is considerably greater in patients in Britain than in Ecuador. Low salt intake was noted and may be a factor in the local avoidance of stroke. Some populations in Amazonia and Africa with the lowest salt intake do not develop hypertension in age. A low-fat diet was also observed, heavy smoking was rare, and most of the older people were normally active. All this contributed to the fact that strokes in the region were remarkably rare. However, there may be some incidence of minor strokes which might not be recorded.

Few studies have been undertaken in developing countries as to the effect that activity opportunities have on older people.

Frequently, the older person has to earn in order to eat so that other aspects of activity become relatively important. One study in Colombia did try to assess the impact on intellectual conservation of the old person of the provision of work activities within residential institutions. This failed to prove any direct correlation, partly because the period between commencement of activity and final assessment was too brief and possibly becasue the measurements of intellectual conservation for younger groups are not subtle enough for older groups.[10]

What the study did most clearly record was, first of all, the ability of the older person to achieve a high quality of work, and secondly the ability of older workers to become engrossed in work for work's sake. Thus the introduction of financial rewards for the second phase of production actually caused no increase of productivity. The incentive was in the act of work itself. The researchers therefore presumed that the opportunity to become involved in meaningful activity is a prime requisite of older people in a developing country situation, irrespective of financial considerations.

A workshop was held in Malaysia in 1986 to study curricular changes of training institutes to meet the developing needs of an elderly population. Based on the four-country study referred to in the last chapter, it gave some further insights into developing needs and requirements of an ageing population.[11]

Although the proportion of the elderly is still small, it is calculated that in Malaysia the utilization of the health services by the elderly amounts to 25% of the total resource, and this is compounded by the long period of hospitalization, after-care, and higher cost of care. In developing countries there are 'specific disease patterns related to the elderly and their care requires special skills', but current medical training does not emphasize this element, nor does it counteract false images of ageing.

Geriatric dentistry is another element which needs urgent priority. Some amount of nutrition loss must be due to inadequate tooth structure due to ageing losses. Positive attitudes need to be engendered about the elderly and their teeth. . . .

[10] Dulcey-Ruiz 1985.
[11] WHO Kuala Lumpur, 1986.

No structured training has existed for nurses and health auxiliaries. Apart from knowledge of specific ailments of the elderly, skills are needed in communication with the aged, promotion of self-health and self-reliance, and preventive measures possible at all ages. . . .

Whilst social workers do receive some training in care of the aged there is a wide need to recognise the importance of the inter-disciplinary approach, including especially mental health, physiotherapy and occupational therapy. Communications skills and the process of institutionalization where absolutely necessary are other important elements.

The workshop also pointed to the decreasing contacts between children and the grandparent generation, and the need therefore to include lessons on ageing in school curricula. Students should acquire knowledge about ageing and also skills in contacts with and care for the elderly. This presupposes that teachers will be trained to impart that knowledge and those skills. The same principle applies to the education of the general public with 'Respect the Elderly' campaigns.

African Trends

Existing trends in Africa were summarized in a meeting in Dakar, referred to elsewhere, and organized by the International Centre for Social Gerontology of Paris (CIGS). Various countries summed up the local trends in apposite statements. In Zambia those most affected by migration are the remaining elderly 'who have been left in the rural areas to eke a living from the land with very limited tools'. From Botswana came a report that the problems of those rural elderly are further aggravated by periodic droughts 'which make subsistence farming even more difficult'.

A further factor leading to the breaking down of the extended family systems is the growing tendency of urban women to work, as in Guinea. In Ethiopia the 'living conditions and industrial occupations provided for younger persons are not conducive for them to care for all their elderly relatives'. The Liberian representative mentioned the method used by large companies of housing their workers in camps or 'residence' so that no extended family household was possible.

A Congo speaker cited 'the search for profit . . . competition

. . . and salaried activity . . . militating against the old systems of community and mutual caring'. A Tanzanian saw modern education as fostering individualism and straining the old community ties of interdependence. Zaire expected a 'void through the elimination of the active population' who would previously have cared for the needy elderly.

The speaker from Cameroon blamed modern mass media for eroding the best values of traditional culture and care systems. A Mali report quoted many townspeople so preoccupied with 'material constraints . . . [that they] fail to fulfill their duties towards the old'.

Believing that 'the disintegration of the family, its resignation of its social role, and the abandonment of old persons are inescapable results of the model of industrial civilization', the delegates looked towards a reinforcement of kin groups and traditional values. In little more than three years since the Dakar conference expressed these views, many African communities, which were already feeling the effects of migration and the exodus of the middle generation, had to confront the new disruptive factor of the fatal disease AIDS. The main target area of AIDS is again the middle generation and the main surviving burden bearer is the elder who has to 'pick up the pieces' of family care, food production, and community roles.

The main impact of AIDS so far has been in certain areas of east central Africa and highly populated locations in Latin America. However, reports of cases from other areas of Africa and from Asian countries suggest that few countries may expect to avoid what is now, in some specific communities, an epidemic of major dimensions. This is discussed further in Chapter 10.

6

EXISTING SERVICES

THE present state of underprovision of services for the elderly is often obscured by the ambivalence of countries and organizations in reporting to the United Nations and other world conferences. It is understandable that a nation wishes to present itself in the best possible light in respect of the care of its aged, and reporting often shows a bias towards optimism.

For instance, in recent updating, one country blithely reports inter-generational contact 'as satisfactory at 58.3%'.[1] It totally fails to observe that this leaves an enormous 41.7% of old people with no inter-generational contacts. Another country reports that it is common for older women in rural areas to assume responsibility for rearing grandchildren when adult children migrate, as though this were a simple, happy process. No mention is made of the extreme poverty suffered in those areas as part of the process.

A third country reports its efforts to produce incentives for older people to remain in the labour force by giving pension increments for each additional year worked over retiring age. The report omits the fact that less than 10% of workers qualify for a pension and that at least 75% of older men can never retire.

Such reports tend to give a falsely optimistic impression of existing services although a survey made by the United Nations itself gave a very pessimistic picture. Out of 23 developing countries, only 9 had 'some kind' of social security scheme, 6 had pension schemes for a small minority, and 3 maintained government-run institutions for the elderly in need of such care. None had special geriatric medicine, none had special housing, none had employment after retirement on an official basis,

---

[1] Examples are taken from 'The World Aging Situation: Strategies and Policies' (UN 1985) described in para. 5 below.

and none had domiciliary programmes. In fact, 8 had no governmental services of any kind for the elderly.[2]

The extensive review document issued by the United Nations in 1985, *The World Aging Situation: Strategies and Policies*, gives a misleading and unduly optimistic impression although its details are accurate. Firstly, it is not a 1985 update but a collection of reports to the 1982 World Assembly, some of which were prepared on data from well before 1980. Secondly, a number of countries tended to report future aims as though they were present realities and past achievements. In many cases the observer in the field will find that the hopes expressed in 1982 are no nearer achievement and in some cases, due mainly to economic restrictions, are actually farther from reality.

Pensions Only for a Few

A further impression given in World Assembly on Aging reports, that old age pension schemes are abundant in the Third World, needs to be adjusted to reality. While many Third World countries do have some kind of pension or social security schemes, those schemes are often restricted to a small minority of people who, in any case, enjoyed superior income provision during active life.

Pensions are no novelty in developing countries. The Colombians somewhat humourously claim that Simón Bolívar himself became the first pensioner in Latin America, by national decree of 23 June 1823, when he was awarded 30,000 Colombian pesos a year. Certainly in that country and others, individual pensions were voted from the earliest days of independence.

In Brazil in 1888–9, a law was introduced to set up a pension benefit fund for state railway workers. The Decree Law 72 of 21 November 1966 replaced six former Brazilian retirement and pension institutes—all for classes of urban workers in private firms or some public services. By 1975 6 million workers in Brazil were insured together with their 18 million dependants out of a total population of about 100 million.[3]

[2] UN General Assembly, A/9126/1973, Annex II—a little dated but still contemporary to some data used in the UN 1985 publication cited in n. 1 above.
[3] Brazil, Ministry of External Relations 1976.

In Colombia, Law 6 of 1945 created a Social Insurance Fund. Law 171 of 1961 indexed pensions to prices if inflation rose over 5%. Law 4a of 1976 fixed minimum pensions at the level of the highest minimum legal salary, and the maximum pension at 22 times the minimum. These were all well-meaning pieces of legislation. However, in 1978 there were still only 135,258 persons pensioned, rising to 184,569 at the end of 1981—6.45% of those over 55.[4]

In Peru in 1982, a HelpAge report estimated that out of 938,000 persons of pensionable age, only 90,347 were in receipt of pensions and the rest were considered *carga económica*—a non-productive, economic liability. Often in those countries the law has little powers of coercion; another report from Colombia revealed the San Jose de Suaita Company owing 120 pensioners a total of 12 million pesos (about two years' payments).[5] In Mexico, where civil servants have been covered for pensions since 1824, only 16% of about 4 million people aged 60 years and over received pensions in 1982, and disquiet was expressed as to the adequacy of those pensions, especially when related to soaring inflation.[6]

In Ecuador in 1980, when the over-60 population was recorded as being about 488,000 people, the total number of pensioners was about 84,000, comprising nearly 77,000 retired workers, 5,000 retired soldiers, and 2,000 retired policemen.[7]

Among countries with higher pensioner percentages are Argentina and Costa Rica. In Argentina attempts have been made to introduce some form of global pension, but an Argentine gerontologist comments that the amounts received varied with the passing of time and very rarely did they cover all the needs of the recipient.[8] In Costa Rica 'some form' of income maintenance is available to all workers after 60 whether or not they have contributed, and the official retirement age of 60 years is not negotiable for government workers. However, the government, which is the largest single employer in the country, has not always been able to maintain its contributions to the Social Security Institute, and there are doubts about the long-term efficacy of the programme.[9] This is most significant for Costa

[4] García 1981.   [5] Ibid.   [6] Contreras de Lehr 1986.
[7] Merchan 1984, pp. 11, 85.   [8] Carbal Prieto 1980, p. 159.
[9] Denton 1982, p. 94.

Rica has no military establishment and is able to make a far larger relative contribution to social budgets than many other American developing countries with their excessive military commitments.

A Latin American conference on the aged calculated that formal social security coverage varied widely from country to country ranging from (then) 80% of the elderly in Costa Rica to 1.5% in Haiti. They observed similar characteristics throughout the countries, such as limited coverage, inequality between different groups of workers, delays in adjusting contributions actuarily, and use of long-term financial reserves for short-term programmes.[10]

A Nigerian comment sums up the pension situation for most of the developing world: 'In non-industrialized countries any official retirement age affects only a small proportion of the population and leaving the labour force is often a gradual process of declining commitment as age takes its toll.'[11]

The retirement age in countries where pension schemes are available, varies wildly. Government pensions can be taken in The Gambia at any time after 45. In Nigeria the official retirement age varies between 55 and 60 and in Sierra Leone it is 60. However one study in Ghana found an average age of retirement for those with pensions of 56, as compared with the official age of 60. Yet the actual age at which persons in the sample had retired varied between 31 and 75. Ill health or conversely physical and mental vigour appeared to be the main determinants of date of retirement.[12]

In Kenya the government's Social Security Fund, which is a form of pension scheme, provides wage-earning workers with benefits after 55 years of age. At a recent conference in Zimbabwe, government ministers from a number of countries expressed commitment towards the welfare of the aged but remarked upon the economic problems of providing global benefits as well as the recent emergence of the abandoned aged as a national problem consequent upon the gradual breakdown of the extended family system. Zimbabwe itself has promoted 'a significant expansion in the membership of pension schemes in the absence of a national scheme. The government intended to

[10] UN WAA 1982d.
[11] Ekpenyong et al. 1986.   [12] Ibid.

introduce such a scheme, but this may not be feasible as
Zimbabwe is still a young nation and might not have the
financial resources . . . '.[13] It also inherited the former Rhodesian
system.

In Asia generally, while modern civil services and commercial
enterprises have introduced pension schemes for their workers,
the extended family network still widely continues to be the
means of provision for the elderly. Frequently researchers report
that questions of income and adequacy of economic resources are
closely tied to the issues of financial and other support provided
within the family. Indeed, in many instances, respondents
reported no personal income at all, but were clearly adequately
provided for by the family. 'Pension' assistance is sometimes
afforded in the form of food programmes for the aged and
destitute, as in Sri Lanka. In Malaysia 12% of old people had
monetary pensions or superannuation.[14]

In China, pensions systems are being instituted but are the
responsibility of the communities through the 'brigades' which
provide services. An example of a rural pension system near
Chendu cites women allowed to retire at 55 and men at 60 on a
pension of 16 to 18 yen a month; childless pensioners received 20
yen a month. A bonus of 10 yen was payable at the Spring
Festival. If productivity within the brigade areas was good this
pension might be augmented by 50 yen in additional bonuses.
Only some of the brigades in an area had collective funds
sufficient to pay such pensions.[15] A survey by the Chinese State
Labour Bureau estimated that about 45% of urban dwellers were
covered by some kind of pension scheme. Where older persons
are not eligible for pensions or where pensions cannot be paid,
the state has agreed that they be allowed to engage in private
enterprise in order to acquire sufficient income. Licences are
issued for such pursuits for persons having no employment or
pension rights.

Varying Health Services

In respect of health services the same kind of variations also
exist. American countries have the 'most developed and best

---

[13] HelpAge International 1986.
[14] Andrews *et al.* 1986.   [15] Goldstein and Goldstein 1986.

distributed health infrastructure', but while Argentina's popula-
tion-per-hospital ratio is lower than Spain's, countries like
Bolivia, Peru, and Ecuador are well down the world table for
hospital provision.[16]

TABLE 6.1   *Health-related Indicators, Selected Countries, 1965 and 1980*

Country	Population per physician		Population per nursing person	
	1965	1980	1965	1980
Ethiopia	70,190	69,390	5,970	5,910
Kenya	12,840	7,890	1,780	550
Mozambique	18,700	39,140	4,720	5,610
Chad	73,040	47,640	13,620	3,860
Algeria	8,400	2,630	11,770	740
Lesotho	22,930	18,640	4,700	. . .
China	. . .	1,740	. . .	1,710
Burma	11,660	4,680	4,170	4,950
Philippines	1,310	7,970	1,130	6,000
Bangladesh	. . .	7,810	. . .	22,570
India	4,860	3,690	6,500	5,460
Sri Lanka	5,750	7,170	3,210	1,340
Papua New Guinea	12,520	13,590	620	960
Jamaica	1,930	2,830	340	630
Haiti	12,580	8,200	3,460	2,490
Costa Rica	2,040	1,460	630	450
Argentina	640	430	610	. . .
Colombia	2,530	1,710	890	800
Peru	1,620	1,390	880	970
United Kingdom	860	650	200	140
United States	670	520	120	140

Source: World Development Report (1985).
Note: decrease in 'population per . . . ' is, of course, an improvement in service.

Table 6.1 shows the variations in 'health-related indicators' for
a selected number of developing countries. Some of these figures
indicate a deterioration over a period of 20 years. A United
Nations study says:

[16] Golladay and Liese 1980.

The insufficiency of medical infrastructure can be seen by comparing the hospital capacity of the Least Developed Countries with that of other countries . . . the number of hospital beds per 100,000 inhabitants is only one tenth of that of the developed market-economy countries, whilst the number of doctors is one twenty-fifth. Moreover, the concentration of health services in urban centres leaves rural areas practically without any medical care. Required medicines are often not available or reach patients in a condition which make them ineffectual or even dangerous.[17]

The report, which covers 36 Least Developed Countries, also points out the dangers inherent in widespread food deficiencies, bad sanitary conditions, and lack of primary health care. There is only one health worker (including traditional midwives) for every 2,400 inhabitants in LDCs, in contrast to one for every 130 inhabitants in developed countries. Only 31% of people in LDCs are reached by clean water, compared with close to 100% in most developed countries. Inadequate sewerage systems are aggravated by overpopulation.

A study of South Asia (Bangladesh, India, Nepal, Pakistan, and Sri Lanka) reports that 'in countries so inadequately provided with the facilities to care for the sick, the poor will generally go from birth to death without receiving the administrations of a medically qualified person or lying on a hospital bed'. What medically qualified people there are can usually be found practising in urban areas.[18]

In Bangladesh 'only 10 to 15 per cent of the rural population have effective access to static health facilities'. Major urban areas of Pakistan have one medical or dental practitioner for less than 2,500 people but in rural Baluchistan one doctor serves more than 20,000, 'meaning that in effect for the vast majority, medicine is an aspect of life so remote as to be inaccessible when needed, quite apart from being beyond the purse of the poor'. In Nepal, where most communication is on foot, only 31 out of the 75 districts had any kind of hospital facility.

Pakistan's own Economic Survey has commented that out of 18,000 doctors registered in Pakistan, 'only 10,000 were available in the country, the rest having migrated to more lucrative employment abroad', many to the oil states of the Middle East.[19]

[17] UNCTAD 1985.
[18] Ibid.   [19] Johnson 1983.

In this situation a number of countries are planning to develop the so-called 'bare-foot doctor' programme proven in China to be an asset in rural areas. In 1975 Pakistan initiated a People's Health Scheme to send out 'Health Guards' to provide basic servies to the rural masses. Bangladesh has a system based on Thana Health Centres. In India a similar system has seen the creation of 5,400 rural health centres and 39,000 subcentres since independence. Such schemes have proved that many duties formerly the preserve of fully qualified medical doctors can be undertaken by suitably trained people of lesser qualification. However, the lack of trained practitioners remains an impediment to the delivery of adequate services to all people in numbers of countries.[20]

In Malaysia one national study discovered that 41% of the elderly had seen the doctor during the past month, indicating convenient access to medical attention. Only 1% had seen a nurse and 7% had consulted a pharmacist. There was little difference between urban and rural areas. Fifty per cent of the elderly took medicine as prescribed and another 29% took traditional medicines, mainly herbal medicines. This illustrates something of the variation in accessibility of medical services between countries of geographical proximity, when compared to other South-east Asia studies.[21]

This rate of accessibility was reflected farther east, for in Fiji, 37% of old people in a sample had seen the doctor during the previous month, 15% had seen a nurse, and 14% the pharmacist. In Korea 20% had seen a doctor and in the Philippines 34% had seen a doctor in the previous month. Elderly Filipinos also had a higher rate of consultation with nurses, reaching 20%. In the Philippines and Fiji the accessibility of practitioners was weighted in favour of urban areas but this was not so evident in Korea and Malaysia. Table 6.2 breaks these figures down by sex and age. It should be noted that the apparent decrease among over-80s in the percentage of people seeking the doctor may well be indicative of travel problems.

An Indian study revealed a probable 7.5 million backlog of cataract treatments. In 1982 it recorded a total of 3,470,000 blind people with an average age of incidence of cataract at 55,

---

[20] Ibid.
[21] Andrews et al. 1986.

TABLE 6.2 *Visits to Doctors in Past Month in Four Western Pacific Countries, by Sex, 1986 (%)*

Country	60–4	65–9	70–4	75–9	80+
			Males		
Fiji	40	42	40	42	26
Korea	23	23	18	24	17
Malaysia	35	39	39	54	39
Philippines	29	32	35	43	25
			Females		
Fiji	36	41	33	34	24
Korea	19	19	18	15	9
Malaysia	46	46	42	31	40
Philippines	37	33	33	45	30

Source: Andrews *et al.* (1986).

compared with an age of 65–70 in developed countries. One Indian voluntary agency seeking to combat the backlog has an annual record of over 21,000 ophthalmic patients seen at its headquarters centre, 7,500 treated by its mobile unit, and 1,250 operated on in temporary 'eye camps'. This one set of data from one country reveals something of the immensity of health problems in tropical lands.[22]

Africa is known to suffer from lack of sufficient trained personnel and vast distances to be covered in treating rural patients, but a meeting of African doctors identified another gap in service. This is 'the lack of precise epidemiological data' so that there is a need 'to see research units set up which would focus on socio-economic and medical living conditions of the elderly and the links between the ageing process and the specific pathology of countries with a hot climate'. This would help locate and remedy significant 'risk factors related to pathological or accelerated ageing'.[23]

A World Health Organization representative, speaking at a HelpAge meeting to delegates of countries from Southern Africa, admitted, 'although WHO's activities in the field of ageing began nearly three decades ago, in 1958, we in the African Region have

[22] Project reports to Help the Aged, London.
[23] CIGS 1984.

had no tangible programmes developed; in fact we have been known not to encourage development of programmes in the formal sector on the assumption that all was well and the traditional family ties would take care of the problem . . . I suspect that not all is well . . . '[24]

By contrast, medical provision for the elderly in some developing countries of America (but not all) is relatively advanced. In Argentina, the government-founded PAMI programme for integrated medical attention covers 47.2% of the nation's elderly over 60 years of age as insured under the scheme. Another 13.7% of over-60s use the service as fee-paying recipients.

Throughout the Americas improvements have been made. The population-per-health-worker ratio improved from 500 to about 360 between 1970 and 1976, while population per physician improved from 1,800 to 1,300 between 1964 and 1976. In Temperate South America the latter factor was almost on a par with the United States, at 600; in Tropical South America the figure was 1,600. Two-thirds of the physicians were serving the third of the population resident in large cities.

Throughout the developing countries of America there is a shortage of nurses, partly due to the lower social status of the nurse in the region and partly due to the emigration of some 20% of nurses to the United States or Canada. Thus while North America had 248 nurses and 411 nursing auxiliaries for every 100 physicians (1976), South America had only 32 nurses and 134 auxiliaries per 100 physicians.[25]

In some smaller countries there were some bright spots, as in Antigua where a free health service was available for the over-60s. In Barbados major research had been carried out into health care delivery and attitudes of the elderly. Grenada has a geriatric hospital but with facilities 100 years old which do not ease staff problems. In Trinidad and Tobago, requirements for geriatric services had been well documented; attention has been paid to the phenomenon of deaths soon after admission of destitute elderly (due perhaps sometimes to rapid metabolic changes consequent upon an unaccustomed high calorie diet and drug toxicity related to malnutrition). However, both Dominica and

[24] HelpAge International 1986.
[25] PAHO 1985.

St Vincent had ratios of over 5,000 population for every physician.[26]

Emigration was also a factor affecting the medical services in Haiti. There has been a very considerable exodus of doctors from a service which, in any case, was always inadequate and short of trained staff.

The regional preparatory meeting for the World Assembly on Aging at Villa Leyva, Colombia, in 1981 was disturbed about the 'considerable inequities' in the availability of health services, as between urban and rural areas, and also as between various social groups: 'The economically weak aged have quite inadequate access to health services.' Few people have the opportunity of medical check-ups, and the elderly frequently resort to medical attention only when their illness has reached a stage requiring highly skilled or specialist services which are probably not available. Thus the existing provision of 'general practitioner' or *primera asistencia* services is usually by-passed by older people.

The provision of psychiatric services for the elderly is often very scarce and of very poor quality. A Bolivian study assessed the 'satisfied' demand in Latin American capitals as being between 12% and 23%. In Bolivia itself there is one specialist psychiatric facility, in Sucre, catering for all ages, with referrals from throughout the country. Shortage of trained personnel is a problem superimposed upon the lack of finance and in the Bolivian hospital only 31 out of 40 establishment posts could be filled.[27]

A survey in the regional psychiatric hospital of Chitre in Panama revealed 31% of all psychiatric cases as being between the ages of 60 and 65, with 67% male and 33% female. Of these, 54% came from other provinces and were suffering the effects of institutionalization due to the lack of contact with families and a known environment and culture. Fully 69% had been in hospital for more than 7 years as there were few rehabilitative or community care provisions; 97% had been abandoned by their families, and there were no social service provisions for renewing family links. Thirty-six per cent reported being molested by younger patients due to lack of care staff.[28]

[26] PAHO, microfiche 30075.
[27] Report of Instituto Nacional de Psiquiatria, Sucre, 1982.
[28] Project report to Help the Aged, London.

Few Social Services

The situation regarding structured official social services is even more serious. In Colombia, Law 29 of 1975 required the government to provide the elderly with home, clothing, food, medical service, and funeral costs. Law 2011 of 1976 provided for the creation of a National Council for Protection of the Aged (although no steps were taken to implement this law until a visit by myself in company with the Director General of Help the Aged UK and officers of Pro Vida Colombia when, in a special audience, the President of the Republic initiated the necessary procedures). Yet in 1981 it was calculated that provision was made for only 1.1% of the elderly population (apart from contributory pension rights). Only 0.09% of the annual national budget was allocated to age welfare, and the average government contribution to old people's homes was 27 pesos per capita, then about US$0.55. Yet I perceived provisions in Colombia as being in advance of those in many other developing countries.[29] At the same time the government grant in Bolivia was US$0.22 per capita.

It may well be that certain countries will be led to follow the example of those which have sought to promote age welfare by imposing legal compulsions. Tunisian law requires that children must provide housing, clothing, and food for needy elders of the family. Parents in Tunisia also have a legal right to dwell in houses owned by the children.[30] In Morocco, adult children are obliged by law to provide food for their parents, and the possibility is being studied of extending that obligation to other elderly near relatives. Chinese legal requirements were quoted earlier in relation to the regional study on China. However, some commentators are concerned about the possibility of tensions within families if children are legally bound to provide certain needs of the parents. They suspect that the aged parent may be made to suffer more if legally a ward of the family than if actually abandoned outside the family home. In 1986 Mexico introduced

[29] García 1981. Speaking at the Pro Vida Conference, 1988, E. Crespo cited the Spanish phrase 'candidatura a la muerte' (candidateship for death), as a description of entry into old people's homes.
[30] UN 1985.

a new law of social assistance which is designed to give support to the aged among other underprivileged groups. However, this invoked a kind of general social contract of the nation rather than imposing duties solely upon relatives. In many places the only appropriate provision made for older people is the home for the aged. This is not normally a preferred option but often is the only viable one in view of economic stringencies.[31] The possible scale of abandonment is indicated by the data in Table 6.3.

The situation is probably best summed up by a Kenyan government spokesman:

Although it is a Government Policy to discourage Homes for the Aged, sometimes it is at pains to accept such homes as a last resort, especially for the abandoned aged persons, mostly in urban centres. At present there are about 25 homes for the aged assisted by the Government financially, although it does not run the day-to-day affairs of the Homes. The grant to these Homes has risen from 1 million Kenyan Shillings to about 5 million Kenyan Shillings this year.[32]

At the World Assembly on Aging in 1982 other African countries reported similar intentions, with old age homes seen as a last resort. In many African countries the old age home as such was almost unknown. Malawi had two such institutions. In India most of the old age home provision is provided by religious orders, as also in Sri Lanka, while in other countries the numbers of old age people residing in this way are too few to appear in statistics.

Old people's homes are more frequently encountered in Latin America. My experience in some of these, both as a resident worker and as a visiting consultant, tends to influence me to treat this subject with some emphasis. It is to be feared that, in spite of their inhibitions, some other countries will, as their age problems develop, find old age homes to be the most economic first, as well as last, resort. It is therefore pertinent to point to some of the sad residential experiences of the aged in Latin America to reinforce the negative experiences which developed countries have had with this kind of age provision.

In 1981, I reported on one home, housed in an old prison, where 750 old people, many of them in extreme stages of illness or incontinence, were cared for by a total staff of 13 dedicated but hopelessly overwhelmed religious sisters, none with specific

[31] Ley Sobre El Sistema Nacional de Asistencia Social, DIF, Mexico, 1986.
[32] HelpAge Kenya, 'Seminar on the Aged', Nairobi, 1985.

TABLE 6.3   *Percentage of Over-60s Widowed, Selected Countries, by Sex*

Region/country	Males	Females
Africa		
Botswana	8.5	53.7
Kenya	7.5	51.0
Morocco	8.3	68.2
Uganda	9.4	48.6
Asia		
Indonesia	15.4	68.7
Japan	16.6	56.6
Korea	19.2	70.2
Latin America		
Brazil	14.4	50.2
Chile	16.2	45.5
Costa Rica	12.2	33.9
Cuba	10.6	36.9
Dominican Republic	7.7	31.6
Mexico	10.8	36.6
Peru	18.3	44.1
North America		
Canada	12.7	41.6
United States	13.2	44.5
Europe		
France	14.5	45.5
German Democratic Republic	14.5	48.7
Netherlands	15.0	36.8
Sweden	14.2	34.2
United Kingdom	14.3	41.9

Source: Myers and Nathanson 1982.

training in geriatric care. A semi-official report from Ecuador, noting a total of 30 homes in the country, described the inmates as 'vegetating and waiting for death'. (Ecuador has set up a Servicio Nacional de Atención Gerontológica with the aim of improving services nationally.) The recommendation of a visiting social services consultant for one Central American home was that it should be evacuated immediately, blown up, and burned to the ground, due to untreatable infestation of the building and site with various types of vermin.[33]

[33] My wife readily accepts responsibility for this remark.

TABLE 6.4   *Males per 100 Females among Over-60s and Over-70s, Regional Groupings, 1980 and 2020*

	60 years and over		70 years and over	
	1980	2020	1980	2020
World	79.8	86.3	70.6	76.7
More-developed regions	65.9	78.1	58.4	67.3
Less-developed regions	93.3	90.9	86.0	84.3
Africa	84.4	87.0	78.6	80.5
East Asia	89.7	89.5	81.4	83.3
South Asia	98.7	93.4	93.2	85.7
Northern America	75.3	77.4	64.9	65.1
Latin America	90.0	88.8	84.9	82.7
Europe	70.1	81.2	62.4	71.4
USSR	44.8	70.3	39.5	56.2
Oceania	82.9	86.1	71.1	77.2

Source: Siegel and Hoover (1984).

In a number of countries, isolated initiatives have taken place in types of service available. In Argentina, for example, a magazine for pensioners, *Tribuna del Jubilado* (Pensioner's Tribune) was founded in 1978, and clubs for pensioners have been operating regularly since that time—I initiated the first of such activities in Argentina in 1956, and in Chile in 1959. In Argentina also there have been programmes similar to those known as Universities of the Third Age. Similar variations of services have been initiated in Uruguay and elsewhere.

The contribution of voluntary services has been important, though often unco-ordinated, and sometimes the initiative was from professional or allied groups concerned about increasing problems, such as the initiatives of the Nurses Association of Jamaica since 1982. In Antigua the responsibility for age care 'is placed on charities, of which the Salvation Army plays the major role'. In Dominica services were rendered by a local organization, REACH, Help the Aged and the regional church committee.[34] In many Latin American countries almost the only social service

[34] Fraser 1982.

available to the aged is from a Catholic order of sisters. In Belize City, with 40,000 inhabitants, I found 10 different voluntary organizations carrying out small but effective schemes for the aged, but with gaps in the service provision due to lack of co-ordination and liaison.

Frustrations of Age Care

There are clearly problems in contemplating a total response to the health and social service needs in these countries. One distinguished commentator has concluded that there are insufficient human, material, and economic resources to resolve the problem.

The expert voice of PAHO witnesses clearly to the prejudice against old age, the negative image of ageing, the bias imposed by the age composition of the countries (tending to highlight the apparent importance of younger age groups), and other considerations in resource allocation:

Health measures have focused on mothers and their small children and on the prevention and control of infectious diseases, particularly those which are communicable (and thus leading towards greater longevity). People with chronic illnesses and those in need of long-term attention have been traditionally relegated to the care of their families and of custodial institutions—with minimal access to professional treatment and services.[35]

The PAHO comment also refers to influential sources which 'cast doubt on the economic rationality of allocating resources to . . . an unproductive minority'. The same report also notes that while most older people are always able to engage in some kind of self-health care, and most are also capable of rendering some service to others, this approach is not generally favoured either by professionals or by the general public, due either to rigid views of treatment solely along curative lines or to sheer ignorance of the basic facts of ageing.

There are inherent frustrations of age care. As another report says, 'the complex and sometimes intractable nature of the problems associated with the ageing process is a major source of

---

[35] PAHO 1985, p. 22.

professional tension and frustration'. The 'perceived failure of
the aged to respond to professional care' precipitates a vicious
circle in which the elderly forego the support of influential voices
and, deprived of priority consideration in resource allocation and
individual concern, deteriorate into an even more dependent and
potential chronic care category.[36]

Another identifiable vicious circle lies in the problem of
lessening family care, related to the higher demands made by
elderly dependants in an era when younger carers have less
opportunity, resources, or incentive to continue to care.

As developing countries become aware of the ageing problem,
the tendency is to fall back on the traditional system of the
extended family, and to hope that the family will care for the
increasing number of elderly. At the same time little is done to
curb the mass migration which is splitting up family units, and
little is done to reinforce the individual family which is caring for
an aged parent. Surveying the response of nations to the present
crisis in family unity, one researcher feels that 'though one can
point to programmes in some countries that address family
needs, in the main relatively little has been done to strengthen
the family's capacities to help its elderly . . . excessive burdens in
providing services may become socially counterproductive by
creating family breakdown'.[37]

Institutionalization

As the classic, and sometimes only, extrafamilial provision for
the elderly in many developing countries is the old people's
home, this brief survey of existing services should conclude with
some comment on the problem of 'institutionalization'. This is
the term being used more and more frequently to describe the
effects on the individual when confined to an institution for long
periods, for example, lack of interest and initiative, mental
confusion, loss of appetite and mobility, and unprovoked
aggression in defence of territory or belongings.

It is generally agreed, says PAHO, that admission to an
institution should be put off as long as possible, and more

[36] Tapia Videla and Parrish 1981.
[37] Brody 1981, p. 196.

humanitarian alternatives found. An Ecuadorian report is most scathing about long-term internment in closed residential institutions. It terms them *gerontocomios* (age asylums in the worst sense of asylum), *cronicarios* (chronic houses) and *precementerios* (pre-cemetery houses), and refers to residence therein as the phase preliminary to and preparatory for death.[38]

One report uses the term 'deposits' as descriptive of long-term homes ('deposits' as in rubbish deposits). The same report identifies the individual as being in isolation from society, in total economic and personal dependency, suffering loss of prestige and damage to his/her dignity. Psychologists Rubin and McNeil 'suspect that institutionalization contributes to a decline in intellectual skills among old people. There is a prevalent negative view of old-age residential institutions.'[39]

Dr Roberta Gaskin in Trinidad and Tobago remarked on the incidence of death due to institutionalization, as mentioned earlier,[40] while Aldritch and Mendkoff also found increased mortality rates related to moves out of an institution after long residence. Various studies have identified physical, psychological, and social deterioration at such times.[41]

In other studies, several negative effects of institutionalization were categorized, including low morale, negative self-image, preoccupation with the past, feelings of personal insignificance, docility, withdrawal, anxiety, and excessive fear of death. Erving Goffman coined the term 'total institution' for the barracks type of home, and saw it as leading to equally total 'curtailment of self'.[42]

Esther Contreras de Lehr in Mexico reported 'loss of orientation, motivation, identity and self-esteem; negative attitude towards life and the future'.[43] Another Brazilian report used similar terms of 'trying to hide dotage . . . like rubbish in deposits of people awaiting death . . . ', and also criticized some voluntary homes for having become merely businesses for profit. In yet another Brazilian reference, admission to an old people's home was likened to exile to a Russian *gulag*.[44]

Specific problems of adjustment include a case of an old man

[38] Merchan 1984, p. 42.   [39] Rubin and McNeil 1985, p. 65.
[40] Aldritch and Mendkoff 1963, pp. 185–94.   [41] Liebowitz 1974, p. 293.
[42] Goffman 1961.   [43] Contreras de Lehr 1986.
[44] Professor Antonio Jordaõ Netto, in unpublished speeches.

forced to sleep in a dormitory when his natural custom was a hammock in the open air. This had a paralysing effect on him. I encountered a similar problem in Sucre, Bolivia, where country people, used to sleeping in a small, individual hut-bedroom, were introduced into clean, beautifully decorated but vast dormitories created from former military barracks.

The effect of family contacts during long residence is a vital factor in a person's resistance to institutionalization. In a survey of old people's homes run by a certain Catholic order in Colombia, the following results were recorded. Of the 59% of residents who received family visits fairly regularly, only 2% were uncommunicative, unhappy, and showing classic signs of institutionalization. Of the 41% who had no family, all commenced with appearing lonely and taciturn, but the majority eventually integrated into the peer group; the remainder deteriorated rapidly. But of the 6% who had family who did *not* visit them, all without exception were bitter, never integrated into the peer group, suffered depressive guilt complexes, and deteriorated into the inevitable symptoms of the institutionalized person.[45]

Another effect similar to 'institutionalization' was the impact of waiting for long periods for admission. This produced apathy, self-criticism, depression, bitterness and extreme irritability. Institutions were also hampered by the lack of medical or psychiatric attention for the old person who had begun to show the classic symptoms which often untrained care staff were unable to understand. Of 183 such homes in Colombia, only 98 had the services of any kind of medical practitioner, and attendance of such a practitioner averaged only 207 hours a week total for the 98 homes, in other words 2.1 hours per week per institution.[46]

A most debilitating practice observed in a home in Lima is that of separating husband and wife on admission to closed-off wards, so that from then on they have no normal contact. Thus, although the Catholic church opposes divorce, the religious sisters at the home were, in effect, divorcing the married couples, due to inadequately planned installations and lack of care staff.

Many reports support the contention that care staff are rarely trained and competent to recognize and treat the effects of

[45] Amaya 1981.   [46] Jiménez Gandica 1981.

institutionalization. Some reports show staff as unwilling to allow residents to take part in routine activities, often because the older resident takes more time to accomplish the task. So the resident is left without tasks and without incentive.

Recognition of these factors does not presuppose a general move to outlaw or rehabilitate old people's homes. In some places it is still regarded as a part of local prestige for a town to have an old people's home and an orphanage. Many old people may well live 'in such hardship conditions that even the impersonality of an institution would seem more desirable'.[47]

When I inspected the old people's home in an abandoned prison as described above, where 750 old people were cared for by a total staff of only 13 nuns and expressed grave concern as to the well-being of the residents, the Superior in charge of the home responded by showing me a waiting list of several hundred homeless old people who obviously considered that conditions inside the institution were much preferable to a life of hunting scraps on the rubbish dumps in the streets outside. At least on the inside there was some kind of food and shelter and beds and security, and somebody who cared, even though that care had to be shared out to an impossible ratio of carer/client relationship.

[47] Denton 1982, pp. 102–4.

7

PILOT METHODS OF RESPONSE

THIS study has set out to be positive in its attitudes. While detailing a fairly pessimistic view of the future impact of an ageing population in the Third World, it also seeks to point to ways and means by which a potential world tragedy may be turned into an enduring human benefit.

A number of experimental projects have already been introduced in developing countries to enhance the lives of older people. Although the vast majority of those projects were introduced with the primary objective of rendering immediate aid to groups in dire need, they are termed experimental here because in many cases there was no established precedent, models, or procedure to which to work, and, in most cases, there was no time, energy, or finance to permit adequate prior assessment or subsequent evaluation. They are therefore presented not as perfect models but as pointers proven in certain specific localities in response to particular conditions.[1]

Major Areas of Enterprise

The models quoted cover a number of areas of enterprise and development. Before referring to the individual projects, it might be instructive to indicate some of the major areas in which initiatives have been taken. This list is not exhaustive but is simply intended to underline some problems for which responses are more readily conceivable and viable. It will therefore, by implication, also indicate other areas which may be more

---

[1] Unless otherwise indicated, details were extracted from Help the Aged (UK) or HelpAge International. Further information can be obtained from HelpAge International Secretariat, St James's Walk, London EC1R OBE.

difficult of solution or to which inadequate attention has so far been directed.

A most important type of programme is that which includes some form of income generation. The lack of governmental social security provision in many developing countries means that for the older person deprived of family support, the question of income generation becomes crucial. In some societies the figure of the aged pauper is still regarded as a subject for sympathy and alms, but many other societies regard that same figure as a subject for disdain and rejection.

A considerable proportion of the problems related to seeking an alternative means of income once family support has been removed hinges on the diminishing physical ability of the elder to undertake the normal productive tasks of the culture. Some projects have therefore tended simply to supply materials such as tools, seeds, and so on which are appropriate to the common labour tasks of the region, yet others have sought to find new ways of income generation which are appropriate to the physical strength and intellectual capabilities of the older person. Such activities as bee-keeping, weaving, and basket-making have the obvious ingredients of leisurely, physically undemanding toil, but often the apparently simple individual solution is complicated by the inability of the new cottage industry to achieve viability and open up markets for itself.

Some of the failures in these and other projects have arisen because of the excessive reliance on external, often expatriate, expertise and the lack of involvement of the local community in planning stages. This involvement therefore becomes another major aspect of projects concerned with the older population, especially because the recipient group is sometimes unable to undertake its own planning and organization due to the onset of senility or to an inadequate knowledge of modern market requirements. The willing co-operation of a group of local people at an early stage of a project also induces a sense of local 'ownership' of the scheme and results in a higher possibility of perpetuating the scheme once expatriate involvement is removed.

While still referring to expatriate influence, a very necessary element of an ageing programme in a developing country lies in the ability to exercise critical assessment of any 'Western' model which is proposed. A particular example of dubious 'Western' benefits is the profusion of convent-type old people's homes instituted by agencies from North America or Western Europe in developing countries. In many cases such homes are architecturally unsuitable, impose an alien discipline, culture, and possibly creed, and require programmes of activities, or lack of activity, which are far removed from the customary daily pursuits of the residents. Such institutions may provide the basics of bed, food, clothing, and shelter but they sometimes develop into regimes of considerable personal dependency, oppression, and even at times cruelty.

Other unacceptable Western models include such apparently attractive programmes as pensions insurance, which may be beyond the economic ability of the country to implement or may be so selective as to fail to benefit those who most require aid. Progressive planning for the ageing community will therefore always be alert for the locally feasible and acceptable alternative. In this respect the early involvement of the elderly themselves can often be important (as distinct from a non-elderly group of local charitable volunteers). In most developing regions the elderly are, as a group, most likely to have the knowledge and appreciation of local affairs to be able to criticize an alien scheme and warn of likely impediments or unsuspected by-products. The involvement of the elderly as participants also reduces the aura of dependence which often attaches to so-called charitable programmes based on the donor-to-recipient concept.

Whilst it is a much greater problem than simply as related to the grandparents, the breakdown of the family is also a phenomenon for which provision is made in a number of programmes. Most well-informed projects aimed at helping the aged commence with the question, 'Is there anything that can be done locally to strengthen or rehabilitate the extended family?', yet once the vicious trend of migration has commenced, it is often impossible to restore certain family groups.

Closely tied in to the question of family survival, especially in urban areas, is the problem of unsuitable housing and the need to experiment with new types of accommodation, both for the elderly who have no remaining family and also for the elderly who may still be able to live with or near the family, given suitable accommodation.

Suitable accommodation is related, too, to the development of appropriate technology for problems of ageing. This can involve the adaptation of living space for the peculiar requirements of frail or disabled elders, and it can extend to prosthetic aids of types that can be produced locally at low cost. It should certainly take into consideration simple tools and machinery which would enable the person with failing strength to continue a type of labour which would be impracticable with existing tools. The latter particularly applies where there has been a massive out-migration of working-age labour or, as now appearing in AIDS epidemic areas, where there has been excessive loss of manual labour force due to mortality.

The need for involvement of local groups and of the elderly themselves has already been stressed. To the initial interest aroused in such groups must then be added the skills and resources adequate for supporting and extending new enterprise. Some of the projects quoted will be seen to emphasize training and support, not only in technical and professional subjects but also in the everyday realities of administration, volunteer recruitment, finance, and so on.

Two apparently opposed considerations also emerge from a study of the projects. It seems that it is possible in certain instances to identify programmes which directly, and sometimes solely, benefit the elderly as a group. One such area is in the prevalence of eye diseases, particularly cataract, and the low-cost, low-technology intervention which is possible in ophthalmic treatment. At the same time as 'segregating' the needs of the elderly, it is seen as imperative that the elderly of developing countries be given every opportunity and support to remain integrated or become reintegrated in the family and accustomed community, contrary to the system of total segregation of elderly seen in some Northern societies.

Asia: A Unique Approach

In many respects, the doyen of indigenous 'age action' agencies is HelpAge India, which originated in the mid-1970s and is now a well-established national organization. As a result of a visit by two Indians to study the operation of the Help The Aged head-quarters in London, this organization has from the beginning emphasized the inter-generational aspect. Largely through the enthusiasm of young people and children, but also owing much to the practical expertise of its own directors and project advisers, it has been able to fund many local projects in India. It acts, too, as intermediary for international agencies in many and varied projects, some of which will be discussed.

A high priority within the HelpAge India infrastructure was given to the education and recruitment of schoolchildren and youths in age care and fund-raising programmes. The purpose of this was to lay the foundations for a new generation which will remedy some of the social failings arising from migrations of the present working generation, where younger people, under economic pressures, have abandoned the grandparent generation, either purposely or involuntarily.

There is no lack of commentators who have expressed concern about the breakdown of inter-generational understanding. It is important that children and adolescents get as realistic as possible a picture of old age since the picture of ageing and old age formed in childhood accompanies us throughout our lives and may establish norms and attitudes for our own ageing. In the shaping of society, it is therefore necessary to give the young a realistic concept of ageing in order to minimize the effects of non-genuine age changes.

A Latin American writer has said that 'the preparation for old age must commence from infancy. The habits acquired in the first steps of life, if fruit of a proper formative period, are the determinants of a satisfactory old age.' So, she continues, 'we are seeking to change the idea [among young people] of old age from being passive, useless, dependent and sidelined to being active, autonomous, useful, and socially participative'.[2]

HelpAge India's contribution is therefore unique in recruiting hundreds of thousands of young people both to work directly with older people and (HelpAge India's initial concept) to take a responsible part in the procurement of those financial resources without which no project, however well planned and well intentioned, can hope to get off the ground. The organization is also of significance in that it has been successful in transposing what were originally British models for acceptance and success

[2] Dulcey-Ruiz 1985.

to an indigenous culture, a transplant operation which has been achieved with similar success in the varying cultures of Sri Lanka, Kenya, Colombia, and elsewhere.

The provision of financial resources promises project viability for forward-looking project planners like those of AWARE, CEWA, URDES, and other caring agencies that will be discussed below. The first two projects discussed tackle the basic problem of personal destitution and means of financial support for individual older people themselves.

Rural India

There are many rural labourers in India who spend their lives trying to be rid of debts which never seem to diminish and which they have little hope of ever clearing. In order to try and pay off their debts, labourers are obliged to work on their creditors' farms until the creditors declare that the loan has been repaid. The labourers very often lose track of how much they owe and how much they have repaid, and are therefore very much at the mercy of their employers. During the period of repayment, the labourers do not have the freedom to seek other employment or other means of livelihood.

In general, the wages are so low and interest charges so high that they have no chance of repaying their debts, and often have to incur more debts in order to survive. The period of repayment is thus often passed from generation to generation, with sons and daughters pledging their labour to repay loans when their parents are no longer able to work.

A typical example of these labourers is Guruvayya, who borrowed 300 rupees (about £20) as a young man, to meet his family's basic needs for food, shelter, and clothing. To pay off the loan, he joined his creditor's farm as a labourer. *Sixty years later*, he and his wife are still working to repay the money. They earn only four bags of rice a year, and even their land has been taken as part-repayment. They have little hope of clearing the debts during their lifetime, and it will probably then fall to their children to take on the liability.

Another example is Vadthyia Laxim, a tribal woman, whose husband died 10 years ago leaving her to pay off the remainder of his original debt of 400 rupees. Every time she thinks she has succeeded in her repayment, she finds her debt has increased due to the very high interest charged by her employer.

A Hyderabad organization, AWARE (Action for Welfare and Awakening in Rural Environment) has for some years been involved in publicizing the plight of these rural labourers and helping them in their struggle to free themselves from debt. AWARE is supported in its actions by the Indian Supreme Court as this system of debt repayment is, in fact, illegal.

AWARE periodically organizes large meetings for local labourers, police, and government officials to discuss the problem and suggest ways to overcome it. At the meetings, labourers who have succeeded in liberating themselves are called upon to tell their stories to the crowd in order to give hope and encouragement to others to persevere in their struggle for freedom from debt.

Once the labourers have been released from debt, it is important that they are immediately set up in a money-making activity so that they can become independent earners. Otherwise they face the likelihood of falling into debt all over again. The average amount required to set up a labourer in business and keep him/her going at subsistence level for three months is 3,000 rupees (£200), although this does vary according to individual needs. For example, the labourer may choose to buy farm animals, such as a couple of plough bullocks (about 2,500 rupees), or perhaps the tools and materials for a trade such as shoemaking.

AWARE, aided by a HelpAge India grant, is committed to aiding the release and rehabilitation of 400 elderly people in Hyderabad, in the state of Andhra Pradesh. The elderly labourers are given easy-term loans by the bank where the money is deposited, enabling them to set themselves up independently so that they become self-supporting. As the loans are repaid, the funds become available for further loans to other labourers. The whole operation is strictly monitored.

Novel 'pension' scheme

A disastrous cyclone in the state of Andhra Pradesh, that swept away entire fishing villages was an opportunity for a local agency, URDES, to remedy a state of financial dependency of the fisherfolk and to provide a permanent 'pension' in kind for the aged.

Fishing is the way of life of the men of Pallepalem village. The women grow millet and some other vegetables in plots near their homes, but for men fishing is the only work available. They use fish traps made of reeds to catch small fish in the rivers but if they want to go to sea they must have a boat.

There is no suitable wood for boat building available near Pallepalem. For as long as anyone can remember, the wood for boats has had to be brought from far away Kerala, in the south-west of India. Logs of this wood can be bought in Pondicherry, the capital of Tamil Nadu state which lies next to Andhra Pradesh. All the fishing boats in the region are made in the same way, from five huge logs of a tree which is chosen because it is buoyant and floats easily. The logs are shaped and cut to size with the largest in the middle and are bound together with rope to form a boat.

For generations, the fishermen of Pallepalem have lived out their lives in debt to the merchants who owned the fishing boats. This is still the situation in hundreds of other villages along the coast. When the catch was brought ashore, the merchants' local agents collected a proportion of the catch and bought the rest from the fishermen at a price that *they*, the merchants, fixed, which was well below the market rate. For example, in the early months of each year, prawns can be caught about five kilometres off shore. The agents paid the fishermen 40 rupees per kilo for these, although they sold at 100 rupees per kilo in the market.

After the cyclone, HelpAge India provided funds through URDES to help the fishermen set up a co-operative society which would own and work from its own fishing boats. Funds to buy enough logs to build 33 boats were provided, and a co-operative society of 100 members—all the men of the village—was formed. HelpAge India agreed to finance the operation provided that the boats remained the property of the whole co-operative and that each boat crew agreed to contribute three kilograms of fish from each catch to the widows and elderly of the village. In return, the widows would have the job of selling all the fish each day in the local market at Kavali, nine kilometres from Pallepalem.

URDES staff had never been involved with fishermen before; they usually worked in clinics doing medical work with the very poor, or in village schools. This time the URDES officer in the village acted as an adviser. He encouraged the villagers to accept the grant and to form the fishing co-operative. He went with some of the men to Pondicherry to buy the logs and has helped them to open a bank account. He also advised them to ignore the threats from the agents. He has been threatened himself and told to go away from the village.

Mr Venkatarana, the secretary of the fishermen's collective, described a visit to the village by some representatives of the merchants who had previously rented boats to the village people: 'They threatened us and said we must pay for the boats which were lost. They told some of the men that they should have a share of the catch from the new boats. We refused.'

The support of two national organizations and an international agency enabled the people of the emergent co-operative to resist the malicious pressures of their erstwhile 'owners'.[3]

Self-help communities

CEWA (Centre for the Welfare of the Aged), a well-established organization of repute in the field of urban poverty, was set up in 1980 to help cater for the needs of the large number of elderly people in India who do not benefit from any age care services. It was created with two main aims in mind. Firstly, to initiate services for elderly people in different parts of the country (with appropriate modifications to suit the local conditions), and secondly to function as a research and training centre on ageing and age care.

In contrast to some popular programmes for the care of elderly people in India, which tend to promote institutional care, CEWA believes that the best place for the well-being of elderly people is within their families and communities. It therefore promotes a variety of non-institutional services for elderly people, often run by the elderly people themselves, which enable them to play an active part in the community.

CEWA's work began with the establishment of a day centre in a small hut in Naduvakkarai, a slum area of Madras. Meetings

[3] A special education pack for teachers in schools, *The Pallepalem Report*, from Help the Aged's Education Department, is also a good example of use of project information in an imaginative way.

for elderly people were organized to spread the concept of day centres in the area, and a household survey was carried out with the aim of both spreading the idea of community care for elderly people through day centres and of collecting basic information on the families of the elderly people.

In the areas where CEWA set up day centres, community leaders were involved in the proceedings right from the beginning. At first, the idea of community-based services for elderly people was quite unfamiliar, and the initial reaction from the communities involved, including some of the elderly people themselves, was one of indifference. However, following CEWA's programme of creating an awareness of the benefits of non-institutional care for the elderly, day centres are now accepted and welcomed in the community.

Once the day centres were actually set up, first priority was given to attending to the health needs of the elderly people. As an initial step, a detailed health assessment was made of most of the elderly people in the area surrounding the centres. This was done in collaboration with the geriatric unit of the government hospital. CEWA then set up weekly clinics at the day centres, so as to enable elderly people to avail themselves of medical services near their homes and in familiar surroundings.

A medical officer now regularly visits the day centres, although elderly people requiring more detailed examination are taken to the government hospital's geriatric unit. Here they are regularly attended by CEWA personnel, along with other elderly people and members of the family. The medical officer also visits bed-ridden elderly people in their homes, and, where necessary, arranges special treatment for them, such as visits by physiotherapists. Regular eye screening and special eye camps are arranged to ensure maximum ophthalmic attention for the elderly people.

The overall objective of the day centres is self-help. The centres are managed and run by the elderly people themselves through an Association of the Elderly, with support where necessary from CEWA. At the day centres, the elderly people can become involved in a variety of different activities. There are various recreational facilities available, outings to different places, discussions of daily news and events, family counselling, and celebrations of festivals.

The poorest elderly people are provided with a nutritious lunch, an operation which is fully managed by the elderly people themselves. They buy the provisions and cook and serve the food. Other activities at the day centre include making paper bags and incense sticks, which as well as keeping the elderly people occupied, also give them an opportunity to earn a little extra money. The elderly people buy the raw materials and then sell the goods they make. The profits are shared according to the contribution of each individual.

Eye disease: scourge of age

Eye afflictions and diseases cause more large scale disability and distress in India than any other disease. Up until now, only limited research has been carried out into the long-term effects of such eye diseases. Research carried out by the Vocational Rehabilitation Training Centre for the Blind (VRTC) revealed that out of a rural population of 355 million spread over India's 15 states, 19.9 million people have impaired vision and 3.5 million of these are blind. Eye disease in India has constantly been brought to the public's attention over the last few years; this has led to a reasonable provision of financial aid for cataract surgery, and crucial and highly valuable preventive work is now being carried out in certain areas through village Eye Services. One useful method is to set up temporary but adequately equipped eye camps to which the local elderly in remote rural areas can come for cataract operations.

The Blind Men's Association (BMA) was set up in 1950 as a recreation club for the blind. After many years of struggle against prevailing attitudes towards blindness held by the general public and the blind and disabled themselves, it has become an innovating, modern, and highly effective organization offering a comprehensive range of rehabilitation services both in Ahmedabad and in the surrounding rural areas. The BMA firmly believes that the blind, aged, and disabled have great potential and that they can be valuable and productive members of society.

At its headquarters in Ahmedabad, the BMA provides a wealth of educational services including a Braille and talking book library and an adult training centre. These cater for those who have been deprived of education in other schools, those who are considered too old to be educated elsewhere, those who need further education and training, or those who, because of their background, were not aware of the facilities available for the blind and disabled.

In 1981 the BMA decided that it was imperative to reach and help the blind and disabled in the rural areas of Gandhinagar. A rural rehabilitation programme was devised with the help of HelpAge India, to run initially in 80 villages. The BMA felt that it would be wrong to take the rural aged away from their communities and place them in institutionalized care. It would be more costly and would not provide any solution to the long-term problems of these people, who badly needed to integrate themselves fully into the community and feel a sense of self worth and esteem. The BMA was also anxious that the aged should not be uprooted from their homes.

The new programme aimed to identify the needy elderly in the villages and to offer them a comprehensive rehabilitative programme covering all aspects of medical care, health care, social activities, and economic rehabilitation. Added to this there would be an information service which would spread the word about the BMA and offer advice to the elderly on pensions, transport, and legislation affecting them. Previously there had been no easy way for the elderly of acquiring such information.

The project was initiated in October 1983 with grants from HelpAge India and Help the Aged (UK). By the end of 1984, only a year later, the BMA had succeeded in helping more than 3,000 of the rural elderly in the villages of Gandhinagar. They found that the incidence of disease and illness among the elderly was far higher than had initially been anticipated and, more disturbingly, that many of these illnesses were preventable or curable.

The BMA has given high priority to medical work. The aged blind and disabled are screened by BMA staff and volunteers, and where necessary they are taken to Ahmedabad to receive tretament. Eye clinics are held regularly in the village schools, with the whole community becoming involved; in the first six months of the programme, more than 600 elderly had their sight restored through cataract operations. As a result the Gandhingar district has been declared a cataract-free zone, in the sense that there are no waiting lists for operations.

Tuberculosis camps are also held, and a physiotherapist (who is himself blind) goes from village to village offering his services to those suffering from polio, arthritis, rheumatism, and other crippling diseases. Other BMA staff concentrate on teaching the blind or disabled aged the vital daily living skills, orientation, mobility and vocational skills so that they can lead normal lives.

Those who are able are taught skills so that they can earn a living and thus become more self-supporting and integrated into the community. Raw materials are taken to the villages, and the elderly are taught to make various goods. The finished articles are taken away to be sold, so providing a small income for many of these people. The skills taught include cotton-seed separation, vermicelli-making (out of wheat), weaving, book-binding, candle-making, carpentry, making incense sticks, and cigarette-rolling. The BMA also sees the provision of religious services and material as one way of providing comfort for isolated elderly or disabled and as a way of bringing them together with others. To this end they have provided each village with a cassette recorder along with suitable cassettes. Mobility aids are also provided from the workshop in Ahmedabad.

In 1984 the BMA sought further funding to maintain their programme in Gandhinagar and to expand it to the villages of Daskroi Taluka, and to maintain the Gandhinagar programme until April 1986; and then to cover a new programme in Daskroi Taluka for an 18-month period with the proviso that the BMA should become self-financing and supporting.

The Vocational Rehabilitation Training Centre for the Blind is situated in Ludhiana in the Punjab, India. Its director is Mr E. M. Johnson, an Indian who is himself blind and is qualified in social work and rehabilitation of the blind and handicapped. The centre has a staff of eight and it runs successful and highly beneficial programmes for the blind who live nearby. However, those who live in the country, or who are too old to travel, have no such service. It was strongly felt, therefore, that some provision for these people was necessary in the form of rehabilitation and vocational training.

The Vocational Rehabilitation Training Centre had the idea of establishing Rural Rehabilitation and Home Training Centres.

These would be places where trained teachers would be able to offer their services to impart vocational skills. The first step was to train these special teachers. Each year 30 students are trained at the centre on special courses lasting six months. Three-quarters of them are over 40 years old and they are selected from different areas of the country.

Their training covers mobility, orientation, physiotherapy, occupational therapy, eye disease prevention, rehabilitation and practical aspects of incurable diseases, field work in hospital, counselling and, most importantly, vocational skills. These include rope making, ink-making, rug-making, soap-making, detergent production, candle-making, furniture-making, carpet- and mat-weaving, book-binding, tailoring, home management, light engineering, and music-teaching.

Once trained, these teachers go out as part of teams and set up Rural Rehabilitation and Home Training schemes in other areas of North India. Each team aims to cover about 20 villages a year and train an average of 10 disabled in each village, providing jobs afterwards and ensuring that products are marketed. In this way the blind, especially the aged blind, should receive the care and rehabilitation they need to make them a useful part of the community and to help them achieve more independence.

Towards better housing

A useful service of HelpAge India is advice on constructing modest, inexpensive housing for the poorer elderly, using the best of local materials. This approach is illustrated by an extract from the handbook of guidance prepared on the subject.

Remember that although cleanliness and efficiency are required when looking after old people, they are mainly not happy and do not 'feel at home' in so-called 'modern' surroundings, with a preponderance of glass and concrete and steel. They belong to a generation which appreciated the 'natural' simple direct building materials such as wood, mud, tile, thatch and brick.

'Contemporary' and 'modern' research has been done so that the shortcomings of these 'old-fashioned' materials have been removed and coped with. These new techniques with old materials are undoubtedly less expensive than currently fashionable materials such as cement and steel. It must be kept in mind that India will remain short of cement for quite a long time and it is an essential item for such engineering work, while we have effective alternatives for domestic building work. So use cement sparingly. . . .

Lime is an older and well-tried material for mortars and plasters. It is as good as cement if pozzolanas (such as Surki) are added. A 1-part lime : 2-parts Surki : 4-parts sand gives a first-class mortar. In many districts mud mortars have been used effectively for centuries. Why stop? . . .

Mud walls. Again, these have been in use for centuries and are excellent when stabilised with lime or bitumen, or reinforced with bamboo, husks, etc. The use of a simple removable adjustable frame into which earth is rammed can eliminate that 'old-fashioned' look and give a strong load bearing wall. Burnt brickwork is increasing in cost but 25% reduction of bricks and mortar is effected if 'rat-trap' bond is used. It also provides better insulation and is strong and load bearing. . . .

Plaster. The use of plaster accounts for about 10% of the total cost of a house. Furthermore you are committed to decoration and maintenance costs for ever more! In most districts, if a roof over-hang is provided, plaster is totally unnecessary on the exterior walls of a building. Internally, if colour or white wash is required (again, not strictly necessary) it can be applied equally well to flush pointed smooth brickwork. So don't use plaster unnecessarily.

Lintels are usually overdesigned or even totally unnecessary. Use simple lintels, or use reinforced brick. Save cement, save steel save cost. Timber is now costly. Consider using treated 'country timbers' and use minimum sections ($2\frac{1}{2}'' \times 3\frac{1}{2}''$ is adequate for door and window frames.)

For FLOORING the old-fashioned floor tile, or 'brick tile', or 'quarry tile' is comfortable, homely and 'good for rheumatism'. These tiles are far superior, for old people, to 'mosaic', terrazzo and polishing stone. All forms of cement floor are found to be 'cold' and they 'sweat' badly during the Monsoon.

In districts where it is available and suitable, use TILED roofing rather than reinforced concrete. Where reinforced concrete is considered essential, then make a 30% reduction in cost and in cement by using a filler slab, or a ribbed slab, or any of the cement and cost reducing systems developed by the CBRI [Central Building Research Institute at Roorkee, U.P.]

At Dehra Dun a variant of the inter-generational approach has been introduced. A club for older people has been set up at the local YWCA. Alongside the YWCA a small crèche is being built so that the more active and able grandmothers from the old people's club can look after small children while their mothers go out to work to obtain much-needed additional finance for the family.

Landless in Bangladesh

In Bangladesh, the Humanitarian Agency for Development Services has taken a special interest in the plight of the landless labourers. Their programme has been aided by funds for age welfare on the basis that this is the best help for local old people, especially where younger male members of the family may have migrated in search of work in the cities. The scheme is based on a group of families making very small savings every week. The savings are organized in 10 blocks of 10 villages each. When funds permit, members of the programme borrow funds for purchase of land, tools, seeds, and so on. Two water pumps were installed which have increased the number of harvests a year from one to three. Because of migration, a significant number of the participants are over 40, which, in local conditions is considered the age at which many people become unemployable, and therefore from a work point of view 'aged'.

The Bangladesh Rural Reconstruction Movement is running a special retraining and relocation scheme for fishermen whose livelihood has been destroyed by silting up of estuary rivers. Younger displaced fishermen drift to the cities in search of work. The fishermen who remain tend to be older and are assisted to change over to farming on newly reclaimed land.

More Asian initiatives

In Sri Lanka a similar programme to that of HelpAge India has been developed by another HelpAge organization. Prominent among its innovations have been the first training courses for care staff for the aged, such care staff having, in the past, lacked both training and professional status. The courses are open both to volunteers and to staff of old people's homes. They consist of blocks of training, beginning with a week's residential course followed by three weeks of work experience under supervision. Twelve such blocks of teaching and experience constitute the full course, which carries the first qualifying certificate for this kind of care practice.

In a programme to improve the living standards of the elderly the new Ratmalana Centre will cater for all classes of elderly, aiming specifically at enabling families to retain old people in their own homes, and for old people living alone to do so in comfort and security for as long as possible. Bathing facilities will be provided as well as a hairdresser. A tea bar is to be run by the members themselves. There will be an Old Friends Group which will interact with schoolchildren who visit on a planned basis. Benefits, advice, and legal aid are to be given. Another organization, Suwa Sewana, is upgrading a slum feeding centre—a very necessary, urgent, and interim response to great need—into a day centre with multiple activities and opportunities.

In Pakistan, the incursions of Afghan refugees have added greatly to the numbers of elderly needing treatment for leprosy and blindness. In fact, the extent and seriousness of the leprosy condition of many of the refugees was beyond the normal experience in Pakistan and therefore added to the strain on local services. Many older people have suffered for years without adequate treatment. Duel-purpose programmes (leprosy and blindness) have been set up in Baluchistan and Azad Kashmir, dealing mainly with the older population. One of the essential requirements is adequate transport, for a delay of a few days in giving the monthly anti-leprosy dose may destroy the entire process of successful treatment.

In Malaysia, an expatriate volunteer occupational therapist has been based in an old people's home in a region of Sarawak where rehabilitation of the elderly is an unknown concept. The therapist is training staff of the home at the same time as working alongside them. More general training courses are also carried out for staff from other medical and care institutions.

Recently, a group of retired Malaysian civil servants and similar people formed into a Senior Citizens' Club offered to carry out voluntary service within the community, lending their skills to any task which might improve the circumstances of the less fortunate. Also in Malaysia, a Ministry of Education official announced the planning of a new secondary school curriculum to include 'concepts to effect a value and attitudinal change' towards the elderly'. Schools will be required to reinforce what is taught at home or even to bring forward new concepts of social commitment.[4]

The little-recognized problem of elderly illegal aliens has been taken up by the government of Thailand and the Redemptorist Fathers. Aliens are imprisoned if they are illegally present in Thailand, and often their own countries refuse to recognize or redeem them. Some aliens are elderly and have been in prison a considerable time. Now such older prisoners can be bailed to the Fathers who accept full legal responsibility for them and undertake to give them physical care until death.

Klong Toey is the largest area of shanties in Bangkok, with some 90,000 people, including numbers of destitute and abandoned elderly people, living in dilapidated shacks and huts in and around the Klong Toey port and slaughterhouse area. The environment in the slums is very unhealthy, with poor drainage and no proper sewage facilities. There is also a high density of rats and other vermin and a great deal of termite damage. Shacks are built on stilts in the swampy area of the slum which floods twice a month. The flooding is caused partly by the high tides, but the situation is made worse by the cement dikes built by the authorities to keep the nearby slaughterhouse dry.

The welfare of the elderly people living in the Klong Toey slum is the concern of the Human Development Centre, a Catholic organization providing them with basic housing and living support, including medical care and feeding programmes. The latter are vital as many of the elderly people suffer from malnutrition. The centre was set up by the Catholic archdiocese of Bangkok and is run by a team from seven different religious congregations comprising six nuns, one brother, and one priest.

The criteria for accepting people into the centre's elderly support scheme are that they should be at least 65 years old, destitute, and without family support, although some exceptions have been made to include some younger disabled people in real need. In addition to providing for the welfare of the elderly people in the slum, the Human Development Centre also provides a variety of services for the other age groups in the community, such as slum schools. It also runs a highly successful craft industry producing patchwork, mainly for export. Much of

[4] WHO Kuala Lumpur 1986.

this work is conducted in the Klong Toey shacks. An international grant is being used to provide extra food for the elderly people and to help pay their medical and funeral expenses.

Inter-generational Plans

Singapore stresses inter-generational educational activities. For example, a 'Senior Citizens' Week' is organized each year to promote social awareness of the contributions made by elders and to instil in the young a love and respect for older people. One objective is to show that Singapore is a warm and caring society; another is to focus on changing inter-generational relationships and needs.

Other inter-generational activities in Singapore include Three-tier Family Living workshops, which seek to bridge the gap between people of different ages and to encourage multi-generational living. In one such workshop, participants ranging in age from 16 to 67 met over a three-day period, dividing into groups to discuss the three-generation family and methods of resolving family conflicts. Each group presented its ideas in drawings, case studies, and role plays. Pre-retirement education programmes are also now being offered in Singapore under the auspices of a voluntary organization, the People's Association Retiree Club.

As a rapidly modernizing society, Singapore is also experimenting with some of the educational programmes pioneered in developed nations, such as a pre-retirement education and a Holiday Camp, residential academic programme for the elderly. Modelled after the US-initiated Elderhostel programme, such a scheme, organized by the Department of Extramural Education and the Singapore Action Group of Elders (SAGE), was held in 1987 at the National University of Singapore. It was designed to meet the needs of the growing number of better-educated older adults in Singapore who desire a suitable continuing education programme. It is intended to hold such camps on a regular basis during the long vacation period. The programme includes lectures on the uses of leisure time, nutrition, and environmental health, along with exercise, games, singing, and dancing.

A sensible blend of appropriate technology applied to local

resources exists in Western Samoa where the installation of a solar heating system in an old people's home is expected to reduce heating and hot water costs to half the annual sum charged for electricity.

Promoting activities

An Indonesian organization called Biro Manula BKKKS formerly concentrated on running an old people's home but has more recently set up Home Care centres, particularly in Jakarta, aimed at enabling old people to remain in their own homes and carry on gainful activities there. These are units staffed by about 15 volunteers, with from 30 to 80 old people attending. Midday meals are served, and attention is given to medical care, house repairs, clothing, recreation, opportunities for self-employment, religious counselling, and funeral insurance.

Cebu Caritas in the Philippines sponsors a programme specializing in work opportunities for older people with insufficient income. Types of craft taught and developed include bamboo, shell, and basketwork. Other work opportunities include car mechanics, industrial sewing, basic electrics, and radio and television repairs. The project works with a group of 30 people aged 60 to 80 integrated with 30 school leavers. Six target parishes were selected to commence the scheme, with the aim of extending to 135 parishes over five years.

A very delicate problem of ageing is attended to by the HelpAge organization in South Korea. Etiquette requires that an elderly single man or widower may not speak to a single woman or widow with intent to form a friendship unless formally introduced. HelpAge therefore holds social events, often tea parties, where the attendant is able to make formal introductions, after which men and women can pursue their own negotiations, perhaps towards matrimony. A general information centre and counselling service advise on less delicate problems, and there is also a home visiting service.

Chinese variants

Some reference has already been made in an earlier chapter to programmes in China. Several other ways have been found to utilize the elderly population. Many are used as volunteers to help regulate a range of civic activities. Men and some women help to enforce regulations in free markets. A produce market in Chengdu, for example, that attracts 700–800 vendors daily, has only three paid staff, but several older volunteer workers to help oversee operations. Older men may direct traffic in congested neighbourhoods. Neighbourhoods themselves are also generally run by older persons. They sit on the Neighbourhood Committees, help to ensure neighbourhood sanitation, help enforce family planning regulations, and generally see to it that the neighbourhood functions properly. Others may act as mediators in disputes or act as after-school counsellors.

Because highly skilled workers are still at a premium in China, the elderly skilled are used extensively to teach others. Thus, a factory may ask a technician to stay on for a limited time after retirement to help train younger workers. Other retired workers may be seconded to factories in other cities or towns, and such a sojourn may last two or three years. With the development of light industry in rural areas, skilled older workers are particularly in demand as teachers.[5]

On the coast of China, age care organizers in the enclave of Macau have found language problems in the training of workers. The local academic language is Portuguese. The colloquial language is Chinese, and most potential nurses are Chinese. The language of pharmacology is English. In spite of this, a course for assistant nurses in age care has been set up with a 690-hour duration. To meet the language difficulty, specialist teachers are brought in from Hong Kong. In Hong Kong itself another HelpAge organization is working with destitute old people.

Africa: An Earlier Phase of the Ageing Process

The onset of modern ageing problems began later in Africa than in Asia and Latin America, but in some areas the situation is already severe enough to require developments beyond reliance on the extended family or the residential institution as a

[5] Goldstein and Goldstein 1986.

substitute. In most African countries there has already been some consideration of, and reaction to, the challenge.

However, there is a noticeable difference in the types of programmes being developed as feasible and most urgent in Africa, compared with programmes in other developing regions. This might best be illustrated by contrasting HelpAge programmes in Somalia and Ghana with those in Colombia and Bolivia.

As will be mentioned, a number of programmes in African countries, especially Somalia and Ghana, involve either the rehabilitation of services which have faltered for lack of resources or the input of training and finance to develop new services of health delivery to the old person. In Ghana, a major scheme has been rehabilitating a disused hospital, training local staff to provide an on-going personnel resource, and then extending the hospital service to include a domiciliary primary health component. In Somalia another major scheme covers the training of existing medical staff in ophthalmics.

In contrast, the major HelpAge programmes in Colombia and Bolivia relate to the empowerment of local groups, including the elderly themselves, to set up their own relevant age care and activity programmes with a strong element of income-generation. An important component in these Latin American programmes concerns the training of staff and volunteers in the skills of organization and finance, as well as the setting up of their own training schemes in service delivery.

The essential variations in strategy relate to the degree of modernization and break-down of the clan and extended family systems in a country or region. This degree of social metamorphosis is also closely related to the experience and structures arising out of such change, providing communities with the ability to organize their own fairly sophisticated programmes. In other words, the community with least clan and family breakdown is likely to have least skill in alternative forms of organization, conditions frequently found in less accessible areas of Africa.

The African precursor of the HelpAge family was HelpAge Kenya. This organization, whose development was facilitated by the modernized socio-economic structures of Nairobi was able to develop activities such as a forum sustaining a free interchange of information on ageing as it affects the country. Two of the programmes featured in such a forum were the Joot Social Services of Western Kenya and Undugu Society of Nairobi. They reported on their activities.

The destitute elderly

Ahero Joot Social Services was started in the late 1960s by Fr. Buers with a mere 45 members. The project was begun in order to help to uplift the lives of the destitute elderly in a plains area of Western Kenya where annual flooding sometimes gets out of hand and destroys the vital maize crops. The project has gone from strength to strength and it now has 3,000 members who have taken upon themselves the responsibility of looking after about 1,000 elderly poor people.

Assistance is provided to the elderly women by holding small meetings each month at which food, clothing, and a little cash are collected. The meetings take place at each of nine parish centres, built in traditional style, run by Joot. The proceeds go not only to the residents of homes run by churches but to other elderly people as well who are living in their own villages. The Joot members of each centre are responsible for the elderly in and around its centre. Each centre has its own elected committee which seeks out the needy and the destitute and adopts them either as residents of the homes (in case they have no one to care for them in their own villages) or as protégés to be assisted at their own place of residence.

No one is permitted to live in any of the nine centres unless no relations can be found to look after her. Thus there are only 60 people living in the homes out of 1,000 or so aged who receive some assistance from Joot.

The Joot members pay regular visits to all the elderly under their care and keep their houses well-thatched, clean, and tidy. They look after their bedding and clothes and report any sickness to the Mission. Immediate action involves taking medicine to the sick and transporting the seriously ill to hospital. Sometimes it is required to provide a decent burial for them, a clear proof that these elderly people have had no one who could have looked after them. Joot makes sure that no one goes hungry by regularly taking food round to the church homes, where a fair distribution is made to all the needy living in and around the centres; this is supervised by the committee members.

Besides this, there are common garden-plots at each centre which are ploughed by the Joot and the food grown there remains in the centre. Elderly women themselves help to sow seeds and weed the gardens as best they can. Some pocket-money is provided monthly to each sponsored elderly woman and she is left free to visit her friends whenever she desires. Thus residents of the church homes retain their personal freedom and dignity.

Those who are not too feeble are encouraged to keep themselves busy by doing hand-work such as pot-making, mat-making, rope-making, and basket-weaving. Some of their products are even sold at the local market.

Generational switch

The Undugu Society of Kenya was founded to undertake work with children in slum areas. With the development of an ageing problem, the society moved into programmes which also gave aid to older people along the lines illustrated below. The aim of the programme is to make people generally aware of their responsibility towards the aged in their community so that later on they can take over the local scheme. This particular programme is carried out in the slum areas of Pumwani and the huge area of Mathare Valley, Nairobi.

In Pumwani old people are assisted by Undugu, through St John's Community Centre. Every Friday, 30 people receive a small weekly financial allowance plus a cup of tea and bread arranged by an Undugu social worker. Pumwani's residents are mostly Muslims, so a committee has been formed which consists of prominent Muslim leaders together with social workers of St John's Church and Undugu. The elderly decide themselves who is in most need, for all are basically poor.

The aims of this committee are to discuss problems affecting the old people and to see ways and means of encouraging self help. For example, if it is found out that an old person on the programme does not have any relative to provide adequate care the committee finds a home help or sponsor.

In Kitui Village, 26 old people are being assisted. They receive a weekly allowance through the leaders of a women's group known as Bora Afya. There are record sheets on which the people put their fingerprints after receiving the money. This system has helped to ensure the money is allocated properly. The group will also take an old person to hospital or to a dispensary for treatment.

In Kinyago 33 old people on the programme each get food on a regular weekly basis. This is done through a special committee which was formed to look into the needs of the old people. This committee consists of the villagers only, the elders predominating. Food distribution was introduced because it was noticed that some people, unused to handling cash, were spending their money on alcohol instead of buying food.

In Mathare, Undugu works with the local church and community leaders, to identify genuine cases where assistance is required. Once or twice a year a mobile eye clinic is organized, and useful gifts, such as blankets, are given during Christmas time. Undugu also tries to teach the youth that the aged are equally important. Young people in Pumwani have been responding positively by helping in the building and repairing of the old people's houses. A walk was organized by the youth with the aim of collecting money to help the aged of Pumwani and Kitui Village.

Rural programmes

Away from the big city in Kenya, the Fundumi Rural Life Extension Society has been active in promoting bee-keeping and dairy farming projects in which older people can participate, as well as in developing schemes that utilize their traditional pot-making skills. For some years the Kenyan clay pottery industry had been neglected owing to the availability of cheap tin and plastic articles. However, inflation had made these products very expensive for rural people. The aged still retained skills in the making of clay pots. Fundumi helped to develop improved types of clay *jikos* (traditional pottery ovens) with which older people were able to revive the almost forgotten craft, with obvious economic advantage to the elderly section of the population.

A welfare scheme run by the Église Protestants Episcopale du Burundi was set up to distribute food and soap to destitute elderly. It was seen by the organizers as being an ideal focus for an ongoing monitoring of the 125 widows regularly attending, keeping a discreet watch on their health and social conditions.

Expatriate expertise

HelpAge programmes normally promote the initiatives of local people and avoid a dependency-creating involvement of expatriate staff on a long-term basis. However, it was considered necessary to introduce expatriate professionals in order to rehabilitate a hospital in rural Ghana which was in a state of disuse. It is not an infrequent experience in developing countries to encounter a hospital, clinic, or other institution founded with good intentions but without the basic resources to run the programme at a permanent level of viability once the initial construction and equipment costs have been paid off.

In the case of Asankrangwa Hospital, the challenge of renovating the building and relaunching the hospital programme was linked to the possibility of using the hospital as a base for a domiciliary programme for the older inhabitants in an inaccessible area and with many small scattered communities. A team comprising a medical director, nurses, and administrator, was recruited in London. Its first task was the mundane physical work of cleaning, adapting, and replenishing the premises. Once the medical and nursing programmes had commenced, the team then moved to the second phase which included developing a good professional service, training local staff to take over the hospital in due course, and exploring the opportunities for carrying a domiciliary service out into more distant villages. It was hoped that the hospital would also serve as an initial base from which to investigate other initiatives for working with the elderly of Ghana as well as inducing local communities and organizations to develop their own specific schemes of aid to the elderly.

The elderly remember

An International Federation on Aging bulletin reported a new outreach in Ghana:

As urbanization, formal education, and technological and social change alter the face of Africa, there is danger that the traditional unwritten knowledge will be lost. In the Volta region of Ghana, a pilot UNESCO-sponsored project has collected and documented the unwritten customs and folklore of the elders of the Awudome traditional area. Interviews were tape-recorded by a dozen specially trained young persons from Awudome, who assisted the University of Ghana's Institute of Adult Education. The 50,000 people in the Awudome area were given advance knowledge about the project through the traditional hierarchy, from the paramount chief through the clan chiefs and family heads.

The Awudome project was thus a collaborative effort between the formally educated youth and elderly persons still living in traditional settings. The information collected will be used in a literacy drive and to provide documented reference material in Ewe, the local language and in English. Six topics received specific attention: pregnancy and child-birth; marriage, married life and divorce; death, burial and funerals; chieftaincy; proverbs; and folklore.

The experience showed that the elderly are worried they will die without passing on their wealth of information. The project's co-ordinators believe that persons in academic life and educated young people in non-literate societies should be more attentive to documenting the traditional sources of knowledge and wisdom.[6]

Meeting basic needs

Southern African countries have been adversely affected by the migration of workers to the mines of South Africa which, while it might suggest increased wealth from the miners' remitted earnings, in fact frequently means the disruption of the family and clan, and the isolation of older people who are left to fend for themselves in the home country. The Iphepeng group in mountainous Lesotho planned to combat this problem, made even more grave by poor harvests, with a garden and seed programme for 2,000 families, the elderly being conspicuous members of the population served. During the interim of garden sowing and harvesting an immediate food distribution scheme was introduced.

The elderly in remote regions are much affected by considerations of accessibility and purity of water. Often they are fully involved in carrying water long distances from not always

---

[6] *Ageing International*, quarterly review from International Federation on Aging, Washington, DC, 1986.

reliable sources. They also tend to succumb rapidly to a variety of water-borne diseases entering the body in the form of bacteria or parasites. So water supply is perhaps even more important to the elders than to other groups. The Christian Service Committee of Malawi sought to ameliorate some of these problems in Mzimba district by opening shallow wells where the high water table facilitated this. Such wells needed to be properly protected which meant that, apart from local labour willingly given, there was expenditure to be met on well linings, well caps, hand pumps, filter stones, and other essentials, including tools.

With 8% of the population already over 60, the government of Mauritius responded by instituting a Senior Citizens' Council to promote the welfare of the aged by involving older people themselves, arranging an exchange of contacts inside and outside the country, and also providing information about ageing.

Training specialists

Somalia, primarily a nomadic country, has recently had to cope with a massive influx of refugees from beyond its borders. Even for the normal population there is lack of health services and a shortage of skilled health personnel in the country. The Somali government is very aware of this and is keen to try to overcome these difficulties, both by extending medical facilities and by providing vocational and on-the-job training for medical staff. The Somali government, in conjunction with the World Health Organization, has planned a National Programme for the Prevention of Blindness.

Help the Aged has provided medical and ophthalmic services and training in Somalia since 1980, initially in refugee camps in the north-west of the country. The first expatriate team conducted medical surveys which revealed a high incidence of preventable eye disease and blindness among the elderly people and other refugees. As a result of these findings, Help the Aged became increasingly involved in ophthalmic training and support work in the region, and by 1982 was running an intensive ophthalmic training programme based at Hargeisa Hospital.

The programme at Hargeisa initially entailed the rehabilitation and upgrading of the Eye Unit. Once this was completed, the hospital functioned as a base and referral centre for the provision of ophthalmic services for the town and the surrounding area. Training in various skills, both ophthalmic and administrative, was given to local personnel, including doctors, nurses, administrators, and community health workers based at the nearby refugee camps. At the end of 1984, the expatriate team was able to hand over the programme to the trained local personnel, who continue to run the Eye Unit themselves.

In July 1984, the Somali Ministry of Health made a general assessment of the feasibility of Sheikh as a centre for ophthalmic training and services. In view of the successful experience at Hargeisa Hospital, the ministry proposed that Help the Aged become involved in a similar programme at Sheikh Hospital.

Sheikh is a village of some 5,000 inhabitants, situated in the centre of the Tog Dheer Region in Northern Somalia. The hospital was built in 1962, but then abandoned. The main part consists of a two-storey block with a number of small wards. Other facilities include an operating theatre, laboratory, autoclave room, and various store rooms and offices. The physical condition of the buildings, despite disuse, was reasonable, although some rehabilitation work was needed in the parts designated for use as the Eye Unit. (The international agency is not responsible for the running costs of the hospital, other than providing the material support needed for the functioning of the Eye Unit itself.)

The aim of the expatriate team's work at Sheikh Hospital, as at Hargeisa, is to establish a sustainable ophthalmic programme which will continue after the team has withdrawn. The main emphasis is being placed on training Somali staff at all levels and in all aspects of eye care, both preventive and curative. Preventive eye care training is of major importance as it will benefit the greatest number of people. Practising Somali health workers are to be trained in basic ophthalmic skills, which will enable them to teach people in the community to adopt simple but effective measures to prevent eye disease and blindness. A comprehensive training programme has been devised by an international consultant ophthalmologist, and this has already proved effective at Hargeisa Hospital. The trainees at Sheikh are to include physicians and surgeons who intend to specialize in ophthalmology, nurse tutors, nurses, auxiliaries, technicians, and auxiliary workers.

More specialized facilities are to be developed at Sheikh Hospital to care for more complicated cases and to ensure continued training and professional stimulation. The plan is to hold mobile clinics in order to extend ophthalmic care throughout the region. This is one of the best ways of reaching elderly or disabled people, who are not always able to travel long distances to the main hospital. It is hoped that with these mobile ophthalmic teams it will be possible to deliver both primary and secondary eye care in areas where such a service is lacking.

A very different approach to the ageing trends in Somalia has been taken by the European voluntary agency consortium ACORD in Sablaale. An extensive scheme to assist the landless had included irrigation, agricultural productivity, and various small business opportunities. In all of this the elderly were very much involved, their wisdom and experience allowing them to make a significant contribution in the decision-making on details of the scheme.

A new feature of the Sablaale endeavour was an afforestation scheme, promoted by Help the Aged (UK). It included the planting of small trees and subsequent care of them, work well suited to less mobile older people. The trees included varieties useful for fuel, for shade, and for timber, all of which stocks had been depleted over the years. New tree types were introduced to be tried out for ecological suitability. With life expectancy in the country averaging somewhere around 45, people of 40 years and upwards were considered for inclusion in the 'older group' engaged on this project.

Rehabilitation introduced

A major enterprise dealing with refugees in the Sudan will be reported in Chapter 10. One effect of international relief for refugees in the Sudan was a feeling on the part of some local inhabitants that they were being relatively neglected and forced to accept lesser services than the refugees who had settled within Sudan. The introduction of a physiotherapist to the central Gedaref Hospital had therefore a dual purpose. Recruited by VSO (Voluntary Service Overseas), the physiotherapist would set up a rehabilitation service in an area where no previous consideration had been given to the possibility of rehabilitation of ill or injured old people. In-service training would enable the volunteer's eventual replacement by local staff. At the same time the rehabilitation would, as proved elsewhere, 'empty beds', enabling older patients to escape from a chronic fate and relieving the pressure on bed occupation and hospital admission waiting lists.

Less accessible areas

An old people's home in Uganda was fortunate enough to receive a donation of five acres of land. This was put to the best use by planting bananas, potatoes, and cassava, partly to feed the residents of the home and partly to sell the surplus at a profit. The elderly themselves participated in the scheme by helping with the harvest, although they were supported by younger workers for the heavy tasks of clearing and ploughing.

Groups of abandoned elderly people may be found in even the most isolated of tropical regions. The Tondo Hospital, near Lake Tumba in Zaire, is 130 kilometres from the nearest town of any size. The nurses from the hospital launched a domiciliary 'seek and care' scheme which identified 30 old people locally who needed their visits and 100 more in surrounding villages.

The well-known Ecumenical Centre of Makeni in Zambia maintains a leprosarium where a training system is available for older people needing rehabilitation into daily living after treatment for leprosy. Couples are given 12 months' training in poultry-keeping, animal husbandry, and farm management. Initial tools, equipment, seeds, and fertilizers are also provided.

The salient point about this particular plan is that until comparatively recently, many agencies, restricted by financial stringency, considered that such skills should be taught only to school-leavers and younger workers who could make 'economical' use of the training, whereas the training of the elderly was considered to be an uneconomical distribution of funds. Now it is recognized that in many places it is the older farmer who has the skills and influence to put new ideas into practice and so maintain, or even improve local productivity, despite the workforce being depleted through migration. Hence support for the older farmer is an investment in posterity for the area.

Extending local skills

The Harare School of Social Work in Zimbabwe has demonstrated an outstanding commitment to the welfare of the aged in recent years. In 1986 it held its second 'workshop', which gathered together social workers concerned with the aged both in Zimbabwe itself and in surrounding countries, including Zambia, Malawi, and Tanzania. Such workshops give carers an opportunity to extend their own skills and also to unite in expressing informed judgements on present conditions for the aged and future policies required to meet those circumstances. The 1986 workshop was notable for the serious interest in it and for the contributions to it made by the government, from Comrade Mugabe the Prime Minister down. Some of the recommendations are included in Chapter 9, on national strategies.

At a more immediate and practical level, the Dete Old Age Association was preoccupied by the plight of retired miners in Zimbabwe, some of whom had originally come from surrounding countries—Zambia, Mozambique, or Malawi—but would never return to their homes. Many still had no local links, no local resources, and no local rights. The association opened a home for these people, with extra nursing care provided where necessary and with an attached garden project for the more agile.

In a number of African countries, lack of finance and planning resources have made it difficult or impossible for governments to take any effective action. Some governments have announced measures to attack one aspect or another of the problems, either as a state enterprise or in collaboration with voluntary agencies, and a United Nations report cites a number of these good intentions.[7]

Good neighbours to the aged

Aiming to support the aged at home, the Caritas Malta Good Neighbour Scheme was initiated in 1986, although the original idea and initial planning started as early as 1982. The first area chosen for the pilot project work was the diocesan parish of Zejtun. The Good Neighbour Scheme is aimed at providing

[7] UN, 'The World Aging Situation', Strategies and Policies, 1985.

practical volunteer help at the parish level to frail, elderly persons and lonely people needing assistance.

Through the initiation of such a scheme in several of the Malta Catholic diocese parishes, Caritas Malta hopes to enable more elderly lonely people to remain in their own community—a milieu they identify with and are attached to—instead of having to live in a residential home for the elderly.

The main features of the scheme are:

1. *Visiting*. Aimed at alleviating loneliness, this service is based on the development of a one-to-one relationship through regular visits by one volunteer (a friendly concerned neighbour) to one lonely elderly person in need of some kind of assistance. Visits are centrally (parish-level) organized, with a check kept that visits are maintained. Visits are long term so as to provide a worthwhile service.

2. *Practical help*. The aim is to provide practical assistance for those people who are unable to undertake certain everyday tasks because of a short- or long-term disability. Such tasks include shopping, cooking, cleaning, gardening, decorating, transport to bank, post office, or hospital, etc. Such a service can provide long-term, short-term, or one-off help. The service is usually based at the parish level but co-ordinated at Caritas central level.

3. *Check calls*. This is designed to provide an early warning system for those frail elderly who are at risk in their own homes. Volunteers keep a regular eye on elderly neighbours living alone and summon help in an emergency. Check call services are based on a very small number of dwellings and can provide a short-term service for those temporarily at risk or long-term help for those permanently in danger.

How does the scheme start? Whenever the need is felt by a parish priest to start a Good Neighbour Scheme within his parish, Caritas steps in to help in the following way:

1. Create public awareness among the local community members about the problems and needs of elderly persons and those living alone (through public seminars, house-to-house leaflet drops, direct contacts with local groups, circulars, etc.)

2. Appeal for volunteers to co-ordinate the Good Neighbour Scheme at the local level. Identifying a resourceful and committed person who is capable of working as a volunteer organizer of the

scheme and to continue to recruit other dedicated volunteers to help get the project off the ground.

3. Formation of a team of volunteers to assist the organizer in planning and co-ordinating the scheme.

4. Preparation of a list of elderly people living alone in the neighbourhood.

5. Identifying volunteers who are willing to assist a neighbour in need.

6. Training of the parish-level co-ordinating team as well as of volunteer visitors.

7. Follow up activities: visits, follow-up planning sessions, support training sessions, publication of literature, evaluation meetings, etc.

The Qormi parish Good Neighbour Scheme has also helped people who live alone to apply for a telephone and initiated a Telephone Call Service: 10 volunteers regularly phone up 12 lonely persons. Both volunteers and these elderly lonely persons usually meet in church every morning. Whenever a person misses Mass, one of the volunteers phones up immediately or visits the house. Four of the 12 elderly persons benefiting from this service are themselves members of the Parish Social Club for the elderly. The parish priest himself is a volunteer within this group. In Zejtun Parish more than 50% of the Good Neighbour team are over 65 years of age themselves.

Some 17 teams of volunteers run old people's day clubs within the overall programme of Caritas Malta, which also includes residential provision. The directors of the programme are well aware of the problems of running such a scheme and have identified some of the main troubles encountered, both in the elderly themselves and in the delivery of the planned services by volunteers.

Some of the types of problems club members have approached volunteers about are dementia; need for someone to sleep in the house because of fear; sickness; government procedures for applying for a particular social service; personal problems (unspecified); family-related problems; a court case; fear of old age; loneliness; not having been admitted to a church home.

Asked whether any of their club members have been the target of break-ins and violence, it was found that four members from four different clubs had been. Seven teams have referred to a total of 19 elderly persons from their parish who have been victims of crime. The other 10 teams said that no cases had come to their attention.

As to the difficulties faced by the volunteers, some of the types of problems mentioned by the 17 teams were inadequate premises; need for more tables; need for a priest to help; lack of funds; activities not always appealing to elderly members; irregular attendances by members; lack of encouragement; dependency of the elderly on volunteers.

One of the most puzzling and saddening factors was the lack of attendance by elderly men at the day clubs, which tended to be utilized mainly by women. Various reasons were adduced for this and various suggestions put forward for making programmes more attractive for elderly men, especially as it was felt that elderly widowers living alone were among those most needing social contact and guidance.[8]

Latin America and the Caribbean

This is the region where I have most personal experience, having been engaged for the past seven years in setting up ageing programmes, both by personal consultancy in the field and by seeking the necessary resources with which national and local groups might implement the new approaches.

During that time a priority objective has been to set up Centres of Excellence. Such centres would not necessarily be built institutions or academic establishments as such. The intention has been rather to set up, in a few widely differing locations, a concentration of pilot schemes to which representatives of agencies from other areas could come in order to review their applicability to their own localities and circumstances.

Such Centres of Excellence have been initiated in a number of widely differing environments, ranging from the metropolitan area of Bogotá, which displays many aspects of modernization and sophistication, through to an area of the very sparsely populated and economically neglected lowland regions of Bolivia at the headwaters of the Amazon.

[8] Further details in Caritas Malta progress reports.

The Pro Vida model

In Colombia, at the time of the first contacts with HelpAge International, there existed a small group of volunteers associated with the committee of the national association of private establishments caring for the elderly. The group had taken the name Pro Vida (For Life—a longer life and a better life). It consisted of some elderly, retired people, a number of active professionals, and a core of housewives with time to spare. Its work consisted mainly in visiting old people's homes and endeavouring to improve the life of the residents by personal visitation, small individual gifts, minor repairs and improvements, and a very modest amount of fund-raising.

The first major development of Pro Vida reflected the urban environment within which it worked. With its existing resources it could never have hoped to extend its services to reach out to the hundreds and probably thousands of destitute elderly for whom there was no place in the institutions. At the same time, the relative commercial wealth of the central sections of Bogotá suggested that some kind of self-financing project might be set up with hopes of providing support for successive generations of elderly for posterity.

International funding was therefore sought to purchase the necessary equipment for a commercial bakery, while Pro Vida worked to obtain premises and, from its own volunteer pool of expertise, design and adapt those premises. With the willing help of local bakery firms, suitable equipment was selected and purchased and technical instruction was planned. The premises secured were conveniently placed on a main arterial avenue with no bakery competition within walking distance.

Soon, good bread was being produced and was on sale to customers from the street. A certain amount of bread was made available to elderly unemployed who agreed to work as itinerant bread vendors. Elderly people were also employed in the bakery itself. With a night shift operating, half of the weekly production of bread was sent free of charge to 30 old people's homes which catered for destitute elderly. Financial conditions in the homes were so bad that on occasions there was literally nothing at all to eat in the home until the nuns could go out and beg a new day's rations.

Some problems were experienced, partly due to insufficient staff training and partly due to an over-enthusiastic donation of bread which left the bakery short on cash flow. At the end of 18 months operation, Pro Vida was able to report that Pan Vida (life bread) was making a profit which could be used to subsidize a free medical clinic above the bakery.

The professionally planned bakery scheme was considerably enhanced by an initiative of the women's volunteer section. They organized a competition among residents of old people's homes to make *Delicias de Antaño* (delicacies of yesteryear)—in other words cakes, biscuits, and sweets 'like grandma used to make'. The winners of the competition were then contracted to supply quantities of the product to the bakery. A separate counter was opened for the *Delicias* which quickly became famous—served by elderly women in traditional costume—and provided another income source as well as considerable work involvement and personal profit for old people who had previously been mouldering without hope or interests in an old people's home or in a shack in a shanty town.

As the bakery was seen to be nearing success, further funding was sought overseas to set up a similar commercial laundry to take from the old people's homes the heavy chore and expense of the laundry. This scheme was first suggested as the result of an application from two homes for commercial-sized washing machines. It was judged more economical in the long run, and infinitely cheaper in initial capital expenditure, to set up one central laundry than to purchase 30 large washing machines. The laundry also serves customers from the street, so that 80% of its dry-cleaning business and 20% of its 'wet laundry' pays the cost of servicing 30 homes and also leaves a profit margin for central welfare funds of Pro Vida.

At the same time as these major innovations, Pro Vida was setting up a network of 12 handicraft workshops in old people's homes. The workers were rewarded with vouchers and later with cash relative to their productivity, while a portion of any income was reserved to the general welfare funds, available to enhance the life of those unable to work or not yet having the opportunity. Very early in the scheme it was realized that the output of these work centres could not be disposed of through casual sales and an occasional bazaar.

Pro Vida therefore set up the first charity gift shop in Colombia, again near a main avenue, and this shop, called Canitas (silver hairs), produced results both in cash and public interest. Typical of the thrift with which the local group works is the fact that the large wooden containers in which the bakery and laundry equipment had been imported from Sweden and Italy were now dismantled by a volunteer carpenter to construct magnificent shop fittings—counters, shelves, and cupboards— on which to display the handicrafts.

These schemes provided the possibility of an enduring economic basis for Pro Vida's developing programme, which also included a growing domiciliary visitation work, the opening of branch groups in other towns, and an excellent volunteer concert party (now two groups), which spent all their time rehearsing and entertaining at old people's centres. A number of the volunteers involved are retired people themselves. It was evident that even the new sources of income would not be sufficient to finance considerable additional development.

Another source of international funding was therefore found to take a selected Pro Vida promoter to Britain, the United States, and Canada in order to study fund-raising, publicity, and campaigning methods, and then to return and adapt them to Colombian use. Special attention was paid to inter-generational schemes and the strategy of educating a new generation to a better appreciation of the growing problems of an ageing population. Within two years, Pro Vida had established a regular arrangement with some 160 schools whereby a trained Pro Vida teacher–promoter visited the schools to give lessons on ageing and involve pupils in initiatives for working with and on behalf of elderly people who had no grandchildren contacts of their own. In addition to the valuable personal contacts established, the scheme produced many youth initiatives to raise funds for age care as well as attracting media, public, and government attention to the problem.

Developing the schools contacts further, after some negotiations Pro Vida was recognized as an authorized teaching institution. Senior school pupils may select to study practical social services as part of their social science examinations, for a half day each week. More than a hundred Bogotá pupils a year are now attached to Pro Vida, to study and take part in the organization's regular programmes and to attend lectures. At the satisfactory conclusion of a pupil's studies, Pro Vida issues its own certificate of competence which rates a credit towards the appropriate school-leaving examination. Similar arrangements have also been made with the schools of social work, especially in the areas of recreation and rehabilitation.

A development scheme of five years' support from the international funding and expertise was thus able to establish a viable national voluntary programme on ageing. In addition, during the national emergency following the Armero Volcano disaster in November 1985, Pro Vida was able to mobilize a relief and rehabilitation programme which led to its being appointed by the Colombian government as the authorized agency for the rehabilitation of elderly people left in need of care by the disaster.

Having set up a small teaching centre at the Pro Vida head office it became possible, in 1985, to invite delegates from age care groups in surrounding countries to attend a two-week seminar that included practical experience in the local age care programmes. Since 1985, in six-monthly 'crash courses', age care organizers and workers from 12 countries have attended the Bogotá Centre of Excellence. All of those who attended returned to their own places to hold seminars and initiate similar groups and programmes, adapted as necessary. The teaching centre now has a permanent form as CIGAL (Centro Internacional de Gerontologia de America Latina).

Applying the model in the remotest areas of Bolivia

The remote Bolivian town of Trinidad, Beni, illustrates some of the consequence of migration. With some younger workers making the extreme effort to get out of the area, their elders are left behind with no support in their old age. An aged person who can no longer bear the savage life of the jungles or the cattle-ranching plains has no alternative but to move into the shanty towns around Trinidad.

In 1981 it was reported that because chronic geriatric cases tend to block beds, the local hospital in Trinidad, badly underprovided with both beds and staff, could not admit anyone over 50 years of age. A patient over that age might be treated in the operating theatre or consulting room but could then be quite literally deposited outside for a relative, a passing citizen, or a policeman to succour. The only resource available to the 'good Samaritan', citizen or policeman, was Sister Pacifica McKenna's tiny old people's home.

Sister Pacifica is a devoted nun of a well-known religious order. Trained as a nurse, teacher, and physiotherapist, she has spent 40 years in the Beni opening up social initiatives. Although now in her upper 70s she is still actively running the only old people's home in the area. When she took it on the home consisted of two dormitories, male and female, where normally healthy old people had perforce to share accommodation with others in advanced stages of leprosy, tuberculosis, cancer, or dementia. Local doctors were unwilling to visit the home owing to the cramped conditions of consultation, although in terms of cleanliness, nutrition, and personal care, there were no complaints. In the extremity of her financial need Sister Pacifica appealed to Help the Aged for support.

After a visit and consultation an additional wing was planned, of the simplest constructional design but with basic care standards clearly identified. At a cost of about $60,000, this wing was to comprise eight individual nursing bed units, a consulting room, pharmacy, and sanitary installations, a treatment room, activities room, and dining room, and a new kitchen, plus a wide verandah providing leisure space. This immediately enabled the isolation of contagious and disruptive cases. Doctors were happy to give time free to serve in the pleasant new consulting room for both in- and out-patients. Much local interest was stimulated.

The small voluntary support group associated with the home was enthused and encouraged to look beyond the confines of the home in order to give support to non-resident old people without families. A younger nun had observed that many older women could only offer services as laundresses in the town. Because of the unreliability of the water supplies it was often necessary for them to trudge long distances to carry out their work or to spend much of their tiny incomes on bus fares. A small international grant enabled the nun to set up a permanent base of water troughs with a piped water supply where the old women could work only a few paces away from their homes and their customers.

The next initiative was to provide a large weaving loom, suitable for products up to the size of a poncho or blanket, so that many of the abandoned elderly women might come and share in the weaving at which so many of them are adept. When the new loom was delivered, the younger nun displayed further ingenuity. She gathered the local church youth group together to dismantle the loom and discover how it worked. The youths then went into the woods, cut down branches of appropriate type and size, and constructed another 10 looms. These looms, which work efficiently, now dominate the thatched huts of a number of elderly women as they sit on the beaten-dirt floor and weave their products.

Other groups in Trinidad began to plan similar responses to the now apparent problem of abandoned elderly. On my return after 12 months' absence, I was greeted by news of 14 new groups operating age opportunity programmes, 8 in Trinidad and 6 in remote villages. In one such village, a thatched hut had been built as the Day Centre where older people could sit and have company during the heat of the afternoon. At the official opening ceremony, as there was no door to open and very little wall, the traditional ribbon was strung between two support posts before being cut and the centre duly opened.

The Centre of Excellence in Trinidad has been visited by organizers and workers from other areas anxious to observe and replicate the programmes. It has also served as the starter point for similar movements of community response in other departments of Bolivia. On 14 and 15 December 1986 these new departmental action committees met in Trinidad to establish a Bolivian national Pro Vida and plan future programmes.

The autonomous national Pro Vida organizations are linked into the HelpAge International network where they enjoy an exchange of information, discovering modern methods of practice and also the way in which age care has been adapted in a variety of developing countries.

Belize: a national plan

A similar initiative in Belize was hastened by a positive invitation from the Belize government to Help the Aged, requesting a study of ageing problems and possible methods of response. Myself and my wife, a Principal Officer in Social Services in London, carried out a study as requested, produced a report and proposed a plan by which local and international voluntary agencies could temporarily fill the gap in age care development while the government, making the best use of scarce resources, concentrated its funds on other areas of need.

Belize is divided into districts, which are the equivalent of counties. Historic influence has left Belize with possibly the most heterogeneous selection of races, cultures, languages, and living styles in the world relative to size of population. Each district possesses its own profound degree of distinctiveness and independence, so the blueprint plan envisaged the immediate promotion of a HelpAge committee in each district. These committees were to report in to a national committee composed partly of District representatives and partly of ex-officio national delegates, including Permanent Secretaries of the government, attending as observers. Thus, in Belize, as distinct from Bolivia, the organizational infrastructure preceded the mainstream of pilot project activities.

Existing residential accommodation for the aged in Belize was centralized in Belize City on the coast and related closely to the discharge of elderly patients from the Belize City Hospital, the only general hospital offering an entire range of medical and surgical services. Because of the cultural variations among Belizeans, people from San Ignacio and the surrounding District of Cayo, often Spanish-speaking, regarded Belize City as an alien environment.

It seemed logical, therefore, to decentralize the residential accommodation and enable old people to remain in their own districts when they came to the point where they could no longer survive in their own homes. However, it was hoped that the provision of new accommodation facilities would not lead to the former type of old people's home, which was virtually cut off from the community and where the residents had little activity or incentive to live.

The new centre in San Ignacio was planned to include both accommodation and space for communal interaction with non-residents. A considerable amount of garden space was provided so that some livestock might be kept and food grown by the elders themselves. The cost of the construction was reduced by the intervention of volunteers from Britain. First a group of youths from the Operation Raleigh adventure team helped to dig the foundations. Then a group of unemployed craftsmen from the city of Birmingham worked alongside local volunteers to complete the building. These overseas volunteers reinforced a local volunteer capacity greatly reduced by the emigration of working age men, especially skilled craftsmen.

Through the operation of other local committees it was possible to make grants for seeds and tools for displaced or indigent old people to commence small gardens under supervision in rural areas. In towns, day activities and visiting schemes were established. One such group of old people worked out its own plan for activities linked to income generation. Discovering that there was no catering establishment within reasonable distance of its meeting place, the group decided to start its own fast-food business, retailing home-made pies and similar dishes of good quality.

In another district of Belize, where the secondary school headteacher happened to be the HelpAge committee chairman, the woodwork and metalwork classes of the school were recruited to work on repairs and improvements to old people's shacks. Elsewhere an old indoor market which had lain unused for years was taken over and renovated for a centre of activities. In other areas, in accordance with local culture, dancing and music were given prominence, with one elderly man given the opportunity to exercise his talent for making drums for calypso music.

Activities in Peru

The second city of Peru, Arequipa, suffers from the effects of both immigration and emigration as rural mountain Indians move into the large city while ambitious young Arequipenos move out to the capital, Lima. A well-meaning plan sought to set up one central facility where old people with no stable income might find work opportunities. A certain amount of success was experienced and a certain amount of benefit accrued to those attending. However, shortage of funds and the large space required meant that the centre had been established in a disused assembly hall of a religious seminary. After a while the members from outlying districts found it uncomfortable or expensive to travel what, to them, were considerable distances in order to attend.

At this point the originating agency, Caritas Diocesana de Arequipa, altered its strategy. While retaining some activities at the original centre, it began to set up satellite centres in the outer districts where most need was found. The workshops were much more modest but were more conveniently situated for the members. This meant some replication of capital requirements in providing separate tool kits for the various centres. On the other hand, revenue produced would much more quickly and adequately provide the actual on-going requirements of the smaller centres and their members.

Abandonment in Panama

One of the minor tragedies of Panama is the fate of people imported from the then British Caribbean and African colonies to dig the Panama Canal. On the completion of the canal, many of the labourers settled in Panama, perhaps continuing to work on the canal and docks. Many of them never acquired Panamanian citizenship or even learned Spanish. They retired without any legal rights and continued to live out their lives in the most abject poverty, remote from their homelands, cherishing some kind of mystical loyalty to a vanished British imperial system and unable to integrate into the local population. Often even the children of the original canal diggers, came to retirement age without the means of continuing to sustain themselves.

A group of volunteer visitors called upon these aged recluses and provided them with the minimum necessities of life on a regular basis. When these aged people became unable to look after themselves the problem was acute, for the only remedy appeared to be to pay for very expensive institutional care. Then an elderly woman, herself suffering from diabetes, offered to open up her rambling but spacious house to one or two of the aged as her guests. She came from the same social background and was not herself particularly well endowed with material things except for the extended house and garden.

Over a period, a number of the abandoned old people of the canal digger category moved into the woman's house. The voluntary visitors were worried about the possible inadequacy of the premises and the service. But the old people themselves were perfectly at home in similar conditions to those in which they had always lived. Meals and basic care were provided, and they wanted little else. The group of visitors decided therefore to do what they could to improve the condition of the premises and support the basic services which the owner could offer.[9]

This case is included because of the number of instances where, on admission to large buildings to which they are unaccustomed, old people have either left the home and returned to their abandoned condition or have been restrained by the provision of locks and sometimes guards on the outside doors of the home. Whilst some old people's homes run by religious sisters in quasi-convent conditions are almost palatial and beautifully maintained, there is an argument for the old person being allowed to live out his or her existence in accustomed surroundings. The example of the rough and ready little home in Panama is one which bears consideration as a possible starting point for remodelling residential provision.

Smaller projects

Two large convent-type homes in Peru applied at various times for international aid to extend or rebuild the residential accommodation. This enabled the funding agency to launch a discussion with the directors about the development of a new style of care, both within the respective homes and in the local community outside the walls. The discussion was influenced by the fact that substantial grants could only be obtained for developmental projects involving non-residents as well as residents of a home.

At one home a small farm was set up, with livestock which the residents could themselves tend. Part of the products of the farm and part of the proceeds from sales were covenanted to meet the material needs of destitute old people for whom there was no room within the institution's walls. In the other case a large rebuilding scheme was to include a health centre and an activities centre which would be open to older people from the surrounding community as well as residents of the home. (Cases are known of large homes equipped with excellent medical facilities where the directors refuse to open their facilities, even to residents of homes run by other sisterhoods).

[9] The 'Canal Diggers' are cared for by the British Aid Society, a group of volunteers based at the British Embassy in Panama.

In El Salvador an initial proposal was made to provide a few trial houses for elderly people displaced by the civil disturbances in rural areas. In the course of project development the proposal was enhanced by two amendments. The dwellings were to be sited among other rural houses of a large community building scheme so that the abandoned elders could be integrated into inter-generational neighbourhoods. At the same time, each small house was provided with a work space and a plot of ground. Technical advice was available for a period to enable the elderly occupiers both to till the land successfully and also to set up some kind of cottage industry.

The bakery idea carried out on a truly commercial scale in metropolitan Bogotá, as described above, has also proved useful in other types of community. In the southern Colombian city of Pasto, with 200,000 inhabitants, the establishment of a scaled-down version of the Bogotá bakery has provided free or low-cost bread for old people, employed some elderly unemployed, and made a profit for the general welfare funds. In remote Vilca-bamba, the 'Valley of the Aged' in Loja Province, Ecuador, there was no bakery within 40 kilometres so the establishment of an old people's bakery was a most useful innovation. The ovens in this case were of simple construction and utilized firewood. A tailoring workroom was also established, and consideration was also given to the possibility of preparing and marketing of herbal remedies.

In other locations use has been made of the profuse quantities of sisal available in rural areas to set up small industries simply equipped with hand-made looms. In one of the sisal programmes a further development was related to the cultivation of Caturra coffee. This strain of coffee has the advantages, especially for elderly workers, of being mature and ready for drinking in two years as well as being a very low plant, which eliminates the need for ladders when collecting the crop.

Consideration is also being given to extending the range of income-producing handicrafts at which unemployed, non-pensioned old people might work. A Belize City group is looking at the viability of exporting shells and coral. An example can be taken from the success of Yanoski's Creations in the Bahamas. These are based on coconut-shell jewellery which requires minimal expenditure in raw materials. It is a simple process involving the cleaning, carving, and varnishing of shell which can be undertaken in a house or a shed with minimal machinery. In the south of Colombia, Pro Vida Nariño is also hoping to work in a form of lacquer used by the old-time Indian craftsmen, involving the decoration of plates and similar objects. The lacquer is produced by chewing the buds of an indigenous and localized bush, and using largely root and berry dyes.

After the major earthquake in Mexico City in 1985, in a combined operation on behalf of the elderly, the Salvation Army established a low-technology brick factory which was soon producing good-quality cement bricks small enough to be used by older people engaged in rebuilding small houses. Although this operation was introduced in an emergency situation, it is the type of scheme which could be applied in many conditions of inadequate housing as an initiative of ageing groups.

Cultural relevance

A salutary experience for aid organizers related to an initiative of workers in the diocese of Chachapoyas on the reverse slope of the Andes in Peru. A proposal was made to set up a small farm for elderly people where the main meat product was to be guinea pig. This proposal was greeted with disgust in some quarters of the funding agency, for in Britain guinea pigs are regarded as children's pets and the idea of eating them was repulsive. However, the workers in Chachapoyas insisted on responding to local culture rather than introducing a source of meat that might be unacceptable to the local population. In addition, the animal might not adapt itself to the particular environment. Funding was provided, with a minimum of publicity in the donor country, and the early results quite justified the estimates of the local planning group.

A health organization in Haiti was worried because few old people appeared at health centres in a region where the rugged terrain prohibited any other form of transport than the donkey. The existing rural health centres were too far apart for the majority of older people, especially if suffering from painful or disabling diseases, with a journey of up to three days on foot. The problem was tackled by training young health workers who could travel on donkey-back to the old people's houses and also by constructing small, inexpensive, intermediate health centres that could provide a minimum level of treatment and waiting space for those who could travel no further.[10]

A volunteer in Rio de Janeiro co-ordinated teams of professional hairdressers and manicurists to visit old people's homes on Mondays, when the beauty salons are generally closed. These visits help restore the old people's physical decency as well as their personal esteem. The initiative arose out of a single volunteer's response on observing a fundamental need.

A Brazilian group of elderly women volunteers run a day crèche for children up to 6 years of age. One of the elderly women, a retired psychologist, is able to make a valuable contribution in resolving any inter-generational misunderstandings. Each older woman is able to take charge of seven children on average. The working mothers who leave their children at the crèche are happy to make modest financial contributions which are then shared between the elderly carers and the scheme as a whole.[11]

Enabling the deprived

Mention must be made of the rehabilitation work of the Guatemalan organization which works with the blind, Comité Nacional ProCiegos y Sordomudos de Guatemala. Deeply concerned by the total destitution of elderly blind people, the organization decided to set up its own pilot project for the elderly. As in so many developing societies, old people who become incurably blind are a heavy burden on the family. Sometimes, in total economic desperation, the family eject the blind elder, who then lives as a beggar on the streets of a city or in the ditches of the countryside.

At the Guatemalan centre a simple scheme required relatively brief but very specialized training for a small number of staff and volunteers. Blind old people were then taught two areas of usefulness. They were given a simple trade, such as manufacturing Christmas decorations. They were also taught household skills, such as cooking, child care, tailoring, and so on. Very

[10] The work of GARD, a French-speaking voluntary organization supported by France and Canada.

[11] CERIS, report on old people's homes in Brazil, 1981.

soon, repentant working-age children were knocking on the doors of the unit, requesting the return of their now productive, active, and clean elders. But the scheme did not end there. The children were required to attend their own rehabilitation course! They were given counselling on family responsibility, and they were also taught skills which would help them to integrate the blind person back into the home.

Often the problem of blindness is purely economic, for in many areas of Latin America the cost of a pair of cataract glasses may be in excess of the annual monetary income of a peasant. An organization like Pro Vida (Colombia) therefore meets the problem by forming a bank of good, used lenses and frames, donated from Britain or elsewhere. The lenses are professionally measured, recorded, and prescribed by qualified volunteers. Each old person attending the eye clinic is given a precisely prescribed lens for each eye and may enjoy a choice of frames, either free or at an assessed low cost.

Reference has been made to volunteers on several occasions, and in almost all countries there is now a proportion of the population which enjoys retirement pensions and is therefore relatively leisured and able to form an additional pool of volunteers. A Costa Rican report describes elder volunteers 'who are doubly motivated in being able to render a service to their contemporaries who are in such need of help'.

The system of Senior Citizens' Councils is well known in developed countries, as are associations of pensioners. In developing countries, the traditions of this type of organization are slender. However, in Chile and Belize, national conferences of the elderly have been held to discuss their own problems and make recommendations. In Belize the discussion has been developed by the incorporation of elder members on to the District Committees. In Mexico a number of Senior Councils have been set up by the welfare agency DIF.

Valuable age assets

In Jamaica a Memory Bank was founded as much of the nation's cultural heritage is unrecorded and lies in the memories of senior citizens, knowledge which is often unique. Another aspect of the Memory Bank is the recording of 'oral history'—facts, knowledge,

and even subjective impressions retained in the memories of
people who were either participants in historical events or were
sufficiently close to form an impression, or who have inherited
knowledge from previous generations. The Jamaican Memory
bank project is operated almost entirely by volunteers who
interview senior citizens throughout the island about all aspects
of life and customs which have a bearing on the cultural heritage
and history of the island.[12]

The project is managed by a steering committee of volunteers
chaired by the director of Arts and Culture. In each parish, a
volunteer co-ordinator recruits interviewers who are trained and
provided with tape recorders. They in turn identify old persons
in the communities with whom they conduct taped interviews.
The material collected is stored for reference in the National
Library, with suitable safeguards, copyright, and confidentiality.
The elderly who participate are given certificates indicating that
they have contributed to a significant national project.

A Jamaican project of a similar nature, which involved a joint
effort of the young and old, was the Village History Project,
conducted in 1983 under the auspices of the Ministry of
Education, with private-sector funding. A competition was
organized for senior pupils and their teachers in 39 rural primary
schools. After receiving training, the youngsters interviewed old
persons in their villages and compiled histories of their villages.
The response was good and the material was compiled in booklet
form. It is expected that these will eventually be a part of the
reading material in schools throughout the island. A video has
also been made of the project.

This project not only serves to enhance the self-esteem of the
elderly who participated, but created a new relationship between
the young and the old. It also gave the young people a greater
pride in their villages, and understanding of their history.

An unusual idea from Argentina that could be repeated in
many hot countries is to hold weekly open-air meetings with the
elderly as the main focus but the whole family invited. In
Argentina this project is known as 'City Meetings in Dorrego
Square'. During a six-hour period, activities take place in
different parts of the square, including handicrafts, painting, skill

---

[12] Report by Jamaican National Council on Ageing.

games, cultural games, theatre, music, and so on, all co-ordinated by older people. The sessions end with a huge family dance involving hundreds of people. This project has generated great interest in the elderly and a recognition of their varied abilities.[13]

When a lunch club was set up for the elderly alone in Argentina it was found that the elderly did not wish to eat without their grandchildren accompanying them. The club was therefore successfully adapted to cater for grandparents and grandchildren together. A significant factor in Buenos Aires city is that while many older people now live alone and choose to be independent, the majority still enjoy an integrated family experience through accessibility to relatives living near or within travelling reach, as has happened in USA.[14]

[13] Posadas 1987.
[14] From reports by R. Barca, R. Kaplan, and J. Oddone at University of Florida Conference, February 1988.

8

A PROGRAMME CRITIQUE

THIS chapter will commence by looking at some age care ideas which have evolved in Europe and North America and which might be applied in certain developing country progrmames. It will then go on to an examination of some of the problems or errors which have been identified in existing projects. A further section will attempt to summarize this and the previous chapter by outlining three model formats of voluntary-sector age care organizations in varying community situations of certain developing countries.

Learning from Western Models

Some types of project which have not been introduced into developing countries might well be studied as to their relevance. For example, there is considerable current development in the United States of inter-generational schemes, with organizations like the Elvirita Lewis Foundation making substantial contributions. In San Francisco there are the SEER programme (Seniors Enriching Educational Roles), in which 200 volunteers aged 60 to 90 share experiences, over work programmes ranging from 10 to 40 hours weekly, with children in schools. The volunteers are not all trained teachers, or even professionals, but have some aspect of experience to impart and are specifically trained for sharing them with the class of children. Twenty per cent of the SEER volunteers have been working on the scheme for more than five years. This is a scheme which could most aptly be applied in developing countries where there is a shortage of both teachers and professional experience available to schools.

The RSVP programme (Retired Senior Volunteer Program) is another model developed in the United States that bears adaptation in its strategy of utilizing the elderly volunteer. This programme, which operates on a national scale, reaches into almost every aspect of human experience and covers shared knowledge in aspects as varied as blood-pressure testing, creative writing, legal assistance, and all types of recreation. In the Coachella Valley alone, in 1985, 493 volunteers gave a total of 120,530 man-hours of service. Programmes in Spanish-speaking areas of the United States have special relevance to kindred communities further south.

In the atmosphere of crime and fear which characterize some urban communities, another Californian initiative in the Tenderloin district of San Francisco is of interest. Elderly people living alone and in jeopardy grouped together to ask the public authorities for more protection, and the police responded with increased patrols of the affected areas. Of even greater consequence, however, was the Safehouse Project, planned and supplemented by elderly residents. Through this project, the residents recruited local businesses, agencies, bars, and restaurants to be places of refuge, designated by a symbol in their windows, where community residents could go in time of danger or medical emergency.

In the first two weeks, the elders recruited 14 different safehouses, the first of which were officially opened by the mayor in November of 1982. Over the subsequent year, crime in the Tenderloin dropped by 18%, and police in the area have attributed the drop in part to this highly successful programme. By the following year, 48 safehouses had been established, and they together were responsible for deterring crime and in other ways assisting community people in 56 different medical and police emergencies.

A useful contribution to the security of old people is found in a variety of alarm systems which could be adapted for developing countries according to the local level of electronic development. One of the most sophisticated systems is a simple press-button necklace which automatically activates the central phone in the house. The signal emitted has a range of 20 metres and a penetrating power able to pass through two normal doors. If the old person is unable to speak after pressing the panic button, the phone is programmed to contact a control centre where the old person's details are immediately available on computer. The

phone also automatically signals to other selected numbers, such
as police, ambulance, or family.

An architectural concept developed in Denmark is the
grouping together of inter-generational residential services. In
one instance, a block of sheltered housing for the elderly faces a
block of housing for students, many of them married with young
families, across an area of common recreational ground.[1] A
British residential design, specifically for the highly disabled,
provides separate apartments with the appearance of individual
houses with the front doors opening into a community street
while the back doors of the apartments open into a fully staffed
and equipped extra-care unit.

A study of multi-generational families in West Germany
challenges some common stereotypes about loneliness, isolation,
and lack of competence among the very old, and the disintegration
of the family in the modern world. Much of the new information
was obtained from a recent study conducted by Lehr and colleagues at the University of Bonn that turned up an unexpectedly
high number of five-generation families. A prediction by gerontologists that demographic pressures would result in four- and five-
generation families becoming more common was, in fact,
dramatically confirmed when newspaper advertisements placed
by the university in search of research subjects for a five-
generation study produced hundreds of responses.

The Bonn study stressed that the world of the very old is very
much a woman's world. The vast majority of responses (402 out
of 411 families) identified great-great-grandmothers, whose
average age was 90.5 years. Only 15 of the five-generation
families surveyed had great-great grandfathers. Their average
age was 87.5. Because of the greater life expectancy of women
and their earlier age of marriage, there are also more mother–
daughter generation sequences than mother–son generation
sequences. Only in the first generation is the proportion of male
and female children roughly balanced.

In almost one-third (32%) of the five-generation families, all
generations lived in the same city or town, but generally (49% of
cases), great-great-grandmothers lived in the same place as only
one or two other generations. Only 4% lived in areas where no

[1] The Ensomme Gamles Vaern Organization, Copenhagen.

other member of the five generations was present. The majority of great-great-grandparents lived in rural areas (50%) or in small towns (26%).

This study from one of the most developed countries could encourage developing countries in their programmes to try to maintain and reinforce their traditional family systems.

Problems in Projects in Developing Countries

Need for organizational skills

In some regions of developing countries there is no long-term, deep-rooted experience of organizing of the kind common in the industrialized countries, in particular in respect to political and community development, economic planning, and volunteer work.

A World Bank report, making this point in reference to community health programmes; pointed out that supporting activities such as logistics of supplies, appropriate management, and the quality of supervision are critically important. Discrepancies between promises and achievements result primarily from inadequate management, and this is a consequence of underdeveloped administrative machinery and lack of organization among client populations.

I have noted elsewhere that new methods are being introduced to meet new problems of ageing and, far from concentrating on former paternalistic and non-productive ideas of relief aid, the new co-operation is producing new types of infrastructure appropriate to the needs of varying cultures. In many places there were found people willing to co-operate, many of them elderly people themselves, but always there was the lack of a vital component: capital finance, skilled workers, training facilities, development of ideas, skill in organization, or even the ability to prepare and edit a sophisticated aid application of the type required by (Western) governmental and private foundations.

Thus it was that in setting up the Centres of Excellence in Colombia, as described in Chapter 7, due attention was paid to infrastructure, especially those aspects mentioned in the previous paragraph. The courses now carried out in CIGAL, Pro Vida's

Bogotá training centre, include sessions devoted to study and observation of infrastructure. A new programme of training is under way by which academic and training institutions of more structured societies lend tutors to developing countries in order to teach basic infrastructural systems. As the programmes continue, the tutors themselves will identify the items of practice and knowledge from the 'structured' countries that are of most use in the developing countries.

The HelpAge International strategy depends heavily on combining the enthusiasm and commitment of local groups in developing countries with the know-how and trial-and-error experience of the North. HelpAge India, the first of these indigenous age organizations to be set up with HelpAge International support, is now a fully independent national organization with its own successful fund-raising programme in India itself and a self-financed budget of up to a million dollars annually for local age care projects.

Other similar organizations followed and became independent, as in the case of HelpAge Sri Lanka and HelpAge Kenya, or alternatively, small local organizations were helped to develop into national expressions, as with Pro Vida Colombia and Helping Hand, Hong Kong. In 1983 the organizations came together to found an association of equal members, now with 16 full affiliates and a number of associates, the majority in developing countries. HelpAge International continues to develop age care infrastructures where the local response ensures continuity of purpose.

Roots of failure

Many of the age initiatives already described are of recent development, so in many cases it is premature to make an estimate of success or failure. What have emerged are certain specific problems and roots of failure which can already be avoided or planned for in new projects of a similar kind. The more important and frequent of these negative factors will now be outlined.

Reference has already been made to the lack of 'a body of experience or established methodology to be followed' in many aspects of development. This is particularly true of age care and age opportunity development. The source quoted previously emphasizes the 'extreme diversity of these problems and the inadequacy, indeed the danger, of the narrow pursuit of any single prescription for their solution'. It is noted that less than one-quarter of the studies presented show technology to be the *key* problem, and then usually in combination with other constraints such as finance, infrastructure, or human relationships.

Government intervention can also cause problems, either from lack of legislation, frequent changes of regulation, or oppressive restrictions. It is especially distressing for voluntary organizations to have to record, from time to time, that in a particular country development is hindered by the inability or neglect of a government to plan for its own underprivileged groups.

It has already been mentioned that volunteer work in some countries is hampered by lack of a voluntary tradition. One Latin American gerontologist has said that the concept of voluntary work is unknown in most of the Latin American countries except for groups in the uppermost socio-economic levels; the small number of aged people who, in a local survey, indicated an inclination to use retirement time in voluntary work is a natural outgrowth of this unfamiliarity. A further extension of this factor is that voluntary organizations themselves are consequently less known, less respected, and less prone to make a national impact than in North America or Western Europe.

A World Bank study reported a 'lack of a responsive local constituency for health care'.[2] It also determined that in many Latin American regions 'the absence of a well-developed political mechanism at the village level is also a major obstacle to implementation of primary health care', militating as it does against both action through an established vertical structure of authorities, and action from already well-disciplined local activists.

Where new organizations are in fact founded, there is then sometimes a tendency to incite undue ambitions and ignite personal power struggles. The progress of age initiatives in at least one American country was retarded, though not halted, by the accession to the top responsibility of a non-national with apparent personal objectives. A new national organization

[2] Golladay and Liese 1980.

attracting both local expertise and international support in the response to a new national problem, such as ageing or drug addiction, does offer a forum for articulate speakers and an opportunity for an ambitious person to have access to authority and power. In the case referred to, the desire of the presiding person to exercise total personal dominance in the field was more unacceptable because of his status as an expatriate.

It is therefore important to take into account the question of nationality at the level of national leadership of a community development organization. It is equally important to ensure a level of local acceptability for individual projects, seeking local approval and support from individuals and grass-roots groups rather than through remote national bureaucratic channels. Again, the World Bank study insists on the need to be aware that 'the most important approach is to ensure that new . . . programmes are responsive to locally perceived needs'. Sanitation and preventive programmes are seen by that study as being 'rarely considered important by the beneficiaries' and are 'thus . . . unsuitable for strengthening local response', in comparison with 'popular' curative or water supply programmes.

However, it might be seen as one of the priorities of the sponsoring agencies to promote a level of information which will educate local communities to accept suitable priorities. Courses of action planned by reputable local professionals and experienced workers might then be received, rather than taking the easy line of supporting what is known to be popular. It is certainly the experience of many international agencies that a project pursued without local constituency support is a project doomed to failure from the onset.

Another problem which looms frequently, mainly with volunteers but also with paid staff, is the tendency to offer services only to the well-behaved elderly. Where a person displays unsocial behaviour or fails to project the kind of psychological profile expected from an older person, especially in respect of gratitude expressed, that old person may well be excluded from future benefits or accorded only such benefits as can conveniently be delivered without undue discomfort to the worker.

This kind of worker reaction often arises from inordinately high expectations of the spiritual rewards of working with old people, from inadequate training in dealing with the aged, or because of salary levels which lower the quality of worker recruited. It is important therefore not to engender in the worker too high hopes of such rewards, nor to stint on the employment of trained staff or on the costs of training.

A case of lack of social compatibility within the residents' group in a home illustrates the inherent danger of a certain method of project financing which is often proposed in situations of revenue shortage. In the particular case, a religious sister had financed and built an excellent old people's home with beautiful surroundings and comfortable installations. It consisted of two wings, one of which was to be occupied by destitute old people of whom there were many locally. The other wing would be occupied, almost in isolation, by aged members of 'good' families which could afford to pay fees calculated to meet the costs of the total operation. The financial calculations were checked by competent accountants and approved. An assessment of need by social workers proved that there were sufficient aged people in need of accommodation, and that the installations would meet individual needs.

Within a very short time of opening, the ward for destitutes was fully occupied. In the wing for fee-paying elderly the maximum number ever to be admitted in residence at one time was two. The finances of the home were in a state of total disaster. The forgotten element in planning was the fact that opulent local families considered it an insult to the family to have their elders living under the same roof as destitute beggars. Thus while they, the opulent families, would willingly despatch their aged elders into paid accommodation, the accommodation had to be such as would be in line with the family's prestige in local society.

The strategy of using wealthy residents to pay for the destitutes' accommodation is therefore seen as fraught with problems. Its only general application could be in instances where there are in fact two separate centres of accommodation in entirely different parts of the town, and where the link between the two centres remains a confidential matter of the directors of the programme.

Cultural misjudgements

A rather strange error in judgement arose out of a local planner's attempt to replicate a scheme from another culture. A project promoter from one of the smaller West Indian islands had been impressed by the success of a rabbit-keeping project elsewhere. The fecundity of the rabbits ensured a high return on investment, and the scheme would also provide both meat and income. Breeding rabbits is a light task which most elderly people can undertake easily and safely. An initial clutch of rabbits is an extremely low capital investment cost. The promoter, although a local man, failed to take into account the fact that rabbit meat was not a delicacy beloved on the island. For several years the project yawed between success and failure. The original forecasts of income and project development proved excessively optimistic. To all intents and purposes the project was abandoned, although some elderly people continued to keep the rabbits as a pastime. The rabbits continued to breed without a development plan. Eventually some people took advantage of the cheap food supply. About eight years after inception the project was beginning to achieve success, but at a rate about six years behind schedule.

A failure to respect local technical advice caused a débâcle in a sanitation project in Colombia. Workers on an agricultural programme, horrified by local sanitary provisions, decided to upgrade the sanitation according to the style of latrines in the United States. They constructed outhouses provided with box seats and doors. To their amazement, the local inhabitants were equally horrified at the prospect of squatting over a hole in a seat in a smelly outhouse after generations of relatively healthy use of convenient bushes in the open air. In that particular environment, the habits of the local population in defecating offered no particular risk, and medical opinion considered the enclosed latrines to be much higher health risks. In this case the desire for 'improvement' was mainly a cultural reaction of the expatriate workers.[3]

The same observant Peace Corps volunteer who recorded the latrine project also recorded a food programme imposed on a local population in Colombia after being entirely planned in an

[3] Soles.

office in Europe. All seeds, animals, and tools to be used were imported. The seeds died. The animals became infected. The tools bent on the stony ground. Spades were too sharp for use with bare feet. Instructors basing cooking lessons on prescribed manuals used vegetables which were unobtainable locally and which could not be cultivated in the village. Middle-class girls in high heels and using an excess of cosmetics arrived in the villages, lectured to peasant women on care of babies, and then returned to their city round. One cake recipe offered to the peasant cooking class required three dozen eggs. This was in a village where not every peasant even owned a hen. Examples of erroneous planning of this type are not so common but do illustrate the tendencies which arise in many minor details of expatriate or non-domestic planning. The expatriate technical skill always needs the refining advice of local experts in adapting to cultural and environmental realities.

The human failure

Dishonesty is another problem about which the planner must be alert and against which the plan must legislate. A frank Brazilian study gives examples of this in respect of old people's homes.[4] I encountered a case with a former agency where the local financial controller of programmes made a discovery which enabled him to defraud the agency for some time. International auditors were unable to identify the method of fraud, even after complaints revealed that it existed. In the particular forest area, the financial controller discovered that there were a number of people who could sign their names but could not read or write apart from that. He therefore used that knowledge to obtain authentic signatures of local people on receipts for monies which went into his own pocket. The signatories believed they were signing for other purposes. But at a remove of more than 7,000 miles from head office, the last 100 miles being hard treks through tropical forest, the controller felt that the risk was worth the gain.

The only insurance against this kind of risk—the queue of ineligible but avaricious applicants of would-be project promoters

---

[4] CERIS 1981, ch. 7, n. 11.

which sometimes forms when considerable sources of foreign aid become available is to plan projects which break down into constituent expenses so small that each expense can be easily verified and audited; and to institute a system of careful financial checks which is known to be carried out by independent and incorruptible supervisors. The voluntary programme of low-key investment requires this kind of insurance and evidence of its integrity as much as any multinational commercial enterprise.

Dependency dangers

A more abstract but equally important consideration is that underlined in a PAHO document: 'Services should not generate dependency. The personal health goal of most old people is to remain independent as long as possible, and this objective should be respected by health providers . . . thus . . . old age is valued and not devalued.' The line between dependency and independence is also difficult to trace in the economic sense. A workshop programme could reduce the elderly participant to an automaton, slaving away day after day at a boring, meaningless piece of hand labour whose resultant income does not suffice to liberate the old person from the new drudgery of activity without ambitions, achievement, or enjoyment.[5]

To an extent, this kind of new dependency can be offset by involving the old people in a discussion of means and objectives from the very beginning. Diversification is also important in work opportunities for the aged, as is a continuing say in the government of the project. Effective executive directors and administrators are needed to handle the mechanics of a scheme, but the general principles and overall programme objectives should be a common cause.

Staff shortages

Reference was made to the emigration of large numbers of nurses from certain developing countries. To some extent or other this pattern is reflected in all skilled trades and professions where the possessor of skills might expect to be better remunerated in

[5] PAHO 1985.

North America or Western Europe. The average ageing project cannot hope to compete with these disturbing influences in terms of salary levels or living conditions. Some compensation can be offered in the way of prestige and personal usefulness within the local community. Many people will respond to such values, even at a financial loss. At the same time, each project needs to take into account from the beginning the probable initial shortage of personnel, as well as the problems of further staff recruitment as the project develops.

This requires consideration of several aspects of staff supply, including induction training for the specific details of the project; transfer of the workers to other areas or countries for an appropriate training course in the specialty if none is available locally; setting up of permanent training facilities locally; import of training personnel for an initial period, long or short, where this is more practical or economic; the training of local trainers for future training development; and short-term visits by specialists of the highest calibre when refresher or upgrading courses are needed.

Foibles of beneficiaries

A more tragic type of problem which may arise is the desire of a section of those receiving benefit to seek more than their share of those benefits. This may also be coupled with a hope on the part of some personnel to benefit unduly from the new endowments of finance, opportunities, and authority.

A case of this kind involved a large central day centre seeking to meet the needs of many old people in a large Peruvian city. Within the overall group of aged people there existed a small but highly skilled and articulate group of retired people who were in receipt of pensions. The pensions averaged up to US$25 a month but were in some cases as little as US$6 a month. With the cost of everyday supplies running almost equivalent to the costs in the United States or Britain, such pensions could only be considered pittances, and sympathy could be exercised towards the pensioners in wanting to improve their situations marginally by taking part in the centre. For some time their influence was entirely beneficial and even self-sacrificial, while they were giving time gratis as volunteers to help equip the centre. However, after a while, the work experience and work discipline of the retired pensioners resulted in them achieving first primacy, then priority, then a planned, exclusive, dominance within the centre. Eventually not only was the governing body expected to respond to the will of this caucus, but non-pensioners were gradually excluded from participation in work opportunities (on the arguable basis that they were unaccustomed to work disciplines and had no requisite skills). When it was proposed that all activities and benefits should pertain exclusively to the pensioner group, and when a member of staff took up the leadership of the caucus in contention against the directorate, it was obvious that a positive change must be made. This involved the hiving off of the pensioner group and the reduction of the centre's status to being one of a number of satellite centres. The main objective of the entire programme was to benefit the very poorest and most needy, irrespective of what skills and experience they might be able to offer to the scheme.

One of the most difficult problems inherent in such a situation is the understandable desire of the planning body to utilize the most skilled people within a community. However in many areas even skilled workers earn low wages, receive no pensions, and have fears about poverty in old age. The plan should allow time and furnish resources to give the skilled members sufficient confidence so that even after a lifetime on low wages they are willing to share with less proficient members. Programmes of 'conscientization' can be needed among the aged population as much as among the general public.

Adapting the lessons

In closing these references to pilot methods, their potential, and their problems, it is pertinent to observe that lessons on the ageing experience can be learned at all levels of national development, not simply as an input from the North to the South. Some American developing countries generally stand fairly high in the leagues of economic and social service development compared, say, to some of the newer African republics; they also stand ahead in their experience of the ills of industrialization, migration, the break-up of the family, the problem of ageing, and the organized response to that problem. Lessons can be learned from the experience of other cultures and continents.

In a 1986 conference in Mexico I was one of a panel of speakers and course consultants who came from developed countries at the invitation of the Mexican governmental social services to join in a seminar on ageing. While some of the contributions of the overseas consultants were irrelevant to the Mexican scene, there was repeated insistence on learning about the errors of European, North American, and other welfare state planning as a simple guide to what should *not* be attempted in Mexico or, if attempted, what problems might be anticipated.

A specific area under consideration was the admitted ambition of higher developing countries to emulate the industrialized countries in every respect, including the introduction of global pension schemes. Already, thinking gerontologists in such countries are doubting the appropriateness of allocating scarce resources in such ways. At the lowest estimate, the developed country experience can warn the developing countries as to the pitfalls encountered in pursuing age care programmes.

A number of organizations in developing countries have proved to be extremely receptive not only to advice based on successful projects elsewhere or on errors in 'Northern' projects, but also to constructive and reasoned criticism of projects in their own countries. Workers display such a desire to learn that they are amenable to being made aware of their own errors. A source of such criticism is the mass of confidential reports which pass over Overseas Aid desks in developed countries. Desks of the Commission of European Communities (CEC) have proved particularly sensitive and accurate in their reporting and derived comment.

A critique of small projects

The director of the typical programme on ageing will find useful guidelines in a CEC report on small development projects.[6] Positively the report says that 'one role which small development projects can usefully perform is to experiment with new technologies and organisational arrangements, in the hope that

---

[6] Crombrugghe *et al.* 1985.

solutions can be arrived at which can then be disseminated on a more extensive scale'. But it warns, 'such experiments generally entail *large* elements of risk and uncertainty and it is often unrealistic to suppose that they can be completed within any predetermined time frame'. The report also found that in some cases initial objectives proved over-ambitious, whereas the ideal pilot project attempts only the spread of operations which are essential to yield a reasonable scientific assessment of the value of the type of project.

Remembering that the CEC report does not refer specifically to ageing projects but can have relevance to them, a further comment was that 'relatively few projects set out with the specific intention of working for the poorest groups and as a result they were excluded from a share of the benefits' (as distinct from the ageing project mentioned, where the poorest were excluded by other beneficiaries in spite of the planners' original intentions).

'Women also received relatively little attention . . . '. It is an ongoing subject for debate as to how far projects solely for older women should be mounted. In projects co-funded by CEC and HelpAge opportunities and care needs are balanced to the relative requirements of the sexes, without normally initiating separately prepared and funded projects for a particular sex. The laundresses' project cited earlier was directed at women as a pragmatic response to observed numbers of unemployed, unsupported females rather than as a consciously planned exercise in positive sex discrimination. Had elderly men wished to participate in the laundering, as in the weaving also mentioned, they would have been considered according to urgency of need.

The CEC critique observes in some places that as soon as the external project support was withdrawn, 'it rapidly became apparent that the mangement structure which had been set up was incapable of maintaining quality control, and that the required levels of skills could not be maintained following the withdrawal of specialist technical staff'. In the ageing projects quoted in Chapter 7 more problems were encountered in the development of subsequent management skills, as in the weaving scheme in Trinidad, Beni, where management was effective until the products of the local industry had saturated the national market. At that point a quantum leap in management skills and imagination was required if the programme was to expand into exports, the only alternative market—and such skills were not immediately available.

Turning to specifics, the CEC mentions (again not referring to ageing projects)

a jam and wine making factory in Bolivia, which could not function after project support (financial) was withdrawn; the solar pumps in Mali, which could not be independently maintained; the pumping system in Zambia, which depended upon maintenance services which were far away and insufficiently reliable . . . a textile enterprise in Nicaragua which experienced difficulty in obtaining essential imported components and was able to produce at 50% of its full capacity as a result . . . In Peru, a seed potato bank—although partially successful in meeting a desparate short term need, the selection of a variety [of potato] which people did not like to eat meant that the project was unlikely to prove viable in the longer term . . . terms of trade may turn against local producers as in a Peruvian project . . .

As projects for older people tend to cover every aspect of human experience the Third World gerontologist has to venture beyond the specialized aspects of ageing into agriculture, horticulture, small industrial projects, and management. The above examples and similar critiques are essential study for the gerontologist entrepreneur. From the viewpoint of an inter-governmental co-funding agency the CEC points out that some international NGOs are themselves weak in follow-up of input as also in the initial identification of suitable projects. It is therefore relevant to suggest that developing country agencies should diversify their international NGO advice and consultancy sources.

Devolution of skills

Equally relevant to the Third World requirements are pilot projects evolved in areas of other developing continents at a similar level of economic or cultural development. The HelpAge International quarterly bulletin *Ageways* already provides a means of exchange of such ideas as it is despatched free to some 70 countries world-wide with the most basic advice and information on all aspects of age programmes. The International Federation on Aging and United Nations Aging Unit bulletins serve a similar purpose at a somewhat higher level of development.

A number of leading international development agencies see the eventual end-product of all their activities as working themselves out of a job by enabling the developing country to supply its own expertise. To some extent this contrasts with the experience of the HelpAge network, which, somewhat unusually among similar charities, has been able to inaugurate independent, indigenous organizations with like principles, methods, and objectives. This suggests that, however quickly and effectively the initiating international body is able to withdraw from local control, the demands of the developing group for information support, consultancy, training, assistance in seeking funding, access to international debate, and inter-organizational friendship imposes an ever-growing responsibility on the international network. Withdrawal from local control can mean an *even greater* commitment in the way of international liaison.

The newer participants contribute effectively to the network, as in the case of the Colombian Pro Vida which sends consultants and inspectors to projects in other countries on behalf of the 'International'. But the originating body finds itself required to develop its own organization, both in size and skills, to respond adequately to the liaison and co-ordination aspects of multiple initiatives resulting from filial groups which are themselves creating, expanding, and diversifying in unanticipated ways.

Model Programmes

During a 1987 conference on ageing I was asked to outline a programme for setting up a typical age care organization for the voluntary sector in a developing country.[7] I pointed out that there can be no ideal or general format for this purpose, given the vast difference in environments, socio-economic factors, political systems, traditional cultures, rates of modernization, actual and projected population profiles, and so on, in so many developing countries across the world. However, with that reservation, I did agree to outline a possible organizational design for three distinct and fairly frequent scenarios. Those outlines may help to

[7] Conference arranged by Brazilian Ministry of Health in Brasilia, Dec. 1987.

synthesize and give some methodical order to the various project descriptions and criticisms already given, as well as the national strategic indications to be included in the following chapter.

The three scenarios treated comprise a small community with few official services; a metropolitan setting with scattered and variable services; and a national voluntary sector programme in a 'middle developing' country where economic circumstances preclude early major government initiatives. These are scenarios which can be frequently encountered with only slight variations in a range of countries, although there are many major variations of conditions in other countries which are either well above or well below the median type of developing country for which these present scenarios may be thought relevant.

District blueprint

For the present purposes, the term 'district' may be considered to cover a population of, say, 20,000 to 100,000. It might be a self-contained town, or a shanty town area of a large city, or a rural area with a small urban nucleus. There may be no specialist service for old people except a small old people's home, which may be in an impoverished condition. The other source of aid may be the local priest with very restricted resources, mainly in the form of small sums of cash or basic foodstuffs. It can be assumed that the over-60s would form between 5% and 8% of the population, and perhaps 10% of them may have some form of pension or similar savings system, but at a low rate of income which is not inflation-linked. For the sake of clarity the steps of initiation and development are numbered chronologically but it will be understood that the varying circumstances of each community may require appropriate changes in the ordering of programme items.

1. *Creating awareness.* It is likely that people of the district are not aware of the developing problem of ageing because its origins almost everywhere are recent—frequently less than 10 years ago, and almost certainly less than 20 years ago. Locally, the increment of people surviving to an older age will thus still be almost imperceptible. Likewise, although the populace may be aware of the incidence of migration, this may not have been related in people's thinking to the increasing number of old

people whose sons and daughters have left the aged parent living alone. The first stage in any community reaction is therefore some awakening of awareness to the incipient social problem.[8]

In this phase the awareness may be aroused by a concerned local inhabitant or group. Failing this it may be influenced by the intervention of an 'outsider' of considerable skill and sensibility. In most continents it has already been seen that the factor of sensibility is the major requirement, and that a non-national, acting with tact and understanding, may be more successful than an overbearing, and possibly politically or financially motivated national.

The first step is likely to be a meeting or series of meetings on either a one-to-one or small-group basis. A 'town meeting' is not likely to produce results if no prior research and planning work has been carried out. One frequently productive tactic is a meeting of representatives of groups already involved in caring work, even though not directly related to, or primarily concerned with the aged. While some of the groups may see an Ageing Committee as threatening their own status, it is from such already aware people that most sympathetic support will first come. However, such people are almost certain to be already totally committed to their own cause, and at an early date it will be necessary to recruit into the group one or two 'action people'. These may include business people who have some experience of planning, negotiation, and financing, or retired professionals or other elderly people whose interests may make them suitable.

The first meetings should be fairly unambitious and should concentrate on causing people to consider their own community and recognize the signs of a greying population. A simple reference to international and national statistical trends may rouse interest. An account of activities which have been successful in other similar communities may lead to the group asking, 'What can we do here?' It is at this stage that the external adviser can be particularly useful, outlining possible initial organization and activity as well as counselling against the inevitable well-intentioned but over-ambitious plans which tend

[8] In my own experience from community work in Latin America, abandoned elderly people were very rarely encountered in the 1950s, but are only too frequently encountered in the later 1980s.

sometimes to spring from initial discussions, only to disappoint at later reviews.

At this point it may be possible to agree on a regular group meeting, with one or two honorary officers, but not too complex a structure. The group should then propose its own second phase. At this stage an office will be required; it may be located in space made available by a local business, or it could be in some community building as long as the new committee is able to express its separate identity.

2. *Research at the local level.* Very early in the group's activities where should be a modest element of very basic research. This might be a house-to-house survey of a small section of the neighbourhood or it might be a review of case reports from local sources—old people's homes, churches, hospitals, police, welfare groups. Lacking this basis of local fact, any further action proposals may be voted down by the inevitable influential unbeliever, or may fail to influence potential local fund-raisers or donors.

The first welfare target could be a modest addition to existing resources. It could be to refurnish and decorate the old people's home, or to supply volunteers and materials so that the parish priest can extend his occasional bounty into a regular feeding scheme, or to persuade a local hall or school to open its doors once a week as a locale where older people can meet for social purposes. It may be necessary to warn that the apparently simple gambit of setting up a visiting scheme for the elderly in their own homes can be fraught with problems unless very carefully organized and well supported by referral services and material resources from the beginning. Volunteers may tire rapidly if not well trained and co-ordinated. Demands of the elderly may be excessive if logistics are inadequate. Above all, cash will be needed for various purposes identified by the visitors.

The main purpose of these initial moves is not so much to benefit the major number of elderly in the minimum time but to gain knowledge, build up local skills, and establish the group as a credible local activity worthy of voluntary support as well as official approbation.

3. *Public launch.* Once a small active committee has been set in motion, some kind of local data acquired and edited, and some useful action project, however modest, is available to view, the

moment for a public launch may have arrived. Here the group must balance its inauguration between outrageous exaggeration and undue modesty. A general rule is that a launch may indulge in considerable and colourful display as long as its public declarations relate to reality. There should be a total mobilization of any and every local group which will pay lip-service to the welfare of the elderly, whether or not any further support is anticipated from that source. Choirs or dance groups from schools can join with local musicians of classical or popular style as well as such sporting or other cultural groups as may organize events or exhibitions. Full use should be made of press, radio, and television. An event like the Crowning of the Granny of the Year is often well accepted.

To justify such ostentation it is not necessary to publish a plan which is patently beyond the resources of the group. All that is required, and what is most likely to be acceptable, is covered in five essentials: a brief account of the tremendous world or national trend towards an ageing population; some relevant local data (not so personalized as to embarrass local persons); a 'track record' of the project already undertaken; a sensible plan for extension of activities; and a simple, achievable, local fund-raising target, probably linked to the highest priority element of the action plan.

4. *Initiating the fund-raising programme.* It should be possible to link such an inauguration into an initial fund-raising scheme. It is better to set an achievable target and to move on to a further target once that is achieved than to alienate local people by setting too high an objective initially. One of the most fruitful sources of support for the grandparent generation anywhere is the grandchild generation. Schools and youth groups can provide informal support by organizing fund-raising events or providing some ongoing practical or material aid. The presence of one or two business people on the local committee will ensure both an entrance into the business community and a sensible approach to fund-raising and project financing.

At this stage it is unlikely that the committee will have any paid organizers or administrators, but committee members may be able to obtain administration or accountancy help from local firms or by using retired volunteers.

5. *Mobilizing local support.* It may now be appropriate for the

new committee to mobilize both influence and resources to improve existing local services, whether provided by government, local authority, or some other voluntary organization.

Local government is frequently susceptible to lobbying by, and co-operation with, a group which is catching the public eye as representing an area of real need and opportunity. With a minimal offer of support, or perhaps exposure, local politicians may respond urgently with whatever resources they have available. Individual voluntary organizations are, however, extremely sensitive as to their own independence and specialty, and rarely respond to what might be called 'public bullying' or unwanted advice. Most voluntary organizations are nevertheless in need of additional resources. The new committee will prosper by observing the real needs of such organizations and, as and when possible, reacting quickly and willingly to supply any resource of benefit to older people within the constituency of other voluntary organizations (while refraining from giving advice until requested).

6. *The first project: a day centre.* The committee might now be looking for its first major project. Again, this may not be a totally independent project but may be set up in collaboration with some organization which has premises available. The first project may be a day centre, and the new committee may wish also to locate its own headquarters there for ease of access to old people.

There is no set format for a day centre. It may be open all week or only a half-day a week. It may be a separate building or a borrowed room. It may have skilled permanent staff or it may commence with a small rota of volunteers. It may offer such facilities as therapy, work training, work opportunities, health education, a free or low-cost dining facility, cultural activities, and professional advice service; or it may be simply a chance to sit around and chat over the local brew. It may offer opportunities for inter-generational exchange or it may initially offer a single, specialist service to older people.

The day centre has several immediate advantages. It can give respite to families where friction has been caused by the constant negative presence of a frustrated or worried old person. It offers early identification of individual problems. It forms a gathering place and a substitute family for those who live alone. It enables a small group of volunteers to achieve some benefit for a relatively large number of elders. It can identify older people who can themselves contribute in some way, sometimes as an Old People's Council, to the programme. Above all, for the infant committee, it affords instant and very good opinions about the realities of old people's lives, about the identities of other old people who are too frail to attend, and about the most urgent priorities for the committee's next planned stage.

7. *Expanding the programme: home visits.* Very soon after establishing a day centre the committee may need to move into a visiting scheme because of the numbers of abandoned elderly housebound that come to be known—always amazingly high. The proviso mentioned earlier still applies. A visiting scheme must be organized expertly with a view to perpetuity. There is no worse disillusionment for a housebound elderly person than to be visited by a volunteer with great promises but no ability to fulfil them, especially when the volunteer disappears after the first visit or two.

Reference has been made to a well-structured Good Neighbours scheme in Malta which indicates some of the requisites of the scheme: a sound central planning group; a rota which provides for unavailability of the duty volunteer; a training scheme to impress upon volunteers the need for regular visiting and also induct them into elements of age care; an agreed referral scheme with any official or specialist services in the locality; a network of informal support services such as transport, legal advice, minor household repairs, help with shopping and own domestic budget, cleaning, therapy; a committee fund which will ensure any emergency requirements such as urgent medicines or attention to domestic breakdown.

In the visiting programme as in centre activities, the intergenerational aspect needs to be developed with both sensitivity and imagination. For example, some older people welcome controlled contact with children; others, more fearful, may find nothing more horrifying than an unannounced invasion by a gang of noisy youths, armed with lethal instruments, even if for the meritorious purpose of mending the roof or digging the corn patch. Visits by children need to be planned so that there is true exchange—the youngster perhaps offering some interesting item from the school curriculum and the elder responding with tales of other days or traditional songs, dances, and games.

8. *Increasing mobility.* The development of activities for the aged will soon demonstrate a need for mobility within the programme. One of the objectives of a visiting scheme will be to encourage and enable the less mobile to attend social centres. This will often call for provision of personal mobility aids, such as wheelchairs and walkers, as well as specially adapted vehicles able to lift the physically disabled to a place of meeting or specialist service. Such vehicles, apart from bringing about a radical change in the life-style of the old person, also have an enormous publicity value when, filled with vibrant elderly people, they are seen moving through the streets at all moments of every day—as well as at local picnic places on holidays.

9. *Supplementing old people's incomes.* In most cases, a priority need will be that of providing a basic income for old people who have neither pension nor family on which to rely. Very rarely are active older people intent on being the mere recipients of charity. Most are only too willing to make some kind of contribution to their own welfare. The economic problem usually relates to their lack of physical strength or stamina to undertake the arduous tasks of their normal trade, their inability to upgrade their own skills in relation to the technological advances in industry or agriculture, or the closure of the local job market to older people, either due to false assumptions as to the work ability of older people or because of an excess of younger workers seeking entry into the job market.

Even a fairly modest ageing programme can follow two lines of approach to this problem. The first is to train or retrain older people for available jobs and to carry on campaigns to convince employers about the value of the experienced, committed, older worker. The second approach is to initiate work schemes which either permit older workers to carry on tasks they are familiar with at a more leisurely pace among their peers, or to move into a new type of productive activity which is not currently carried on in the local community. In a number of instances, HelpAge groups have, by a very brief survey of local commerce, identified some activity which was underprovided in the locality—a bakery, a laundry, an ice-cream factory, a herbal medicine garden, small fishponds—which could quickly and easily be established as a work scheme for elders.

Many of the most impoverished of the elderly are those widows who, having long survived the family wage-earner, have no trade skills or family support. Or in agricultural societies, older women who have been main food-producers all their lives may reach a stage of incapacitation for the accustomed task. Some success has been achieved in employing such women to run crèches for children of working mothers, or as helpers at primary schools, or as part of the staff of feeding schemes.

However small and tentative such a work scheme may be, it is always important that, in addition to providing an income for those actually taking part, a percentage of the income should be set aside for those who are too frail to work. In practice this often supplies a further incentive for the elderly workforce, who feel that not only is their independence and dignity being restored to some extent, but that they are also able to be of help to those who are less well-off than themselves.

In such work schemes, the elderly workers should be allowed as much say as possible in decision-making. The assets of the scheme and the final policy decisions should remain with the organizing body so that, when the current generation of workers is no longer able to continue, more young-old persons may move into the same facilities.

10. *Setting up a stable fund-raising structure.* By this stage the district committee will be faced with considerable ongoing expenses in its annual budget as well as a need for more capital to finance such new outreach as may be indicated by experience and research to date. It will therefore be time to look towards setting up a viable and stable fund-raising structure. To an extent, continued project success and good publicity will generate additional income. At some point commitment and future demand will outstrip the fund-raising development open to the district group.

It should take every opportunity of seeking the approbation of the local authorities for its plans. Many governmental authorities will consider it a better economic option to make a grant or a per capita settlement to a voluntary organization than to set up a self-contained official service, especially when both capital and revenue expenditure measures are likely to be very high.

Any district-level group may, of course, apply for grants to national and international foundations. Three problems in this respect would be the complexity of grant application systems, the low priority which many foundations accord to ageing programmes, and the fact that the district committee may not be well-known in wider circles. It will therefore be to the advantage of the local group to have made some contact with, or entered into membership of, some association of wider constituency. This national or international link should provide the local group with advice and guidance in the maze of grant formalities, and also act as a referee or entrepreneur for the local group in the international grant market.[9]

The third major development will be the employment of a skilled fund-raiser and the adaptation of various schemes which combine awareness with the subscription of the means to act. Fund-raising is a very skilled and precarious activity, unfortunately sometimes attracting predators. In this field too the group would be well advised to seek advice from reputable agencies, and it is no coincidence that HelpAge training courses give considerable priority to fund-raising.

At such a point the fund-raising drive might be directed to two rather unexpected constituencies. The first is the school: if the committee can offer a 'pre-packaged' lesson or series of lessons on ageing and the aged, preferably given by a trained educator or promoter, schools may be willing to enter into a programme which includes regular fund-raising events as well as direct aid schemes linking children to old people in surrogate relationship patterns. The other target constituency is that of older people who have some resources. Many cases are known of considerable legacies made to age care programmes by those who, well provided in their own old age, were reminded of the claims of those not so fortunate.

11. *Training*. As a committee's work develops it will also observe an increased requirement for training at all levels, some of it to be provided locally and other aspects requiring study at a

---

[9] There may be some thought (for instance, in the CEC) that it might be preferable for local developing countries' groups to apply direct to 'Northern' governments for aid rather than through international agencies. This procedure would ignore the considerable problems some local agencies have in understanding and complying with complex governmental co-funding systems. As a rule such agencies are happy to work through the rather avuncular international voluntary agency, which can act as an entrepreneur and consultant.

larger centre. The importance of training volunteers has already been mentioned. A permanent system of volunteer training should be developed, using mainly local instructors. The more trained a volunteer becomes, the more commitment will be evidenced. Without a continuing source of training and information, the volunteer may find many causes of frustration and disenchantment in age care.

The group may also improve care services by co-ordinating training courses and experience for professionals and others exercising care for the elderly in other official or voluntary schemes. The group's training and informational activities should never become exclusive to its own workers and members, for its goal should be to enhance the welfare of all elderly everywhere in its geographical area.

Training should not be restricted to obvious geriatric and gerontological subjects. Respective members of the programme should be trained in programme planning, organizational structure, methods of local training, fund-raising, financial control—in fact, a whole range of necessary peripheral activities.

12. *Accommodation*. Little has been said yet about shelter and appropriate accommodation as this is likely to be an expensive activity best undertaken by a statutory or private commercial body. From the beginning of an age care programme, attention can be given to house repairs for those older people who can neither afford nor undertake them. An organized group can quickly recruit teams of volunteers willing to give attention to urgent home improvements or to adapt houses to the specific needs of elderly occupiers.

A small district committee is probably well advised not to become involved in either major extensions to an old people's home or to building a new residential institution.[10] Attention should be focused rather on measures to enable older people to stay as long as possible in comfort in their own homes. Established old people's homes of a closed nature may often be encouraged to improve services by a give-and-take arrangement. The home might open its facilities to non-residents in a common day-centre activity if the district group is able to offer in return services ranging from structural repairs to free hours of therapy.

[10] This point needs to be reiterated because it is so frequently the first response of local agencies and age-care committees to want to build or extend a home.

13. *Sharing ideas and initiatives.* As the group becomes larger and more successful in its own area it may acquire further impetus and advantage by looking beyond its own borders and sharing ideas and initiatives with neighbouring groups, or even initiating them. There is considerable local kudos to be obtained that way, as well as the advantages accruing from being able to study the successes as well as the errors of others engaged in similar work.

Town groups should also have a concern for their hinterland. Outlying villages can be helped to adapt and develop ideas proven in the town. There is considerable logic in such a collaboration, for in many developing country areas the problems of the shanty town commence in the rural experience of poverty. It may be that an improvement in the life of the old person remaining in the rural area may lead to less people migrating towards the dubious delights of the city. This in turn may lead to less problems for the aged in future.

14. *Headquarters.* One word is probably needed about the often vexed question of a headquarters. Some organizations believe it necessary to build a prestige headquarters early in their development programme. A voluntary organization is well advised to make do with as modest a headquarters as possible. Early success in promoting practical projects reaching to the most necessitous of people may lead to a group achieving solid enough backing to embark on the construction or adaptation of a much-needed service premises, such as a day centre, clinic, or complex of sheltered housing. At that time, space could well be allocated also for the group's headquarters office and stores. Otherwise such facilities should be found in the form of loans, leases, or donations from local supporters.

Metropolitan blueprint

'Metropolitan' here is used to describe a conurbation of perhaps 750,000 population upwards, but the term could also encompass some capital cities of lesser population. The metropolitan area is likely to contain several large institutions catering for elderly people, including hospitals and very large old people's homes (400 residents or more). There are also likely to be numbers of smaller homes. It is unlikely that there is any geriatric specialty apart from private practice, although there may be a separate hospital or wing for chronic geriatric and psycho-geriatric cases. The majority of old people's homes may have no regular medical or therapy services and many may have no organized social activities. Perhaps 20% of the elderly may enjoy some level of pension or formal savings, but the elderly, like the population as a whole, will be resident in stratified socio-economic zones. In the poorest of these there may be casual feeding schemes to which the elderly have access. Day Clubs may exist in higher economic zones. A possible blueprint for development might be as follows:

1. *First steps.* A metropolitan-wide ageing programme may originate from a meeting of groups already involved with the elderly or from a group of volunteers initially involved in visiting old people's homes. The first step is likely to be an attempt at listing and co-ordinating existing services. It is probable that some existing services will accept co-ordination only in very general terms. A more effective metropolitan committee may therefore rely on a considerable proportion of persons not related closely to existing organizations and possessing a much wider range of skills than may be required in the day-to-day running of an institution.

Much of what has been said about a District Committee would apply also to a metropolitan programme; however, the latter would have somewhat different chronological priorities subsequent to the formation of an effective steering group, and this section therefore deals mainly with those variations.

2. *Co-ordination with existing institutions.* Despite early disappointments, an immediate priority would still be the co-ordination both of programmes and relevant studies. Many of the failures to provide services in old people's homes are due either to lack of professional training of staff or inability to organize external aid. Where existing institutions were willing to co-operate, a group of external advisers would be able to locate and co-ordinate training opportunities for staff, or to recruit doctors and other professionals willing to give free hours of service and match them up with institutions having corresponding service requirements.

In a metropolitan setting, research and programme studies often exist if only in the form of case reports and seminar minutes. Rather than set up an early major study of the elderly, the new group would be advised to canvas colleges, hospitals, institutions, and welfare organizations in order to collect, collate, and summarize existing information about the elderly. This should produce sufficient evidence on which to base the first steps of a wider programme.

3. *Identification of gaps in existing services.* A most urgent duty of the group would be to identify gaps in existing services. One aspect of this work would be charting existing services and noting their geographic or socio-economic spread, and consequent lacunae. Another approach would be to prepare a check list of essential and preferred services for the elderly and compare this with available services. A third tactic would be to note the existence of services peripheral to the elderly but which might be conveniently extended to include the elderly or develop a specialty.

The group would soon identify conspicuous gaps in service and would then need to decide on a plan of priorities as to how these gaps might be remedied by: (*a*) drawing the attention of official services to them;[11] (*b*) persuading other services to extend or adapt (perhaps with some support from the new group); or (*c*) setting up its own initiatives and recruiting voluntary help, as possible.

4. *Harnessing the media.* At this point, even without a track record of its own, the group in a metropolitan setting, may be able to gain the interest of powerful local media in respect of service gaps and observed needs. It may even be possible to accumulate enough evidence to begin a fund-raising campaign without initiating a project of its own.

Lack of finance is the most frequent deterrent to good service development, yet in most metropolitan areas there are individuals and companies with considerable financial resources. A new group, including members with entrepreneurial skills, may well make its best contribution at first by inspiring and conducting fund-raising to enable the development of existing well-intentioned organizations which lack this type of skill.

In terms of modern publicity and fund-raising tactics, even a

---

[11] Whilst most metropolitan areas have some general services, these rarely have specific provision for the needs of the elderly, and sometimes even actually discriminate against older people, if only because costs inhibit old people with no income from seeking services.

good representative metropolitan committee may need to look beyond its own borders for new ideas and possibly training. The best fund-raising idea is often the most original one, and it may well have to be imported from a widely differing culture.

5. *Training*. Age care in the metropolitan setting may be characterized by lack of trained staff and lack of training facilities. Abuse of old people in large institutions is often traced to the employment of unsuitable staff. While this can be due to financial stringencies, it is equally likely to be due to low staff status due to lack of proper training.

The group should concern itself with setting up regular training courses in all aspects of care and organization. Such courses can at the beginning be mounted at extremely low cost. University or school facilities can be loaned during vacation periods. Suitable experts can be persuaded to lecture, on an expenses-only basis. Opportunities for practice can be offered by the better-organized institutions. A company with interests in the elderly market may well underwrite such courses.

Applications to international organizations may provide expatriate experts to direct seminars on special subjects. The same sources may arrange for local professionals to take courses or gain practical experience overseas. Such interchange enhances the standing of the profession and the programme locally, and also provides the new group with a cadre of skilled people indebted to it. In the general programme of training, an important factor will be the trainer him or herself; in many developing countries the trainers themselves require training in methods as local professional or voluntary training programmes may be lacking or insufficient. In a large metropolitan programme an expert trainer could be a good long-term investment even though the trainer may not at first be a specialist in any of the 'ageing' subjects taught.

6. *Increasing mobility*. Another early priority in the vaster and more complicated distances of the metropolitan setting is for mobility. The expense and cruel crush of shanty town traffic may mean that special transport provided by the Ageing Committee will be an old person's only opportunity of escaping for a while from depressing surroundings. If the committee has achieved some momentum in publicity it may be possible to negotiate with public or commercial transport for loan of vehicles or for

subsidized transport.[12] Local authorities may well legislate readily for off-peak free or cheap fares as being a popular and inexpensive contribution to the welfare of the aged. In most cases the metropolitan committee will need to acquire some of its own specially adapted vehicles for specific journeys and purposes, or give such vehicles to other organizations who may adequately maintain and run them.

As in the district environment, but on a larger scale, a fleet of distinctively painted, easily identified age care vehicles running through the streets has an instant impact in the group's public awareness campaign as well as being a practical aid to future fund-raising.

7. *Expansion of the hierarchy.* When some success and useful experience has been achieved at the metropolitan level, the group may well give attention to extending upwards or downwards in the national scale. If there is no national committee or similar association, the metropolitan committee is in a good position to propose or promote one. Its own proven projects, together with improvements and developments supported in other organizations, make the metropolitan programme an ideal demonstration and schooling ground for groups or potential group promoters from smaller towns.

The metropolitan group should also become involved in the problems of ageing in its own hinterland. As mentioned earlier, many urban problems of ageing commence as rural problems of poverty. Attention to the rural hinterland is therefore a sensible measure for prevention or reduction of future metropolitan problems.

8. *Research and evaluation.* A special contribution of the metropolitan group could be in the sometimes neglected twin activities of research and evaluation. There is likely to be at least one local university and possibly a training school for social work. The committee can guide researchers so that academic aspirations regarding age research are always directed to some eventual improvement in life for the old person. The committee can ensure that useful research is not filed away to the advantage of spiders, but is developed and applied to the general benefit of the elderly.

---

[12] A Pro Vida regional conference in Bogotá in February 1988 reported that excessive distances between bus stops, and bus drivers refusing to stop to pick up old people, constituted major problems.

The question of evaluation of projects is most important. Many voluntary programmes have neither the time, skills, nor cash for adequate evaluation of their operations. Sometimes they may have been doing the wrong things for the right reasons for many years at great expense when evaluation could have shown them a better way. The sensitivity to be expected of the metropolitan committee would enable them to identify and commission suitable researchers to carry out regular evaluation.

9. *Geographical specialization of activities.* A problem which is the particular preserve of the metropolitan group relates to the stratification of society by socio-economic considerations. It is a subject of debate as to whether deprivation and distress can exist in the upper strata equally, or with comparate call for consideration, as in the lowest strata. Some observers believe that the distress of the garbage picker is without equal. Certainly the extent of poverty there is far more acute than in other social classes.

However, some other observers who, like myself, have worked both with garbage pickers and more opulent classes, have sometimes noted more distress and mental suffering at higher socio-economic levels. The work of Luis Ramos in Brazil tends to bear out the thesis that distress can be total for the abandoned or disadvantaged old person at his or her own socio-economic level, whatever that be.[13]

The metropolitan committee may therefore find it necessary, for other than good administrative reasons, to develop a number of subsidiary district groups. In many metropolitan areas, a careful geographical division of such groups may correspond closely to division by socio-economic strata. This would allow the development of specialist functions, ranging from the committed worker trained to cleanse and fumigate the abandoned beggar to the psycho-geriatrician who can deal with problems of lost prestige, or the financial adviser who can sort out the lack of actual current cash in a situation of apparent adequate capital assets.

In city centres where all socio-economic classes exist cheek by jowl, a subsidiary local group would clearly need either a wide range of its own experts or contacts with an equally wide range of

[13] As reported at the Brasilia meeting cited in n. 7 above.

corresponding organizations to which referrals might be made.

10. *Other considerations of structure.* In many other aspects the metropolitan group would conform to the principles and practice of the district group. A major structural difference could be the eventual remoteness of the metropolitan group from individual old people, leading to a bureaucratic tendency not so likely in the smaller community. This might be offset by regular election of old people's representatives to the central committee, or by the inauguration of a lively Council of the Elderly to act as a counter-check.

Another major structural difference could be that, whereas a district community would be composed of locally known personalities who might be easily replaced by similar personalities as years go by, the metropolitan committee might tend to be more anonymous. It would therefore need to provide in its constitution or procedures for a method of recruiting or selecting new members, some perhaps as representatives of supporting institutions, when older members fall by the wayside.

National blueprint

This model too is proposed as a voluntary sector complement to government services, which cannot be expected to meet all the needs of an ageing population in the near future. The term 'national' describes geographical spread and population totals and density less adequately than do 'metropolitan' or 'district'. 'Nation' includes Grenada and Rwanda as well as Brazil and India. It might be thought that the main distinction in ageing problems between the tiny nations and the giants would be in the cultural and racial diversities of the larger nations.

During 1987, I took part in a national forum on the health of the aged in Brazil. A factor which continually surfaced in debate was the vast difference between São Paulo and the rural north-east, and again between a medium-sized town in Santa Catarina and a settlement on an Amazon headwater. In the course of the national study which I and my wife undertook in Belize, during a 10-mile drive they visited a town with Anglo-Spanish cultural influence, an East Indian (original immigrants from India) village, a cluster of Garifuna (black Caribbean) dwellings, and a Maya (aboriginal Amerinds) settlement. Each small settlement was totally distinct in culture. Evidence suggested that there were corresponding health variations of those different peoples living in the same natural environment.

HelpAge Belize and HelpAge India have to contend with similar regional and cultural diversities, differing only in size. Each nation has a government exercising sovereignty in a common world of conflicting political and economic pressures. Recent experience suggests that a national blueprint for ageing will have considerable similarities in countries at similar stages of development, even though of diverse sizes and cultures. Such a national blueprint might include the following components:

1. *Founding a national committee.* A national committee on ageing might be set up by a meeting together of organizations with similar interests, or by a group of concerned private citizens, or by the association of a number of smaller district groups. It might also be instituted originally by government initiative, leaving it to operate with total independence or relative freedom according to the political system. It could also be generated and welded together by the influence of an international body offering consultancy and some initial financial aid.

However the committee is founded, it should endeavour to ensure for itself three essential elements: (*a*) the support or acquiescence of the majority of organizations in the ageing field; (*b*) the approbation or acquiescence of the government; and (*c*) a resource of skills much wider than those specific to geriatrics and gerontology.

2. *International links.* High on the list of the national committee's action, if not already secured, would be the obtaining of firm international links. It is assumed that some age care actitivies already exist in the country, and that deficiencies in services are due largely to lack of skills, organization, finance, and appreciation of the problems of an ageing population. It can also be assumed that none of these requirements can be fully or even mainly fulfilled by the 'median developing country' unaided.[14] European, North American, and other developed nations themselves

---

[14] This was further substantiated by delegates to meetings studying these aspects at Pro Vida, Bogotá, and at the University of Florida in February 1988.

depend very much on cross-national exchanges for development of national knowledge, skills, and technology on ageing.

International links will be of two kinds. There will be an opportunity to draw upon the resources of developed countries concerned to correct the imbalance of prosperity thought to derive from old imperial days. The new 'world village' concept, speeded by considerations like nuclear disaster and AIDS, will gain further relevance as governments and people generally come to understand the full significance of the greying population. So aid will be available from developed countries not only in cash and materials but in skills, ideas, and especially the priceless knowledge of the errors of other societies in trying to deal with earlier manifestations of the ageing phenomenon.

A further invaluable international link will be between countries of similar cultures, or at a similar level of economic and social development, as they share experience of current initiatives. It should also be mentioned that a national committee will be able to establish its own prestige and quality by offering consultancy and training to other countries still approaching its level of ageing and age care development.

3. *Advising government.* The national committee should lose no time in establishing itself as chief consultant, monitor and worrier on government services and legislation related to ageing. It is eventually the government's responsibility to ensure the welfare of all its people, and the national committee should skilfully remind the government of the morally high priority of the aged who are sometimes considered a political low or nil priority.

The national committee can ensure that overlap and duplication between government and volunteer services are kept to a minimum. It can advise how government can encourage and support individuals, families, and organizations working with the aged. It can also advise on, and help to expedite, government legislation. Even if resources are insufficient to implement legislation immediately, the moral and empowering effect of legislation is a tremendous asset to a voluntary organization often sorely tried by bureaucracies and contentious individuals.

4. *Co-ordination.* On the issue of co-ordination of services, the national committee would, like the metropolitan committee, look out for gaps in service. However, rather than itself moving to

supply those gaps, it would point them out to other relevant agencies, possibly set up regional or specialist groups to deal with the gaps, and, above all, seek the resources to enable the closure of the gaps. Again, international links would be useful in this respect.

5. *Fund-raising.* Like the metropolitan committee, the national committee would also give early priority to fund-raising. Its comparatively high status would give it added 'clout'. It would be particularly useful in advising on the preparation of projects for international funding, especially for that most valuable of applications—the project which attracts international governmental co-funding.

The committee would arrange fund-raising training for subsidiary organizations and also itself conduct campaigns at the highest national levels, such as telethons, national days or weeks of the aged, and so on. It would be in a strategic position to promote sponsorship schemes whereby individuals or groups, internally or externally, 'adopt' or sponsor individual grannies or group projects.

6. *Training.* In addition to the types of training courses suggested for the metropolitan group, the national group would soon explore the possibility of setting up a permanent training centre, essentially to train in the basics of ageing and age care delivery. The training centre would also produce manuals and course materials suitable for extra-mural studies or district seminars. By opening its training centre also to people from neighbouring countries it would add to its own store of experience and ideas.

The committee would also encourge the setting up of university chairs or specially relevant programmes in training colleges, although these would have to be financed by sponsors other than the committee. Sponsors could also be advised on establishing scholarships to overseas centres of high but relevant specialist skills.

The national committee could also obtain ministerial support in teaching and promoting age care programmes in junior and secondary schools, with its own centre possibly authorized to hold examinations and issue credits in social science.

An important related endeavour would be to use all means, including status-giving certificates and media presentations, to upgrade the roles of nurses, caring aids, and similar workers from their present lowly status in some areas. A highly desirable and respected geriatric nursing status could help arrest or offset some of the dangerously high emigration of such staff from certain countries.

7. *Public relations*. In most countries today, a national committee will need to have at its disposal skills in the latest technologies and strategies of public relations and awareness campaigns. Wherever television exists, not to mention the ubiquitous radio, the new committee will have to combat many conflicting issues to gain space: political themes, the more insistent clamour for attention of youth, established popular fund-raisers, as well as more beguiling appeals for the purchase of soft drinks, cosmetics, and transistor radios.

To make national progress in the public consciousness, the committee may have to produce its own videos and, in countries where the cinema still reigns, its own short films. It will have to produce photogenic aged personalities and stage striking community spectacles. Such activities are expensive in time and money, but sponsors like banks and insurance companies may be found for a reputable new cause. All this may seem a far cry from the abandoned aged widow lying dying on a piece of sacking in a rough shanty. Yet a one-minute appearance on national television by an aged personality, like Don Jorge in Colombia, may in the long run achieve more for the nation's aged than a year's work of a willing volunteer. (Although both the volunteer and Don Jorge are needed to deliver effective service!)[15]

The first step in this campaign may be the 'conscientization' of the media itself. Like other sections of the public, many journalists and television producers are unaware of the full impact of the phenomenon, but most are ready to pounce on a new idea, especially one so full of pathos as the figure of the abandoned old grandmother. It may well be that the committee's main problem will be to ensure that media images of the underprivileged are presented in such a way that the dignity of the

---

[15] In early 1988 a Don Jorge 'commercial', produced free of charge, was relayed 240 times on four TV channels in Colombia during one month, also gratis, because of media perception of the extraordinary public impact of an aged man speaking simply about the realities of abandonment in an urban setting.

elder is preserved; and that the essential message of activity and independence in old age is not lost in the more favoured media image of starvation and awful death.

The national committee will also consider the question of suitable publications and translations of materials from other countries. Such publications will portray both the needs of the aged and effective ways of meeting them. Relevant publications will be directed both at the general public and at the groups which are working with the aged. The latter will introduce ideas and methods which may be new to the country, such as the exceptional means now available for rehabilitation therapy after stroke and injury, or new concepts of the hospice system for the dying, emphasizing the domiciliary aspect.

8. *Preparing for disaster relief.* A lesser known responsibility of the national committee would be to build up resources ready for one of the natural or man-made disasters which from time to time afflict many a developing country. The HelpAge International movement originated in 1961 because it was observed that elderly refugees were often left unattended in natural disasters and that no special agency existed to care for them.

The *raison d'être* of the specialist organization in a disaster lies in the need to seek out older refugees, even in the family shelters where they literally take the back seat; in the frequency with which older people become detached from families and friends during a refugee trek; and in the way in which the normal requirements of the geriatric specialty are exacerbated and multiplied in a displacement situation. Any consortium of agencies which confronts a disaster situation without the support of a specialist aged agency is both exposing its ignorance of realities and abandoning to an unnecessary fate hundreds or thousands of seniors who, in the main disaster areas, are likely to be the tribe's or the village's repositories of traditional wisdom and skills.

In recent years, in Sudan, Somalia, Mozambique, India, Thailand, Colombia, and elsewhere, the age care agency has proved its value in setting up rescue and rehabilitation schemes for the aged which could not, or would not, have been achieved by more generic groups. While in some instances the schemes have been set up by hurriedly recruited expatriate teams, in India and Colombia established national age care agencies have been able to move into action faster than the majority of generic international agencies.

The national committee will therefore study the record of disasters in its own country, and will work out a plan of action and an inventory of necessary resources.[16] Voluntary response is never lacking at such times, and the two vital factors may be local mobility and rapid communications with international support services. It will not escape the national committee's notice that, after the seven days wonder (or often less) which the disaster evokes in international media, there is likely to be a very long, costly, and soon forgotten period of rehabilitation, sometimes running into years.

9. *Organizational structure.* Where a metropolitan committee has fused into a national committee, it is essential that the distinctive roles of each should be observed. In time, subcommittees might be formed to plan for particular specialty programmes reflecting these distinctions.

As already indicated, there must be an infinity of variations on the above models. These three are offered only as a general guide. If there are a few general points which should be emphasized above all else, they include the need for groups to recruit skills far wider than those related directly to age care; the need for adequate costing and financing, including alternative income opportunities for older workers; the development of intergenerational and surrogate family links; the value of interchange of ideas and skills within and beyond local borders; and, above all, the active participation of the elderly at all levels of the programme.

Experience so far offers hope that, by releasing the powers of the older generation itself, the world can avoid what has been perceived as a potential global problem. The accumulated experience and skills of many millions of elders should be a productive resource rather than a potential problem.

[16] The Old People's Welfare Association of Montserrat, West Indies, wisely maintains a disaster reserve fund because of the endemic nature of hurricanes and earthquakes. International aid often dries up all too quickly after the first disaster sensation.

9

NATIONAL STRATEGIES

A NUMBER of model projects, mostly low-key responses to the problems of ageing, were described in the last chapter. It is also necessary to outline some general principles for the planning of national strategies on ageing. The planning of such strategies would normally be the duty of government ministers, civil servants, and their professional advisers. However, in many developing countries, often due to financial or training constraints, this is not the case. The task devolves upon planners from non-governmental organizations, who then need to think beyond the implications of the particular project in order to set the organization's projects in the context of the national requirement. In any case, where governmental authorities play some part in the national planning, the directors of non-governmental organizations will work towards a more effective co-operation if they have in mind such over-riding principles.

The New Phenomenon

One factor of considerable implications is that ageing is a new historical phenomenon. A United Nations Fund for Population Activities statement says that 'popular dogma fails to recognise the degree to which the sheer numbers and longevity of old people in the present era are truly *new* historical phenomena that require different solutions from any that existed in the past'. The same point was made in the report of the Technical Meeting on Aging for the Latin American Region held before the World Assembly on Aging.[1] In his own frequent travels in developing countries the writer constantly encounters the argument that the

---

[1] Meeting in San José, Costa Rica, 1980; see UN WAA 1982*d*.

elderly are still cared for by the extended family and that therefore no 'problem of ageing' exists.

These considerations raise the requirement of extensive programmes of public awareness and also underline the fact that few precedents are available in planning for an ageing population.

An authoritative United Nations agency, the Pan-American Health Organization (PAHO), criticizes current planning in developing countries where it exists.

Poor programme design and planning results in a confusion of strategies and puts programmers and those responsible for implementing pro-grammes in a difficult position. As a consequence, numerous errors are committed by programmes, included among them: the lack of attention to self-care—that is, failure to take advantage of the individual reserves of the elderly as generators of action for themselves . . .

The PAHO comment lists further errors of this kind.[2]

A principle enunciated in the comment already referred to above is that 'we will have to accept the fact that programmes benefitting the elderly are a right, not an act of charity, and that this right is part of the ethical philosophy that should govern the fate of mankind'. In many developed countries, the percentage of elderly people in the population is such that governments are seriously constrained to remember their right, whereas in many developing countries the smaller percentage of aged people means that the political imperatives of ageing are not yet so urgent or forceful.

One commentator, referring to the increasing power accruing to the elderly by reason of increasing numbers, also makes the point about the inevitable time-lag which will be involved in planning any long-term policies of value to the elderly, including such measures as pre-retirement training. In 1981 he pointed out that political decisions taken on ageing in the early 1980s would not have full effect until well into the 1990s; accordingly, 'procrastination in the 1980s will lead to social and political crisis in the decades hence'.[3]

At the same time it has also been pointed out that governmental policies related to the ageing of the population are frequently 'population responsive' rather than 'population influencing',

[2] PAHO 1985.
[3] Denton 1982.

tending to look for remedies for problems *after* the opportunity to prevent or restrict the problem has passed.

Available blueprints

Large-scale plans, or blueprints for strategies, are already available on ageing. The World Assembly on Aging in 1982 produced the 'Vienna International Plan of Action on Aging', a document with 62 specific recommendations as well as general indications to governments and other interested parties as to how to approach the general problem. A quotation of one of the recommendations will illustrate the extensive nature of the document.[4] For instance, Recommendation 10 states:

Health and health-allied services should be developed to the fullest extent possible in the community. These services should include a broad range of ambulatory services, such as: day-care centres, out-patient clinics, day hospitals, medical and nursing care and domestic services. Emergency services should always be available. Institutional care should always be appropriate to the needs of the elderly. Inappropriate use of beds in health care facilities should be avoided. In particular, those not mentally ill should not be placed in mental hospitals. Health screening and counselling should be offered through geriatric clinics, neighbourhood health centres or community sites where old people congregate. The necessary health infrastructure and specialised staff to provide thorough and complete geriatric care should be made available. In the case of institutional care, alienation through isolation of the aged from society should be avoided inter alia by further encouraging the involvement of family members and volunteers.

The recommendation quoted is by no means the most extensive of the 62, which are also interspersed with other general comment and exhortation.

From the point of view of developing countries, this document, although detailed and exhaustive, is bewildering and lacking in certain important aspects. It tends to assume always the existence of structures similar to those existing in Europe or North America and aims at detailed targets which have generally not yet been attained even in the most advanced countries, after decades of planning and organization, or only in a way that they are not easily accessible to the totality of the aged population of

---

[4] UN WAA 1982*e*.

the country. If this exhaustive array of targets appears unattainable in Britain or the United States, how much more irrelevant and depressing its recommendations must appear to planners in some of the countries which lack the relative wealth and organizational and political structures of the developed countries?

The Vienna document also fails to indicate priorities in such a way that a developing country might easily avail itself of a portion of the recommendations. It further fails to take any serious account of the fact that, unless the document is supported by some significant and realistic financial recommendations and projections, its well-intended principles and recommendations for action might just as well have not been set down. Finance is one of the essential considerations in setting up programmes, and the Vienna conference totally failed to address either the specific elements of financing programmes or the world political concord which would make large-scale diversion of finances into developing countries' social programmes a feasible consideration. However, it was still a watershed in ageing history, and the Vienna plan of action should be consulted by every government and NGO concerned with ageing.

A more apposite set of recommendations has more recently emerged from meetings such as those in Dakar, Bogotá, and Harare, where the vast majority of the participants came from developing countries.[5] The report of the 1986 Bogotá conference was largely the work of an Argentine gerontologist, Dr Roberto E. Barca. Its recommendations are more specific and relevant, such as, for example: 'It is convenient to recognise that problems such as alcohol, loneliness and beggary among the aged are more frequent in urban areas or in areas of rapid urbanization.' In this last phrase, 'areas of rapid urbanization' refers both to the focus of migration and the source areas of emigration.

The Bogotá report has two inherent weaknesses. The first is in assuming that fairly urgent governmental action may be obtained by such tactics as 'seminars for politicians', when several Latin and Caribbean governments considered the entire subject of too little importance to send an official representative. However, the Bogotá conference, like its predecessor, also failed to tackle as a

---

[5] The Dakar and Bogotá Conferences were organized by the CIGS Paris. The Harare Conference was organized by the School for Social Work and HelpAge International.

priority the basic problem of finance, even in respect of the relatively modest costs of initial 'conscientization' and study requirements.

In case this may seem a precipitate and invidious criticism of a successful conference, it must be pointed out that my own study of ageing in Belize did, in fact, make financial proposals commensurate with the various factors studied and identified. Combining welfare and age activity recommendations with estimated costings, response models, and indications of possible source of finance, this report has been instrumental in securing immediate funding for voluntary programmes in Belize of up to US$200,000 over two years. This is a considerable financial input into a very small country, especially when added to the local enterprise which has been stimulated by the international support.

The point of this comment is that all strategies on ageing should proceed from statements on moral principles and welfare programme targets to tackle the most significant possible sources of funding and political (governmental or non-governmental) structures capable of giving practical effect to recommendations.

Having said this, the Vienna plan and others still serve a long-term purpose in providing a check-list of the vast majority of considerations appropriate to meeting the problems of the world's ageing population. The Bogotá and Dakar reports are a good example of how planners from developing countries can reduce the Vienna plan to more relevant detail.

Impossible costings

The Third World government considering a national programme on ageing would first of all be deterred by the costs, especially taking into account the fact that they would probably be commencing almost all aspects of the programme from a state of vacuum. The only accurately evaluated programmes from which the government could deduce probable relative costings would be those of developed countries, which have of course been building up their own programmes and permanent welfare resources over a long period.

One of the countries with most successful national programmes on ageing is The Netherlands. Some of the statistics emerging from its evaluation of services would be frightening to a Third

World government. In the area of health provision, for instance, the average cost per annum for services to people of the 0–19 age band is approximately £225. For the age band 65–79, that cost rises to £575, and for the over-80s it rises again to £2,010, almost nine times the cost of services to young people. A similar British assessment reveals services to the over-75s costing seven times as much as those to younger age bands.

Even at the present stage of development, 90% of welfare provisions for the aged in The Netherlands are still run by private organizations. Only 10% are provided by local or provincial authorities, and only 60% of old people's homes are subsidized by government. At a time when the global pension for a single person in The Netherlands stood at the equivalent of £300 a month (compared to the state pension of £130 at the time in Britain), an authoritative commentator described 'numbers of pensioners' in The Netherlands as being 'threatened by real poverty'.[6] How can a developing country hope to begin to set up a global state scheme of comprehensive benefits?

Yet another indicator of the immensity of the problem is given by a British review of physical disability. The review covered the entire population of a district, not just the elderly, but the above figures indicate that disabilities, illnesses, and costs are very much concentrated in the older age groups. The British survey found that in a typical health district of 250,000 people, no fewer than 25,000 might be found to have some measure of physical disability, of whom over 6,000 would be severely disabled. Up to 50,000 could be afflicted by osteoarthritis, 11,000 with regular incontinence, 1,800 confined to wheelchairs, 400 requiring colostomy, and 200 with multiple sclerosis.[7] If such statistics apply in a 'welfare state' with advantageous environmental and nutritional conditions, what kind of statistics might be expected among an aged population of a developing country afflicted by all the socio-economic problems imaginable?

An American writer has referred to the 'impossibility of supporting existing national pension schemes by the 21st century' in the United States and similar countries.[8] How does the Third World government *commence* such a scheme? On the

---

[6] Driest 1985.
[7] Report of Royal College of Physicians on Disability 1986.
[8] Kieffer 1982.

international scale the prognosis is equally depressing. A World Health Organization ageing programme to provide a training course for 24 participants for four weeks once a year was in jeopardy due to lack of finances. How can the Third World government hope to raise such finances?

The Brandt Commission and others have referred to the developing countries' financial disadvantages militating against a real choice of options for financing welfare programmes. For instance, in two recent years, developing countries lost US$85 billion simply in the devaluation of their own currency. In the same period their export revenues fell by US$40 billion while their debt service payments rose by US$37 billion. And the World Bank, International Monetary Fund, international and multinational lenders see the first step to 'solvency' as the elimination of costs of social services.

From Mexico, González-Aragón has commented that 'state paternalism as it occurs in developed countries and where the children have lost all their responsibility, and where the state totally maintains its pensioners, this is extremely . . . costly and, because of the economic conditions of our country, would be very difficult to attain'.[9] A Costa Rican commentator has emphasized the diverse financial considerations affecting the ability of even that government, which has no military budget, to counter hunger, illiteracy, unemployment, lack of international exchange, lack of medical services, lack of drinking water, etc.

For the time being, most developing countries should give priority to schemes that are low-capital cost, self-financing, self-perpetuating, response-stimulating, and community-mobilizing rather than any high-cost, highly specialist, technological, and dependency-orientated strategies. One of the advantages of avoiding the developed countries' stereotyped and statutory format would be the ability to diversify benefits according to varying age requirements.

The Bogotá conference already referred to emphasized the wide range of age variations encountered within the overall problem of ageing. This present study has indicated the extreme variations between the 'Vilcabamba' effect and the 'Potosí' effect, so that, in one instance, people of 90 and 100 may be seen

---

[9] González-Aragón 1984.

as active and productive while in another, people of 35 are physiologically aged. Academics and national programme planners may need to have clearly definable age groups on which to base demographic data and actuarial estimates, but age programmes will be less costly to mount and more appropriate to the locality if the more rigid age-group stereotypes of Western-style pension and benefit schemes can be avoided.

In a realistic costing of ageing programmes, the government planner will take into account the impact that ageing has on the much sought solution to the increasing birth rate still observed in many developing countries. 'If the first, second and third sons are regarded as being your pension in your old age, given the rate of infant mortality, you must produce eight or nine children to be sure you have three to support you when you are old', said one political writer.[10] The assurance of reasonable standards of living in old age other than by mass production of offspring can be a factor in reducing the present imbalance in younger age bands in many developing countries, and thus a useful inversion today for tomorrow's economy.

Discovering the realities

A primary consideration of every planner of programmes for the elderly must be the allocation of resources to discovering the true demographic and socio-economic realities of ageing in the area. A PAHO report refers to 'the unknown elderly who are not recognised by any agency and who do not participate in any organised programme—those older people who do not read or respond to advertisements, who are not members of self-help groups, who have no families, and who are isolated and insulated from the world'.[11]

The great imponderable in ageing, given the vast lack of research, is this huge constituency of unknown aged people whose presence can be guessed at but whose mass and condition cannot be assessed. The most likely outcome is that research will prove their numbers to be *more* than anticipated, their needs *more drastic* than imagined, and the necessary response measures *more costly* than so far calculated.

Some assumptions can be made from cross-cultural compari-

[10] Hart 1978.   [11] PAHO 1985.

sons, for present experience suggests that the basic social service needs of the elderly population, in a cross-cultural perspective, are generally similar. The older adult population experiences physical, psychological, social, and economic problems which demand either the establishment of and/or the expansion of social service systems in order to secure some degree of functional adaptability. The exact nature of those services in a particular locality can only be ascertained by an investment in accurate and patient research in the locality.

A general guide to a country's phases, or steps, or 'ledges', of commitment to, and investment in, benefits for the aged was developed by the gerontologist Virginia Little. Covering four successive phases, it illustrates the conditions which tend to occur contemporaneously during development. As some of Little's headings are somewhat misleading (e.g. the use of 'institutional' in its very widest use, as opposed to the narrower use as a term for closed residential care), I have added alternative headings. Little's headings are placed first:

1. *Residual (primary)*. Characterized by family care with a few volunteers; some private homes for elderly; lack of public funding, training, and domiciliary services.

2. *Early institutional (basic structure)*. Official social services; some supervision of private homes; some public funding of institutions; an ageing component in training; pilot domiciliary services.

3. *Institutional (developed structure)*. Specialist geriatric services; licensing of private homes; official funding for housing, community centres, and other functions; professional training programme; range of domiciliary services.

4. *Maximum institutional (total structure)*. Range of specialist facilities and centres; leadership in regional and international standard setting; political and other active organizations of, and for, the aged; regional research, training, and services in gerontology; wide-ranging domiciliary services co-ordinated with other subsystems.

Obviously, these are generalizations. For example, some developing country governments which should be classed in Phase 1 make a small contribution to institutions, as in Phase 2, although they may have no structured official social services.

One Latin American expert has said 'The first strategy . . . is the mobilization of national resources. Although individual resources that frequently are used in isolation can fulfil an important role in the immediate environment, their impact can be maximized if combined with others in national and regional frameworks.'[12] The national mobilization does not necessarily imply total standardization or stereotyping. Another commentator emphasizes that in development (economic or social) 'a multitude of small bets, based on different forecasts, placed by a large number of decision makers . . . may be a sounder strategy', needing only co-ordination in order to avoid duplication and waste of resources.[13] Certainly, at the present stage of development of age programmes there is everything to be said for experimental diversity.

An important health organization comment also supports diversity:

those responsible for actual service delivery must tackle the problem of 'individualizing' service packages that will fit, at the individual level, the unique needs and capacity of the older person . . . the number of services to be included in the system is high if one is attempting to secure acceptable levels of competence and independence for the older person . . . and the services must be flexible and accessible enough to respond quickly to changing needs and situations.[14]

A further commentator insists that 'many traditional ways of doing things and old habits will have to be abandoned, and innovation and modernization will have to be promoted'.[15] The context in which this statement occurs makes it clear that 'modernization' does not necessarily mean technological sophistication but rather the use of adequate research, planning, and organizational methods.

Transformation of attitudes

One of the first strategic necessities in planning for an ageing population is to transform attitudes. Many voices have been raised in support of this priority action. A pre-World Assembly

[12] C. Guerra de Macedo in PAHO 1985, p. 166.
[13] Lal 1983, p. 75.
[14] Tapia-Videla and Parrish 1981.   [15] Jiménez-Castro 1985, p. 91.

technical meeting noted that in developing countries 'the population at large is, in general, ignorant of the problems of the aged. This . . . is a problem which will be effectively addressed only through the appropriate education of the entire population.' One gerontologist applied this rule of ignorance to the family unit: 'The family rarely understands the behaviour of the old persons . . . and problems between them stem from deficient communications. The family is ignorant of the biological and psychological changes that take place with age and want the old person to behave and act like someone young.'[16] In spite of professional fears about the effects of institutionalization, one survey (in Costa Rica) found that when asked where an old person should live, 40% of younger people stated that it should be in 'an institutional setting, old folks' home or hospital'. When asked what the state should do to help, 21% said 'build more old people's homes'.

While many governments do not currently have resources available for the immediate implementation of large-scale action programmes, a legal authority gives the opinion that legislation without resources is at least a significant step forward in national awareness of the problem. She says,

a fundamental basis for strengthening protection [of the elderly] . . . is sound legislation. Official policies are generally expressed in laws. When a government adopts an official policy through enactment of legislation, implementation can begin energetically. Even if personnel, facilities and financing for services are limited, steps can be taken to organize and utilize existing resources in improved ways. Highly motivated . . . workers can move forward, and the authorization and direction provided by legislation can provide a strong springboard for their efforts.[17]

Whilst the same legal commentator's recommendations are a general reflection of current gerontological thinking as to care provisions, she has one less common proposal, that 'local councils on ageing should be established . . . to promote, co-ordinate and provide surveillance of services for the elderly'.

Such councils should consist of both governmental and non-governmental representatives, and 'the elderly should be represented' both locally and nationally: 'they should have an

[16] Contreras de Lehr 1986, p. 17.   [17] Roemer 1982, p. 10.

important voice in determining policies affecting options and alternatives in health care of the aged'. Councils of residents of old people's homes have been established in France by decree in October 1985, and in The Netherlands in the same year. In several HelpAge programmes opportunity has been given for the elderly to express their requirements, but only on a voluntary basis, in developing countries.

The legal commentator does not recommend the measures which have been legalized in a very small number of countries to compel children to care for their aged parents. Such legislation has produced considerable private difficulties within the families affected, and, while apparently a preferred option for governmental action, has yet to bear fruit in any country as far as can be ascertained.

Small-scale industries

The encouragement of small-scale industries in which the older person can seek alternative employment is an important part of any strategy in a country which lacks full pension and social security programmes. It is necessary to 'encourage and improve productivity in small-scale and cottage industries, utilizing where appropriate non-governmental organizations'. However, more than one commentator has noted the possible slowing down of the process of industrialization in developing countries, and 'small enterprises may in the future bulk even larger in the economy'.

Although any action taken on behalf of the aged tends to be regarded as charity or 'benefits', it may be that this possible trend to small-scale industry will convince developing countries of the national economic value of a fully utilized working force of experienced older people. In populations where the age profile has been deformed by migration of 'working age' people, it is a negative policy to allow older people to continue to scratch away at barren soil if they can be introduced to more productive alternative methods of agriculture. It is equally negative, where there is a lack of younger people for planned heavy industrial labour, simply to recruit some of the excess number of older unemployed.

It makes sense to provide this large and growing elderly

section of the population with personally and nationally profitable alternate agriculture and industry such as bee-keeping, small-scale fish farming, the collection and preparation of proven herbal medicines, small-scale manufacture of clothing, and carpentry. In the latter respect, the example has been noted of a Caribbean country where older carpenters would be perfectly capable of making furniture of much better quality than the imported plastic and steel types. Another classic case is the Central American scheme which makes school uniforms in a country where school uniforms are compulsory but had previously to be imported. A relatively minor governmental intervention could facilitate the change-over to such fruitful opportunities.

The provision of reasonable socio-economic opportunities for the elderly is interactive with the good health of the elderly. A person who is deprived of the economic ability to purchase food and fuel (and even shelter) will become ill, and an ill person will not have the energy to remain productive. These two factors therefore stand at the head of priorities for government planning.

Without entering deeply into political philosophy, even a regime of democratic liberty is of no benefit to old people who, perhaps because of failures in governmental planning, are bound by the chains of poverty and ill health. From time to time old people have been observed to be relatively better provided for in a politically restrictive regime in a particular location where they had access to health and productivity than in a politically liberal regime where they were denied, by some circumstances or other, the basic requisites for life already mentioned. This is a plea, not for totalitarian regimes, but rather for sensible and determined planning.

Varying health factors

In developing countries it has normally been in the realm of health that governments have been most able to effect certain improvements. But there is no easy blueprint for health planning, for the epidemiology of the older person varies from country to country.

For instance, it might be assumed that Costa Rica, El Salvador, Guatemala, Honduras, Nicaragua, and Panama might be taken together with one common pattern of epidemiology, covering as they do a relatively small area of geographically similar country. Yet Guatemala is the only one of the six which shows influenza and pneumonia as the highest risk diseases. Enteritis and other diarrheal diseases are relatively lesser menaces in Panama and Costa Rica, but they are high risks in the others and constitute the second worst killer in El Salvador. Malign tumours are among the two worst killers in Costa Rica; in the other countries, particularly Nicaragua, they are less fearful. Bronchitis and similar afflictions are significant killers in Honduras, but not so fatal proportionately in the other countries.[18]

This comparison underlines the need not only for each country to carry out its own health studies, but for countries such as India, Nigeria, or Brazil, which have widely varying regional environments to carry out similar regional studies.

The same variations apply to medical coverage. In another study carried out in the same six 'similar' countries referred to above, at a time that Costa Rica had 83.1% of its population 'receiving medical coverage', and Panama 43.5%, the figures for Nicaragua were 9.4% and for Honduras 6.5%, with Guatemala and El Salvador somewhere near the median for the six. There may therefore be possibilities of replication of specific services from country to country, but differing priorities will apply to global planning within countries.

Primary health care has emerged as the leading strategy for meeting needs in developing countries. It offers the possibility of good access to the most cost-effective forms of intervention, even in the poorest countries. 'Primary health care' is defined as 'not physician-centred', and includes the mobilization of the community into health action, universal access to services, health technology at the level relevant to the location, and the community health worker and/or traditional health workers as the main trained resource.

Governments might intervene in such schemes by providing *appropriate* training rather than *prestige* training, and facilitating the necessary supplies, as well as possible economic concessions for communities successfully operating their own schemes. A prime concern of governments in American developing countries, given the great exodus of nurses due to low status of nursing

[18] Denton 1982.

locally (as already referred to) would be to enhance the status of the nurse and community health worker by all means possible. Costa Rica has a far-sighted scheme whereby teams of about five care workers (nurses, therapists, etc.) are given group training together before practising together.

National consideration needs to be given to the types of hospitals and other medical centres needed to meet the growing proportion and gross numbers of elderly. This aspect has both negative and positive considerations. On the negative side is the understandable ambition of governments of all countries to build prestige monuments such as will enhance the national reputation when compared to other countries. This may be politically desirable, but often fails to meet the need of the community or the individual. On the positive side, countries can be well served by planning various levels of medical care.

Dr Jorge Jiménez has identified four types of service centre of maximum importance: the *geriatric hospital* (central, highly specialist, short-stay treatment); the *general hospital with geriatric services* (a regular district hospital, with trained staff and facilities to treat the normal problems of old people); the *day hospital* (for immediate short-term treatment, or continued therapy), which might be attached to a day centre; and the *chronic hospital* (for those comparatively few patients who cannot be returned home and for whom there is no further curative process available). In implementing such a four-tier system, care must be taken that the chronic hospital is allocated sufficient resources so that the inmates do not become mere human vegetables suffering under the worst of environmental and care conditions.[19]

Another facility that could be added to Dr Jiménez's list is the hospice, which combines pleasant terminal provisions with prior counselling and domiciliary treatment; and the screening service, which might be located in any of the other centres or in a normal day centre or temporary location.

The word of warning expressed about financial allocations to chronic hospitals could also be extended to low-cost rural primary health schemes. Although in the long-run these may be more cost-effective and require lesser budget sums, it must be recognized by the planners that they are not easily instituted or

[19] Jiménez Gandica 1986, p. 32.

maintained. They 'require a complex and (relatively) sophisticated administrative superstructure and new procedures for
delivery of supplies, personnel management, utilization and
quality control, institution-building, marketing, and monitoring.
They require an *administration-intensive* approach.' In this sense,
administration-intensive does not mean the development of a
well-staffed bureaucracy which subjects action to procedures,
but a well-trained administrative staff able to respond to the
requirements of the specific service at any particular moment.[20]

Appropriate accommodation

An area of governmental planning on which the Vienna
International Plan of Action on Aging lays great emphasis is that
of housing for the elderly. There are possibly three major
problems to be attacked in this field: total homelessness of old
people, inadequate and inappropriate existing accommodation,
and the new trend of building to accommodate only the nuclear
family.

The first two problems could be approached jointly, with a
wide-ranging programme of experimental accommodation, both
in terms of individual houses within a street community and
also in the improvement of the type of residential accommodation
at present provided in palace-size, although not palace-quality,
old people's homes. The United Nations declared 1987 as the
Year of Shelter for the Homeless (IYSH), with its secretariat
based at the UN Habitat headquarters in Nairobi, Kenya.
Already certain pilot projects for older people are in process,
both within the IYSH and existing HelpAge programmes, and
this offers governments the possibility of early adaptation and
replication programmes.

Governments could also intervene energetically to ensure that
in newly constructed areas a sufficient proportion of houses are
large enough for use by extended families. Such a measure would
be *one of the most prompt and effective* in countering the unwilling
break-up of so many migrant families under the compulsion of
seeking whatever shelter may be available in the migratory target
area.

---

[20] Golladay and Liese 1980, p. 32.

Retirement schemes

In countries where rapid strides are being made towards sufficient pension provisions, there should be awareness, at planning levels nationally, of the detrimental aspects of the supposed panacea of global retirement pensions. 'Flexi-retirement' and pre-retirement training can be planned and co-ordinated at national level with a significant resource input by various interested parties such as organizations of both employers and employees. The participation of trade unions in such schemes is preferable to their rabid opposition on the grounds that deferred retirement is detrimental to the better pay or fuller employment of younger members. Educational establishments can also contribute to such schemes, as well as to alternative continuing training or study opportunities for the retired.

Figures available for homicides among persons over 65 in Middle America (from Mexico to Panama) are alarming, as are the statistics of mechanical accidents and suicides throughout the continent. Governments can introduce legislation with some deterrent effect and preventive potential in these instances. A variety of other low-cost, politically feasible measures are available to governments and other national planners responding realistically to local circumstances. Duty-free shops for the aged, free or concessionary transport and leisure facilities, and awareness-enhancing exhibitions and conferences are among the possibilities.

Supporting the family

The maintenance of the family structure may be a subject which defies direct legislation but must be kept in clear focus in all national planning. 'One lesson to be learned from developed countries', it has been said, 'is the negative consequence of failing to provide all possible supports for a family which wishes to keep an older person in the household. This choice may not be everyone's, or even the most frequent choice, but in many of the developed countries institutions have been made too accessible.'[21]

Another report concludes, 'the target for services to the aged,

[21] UN WAA 1982*f*.

especially in developing countries, is the family. Therefore a criterion for assessing the appropriateness of services, methods, technologies and treatment is whether or not they facilitate self-help, self or family care.' Some kind of official action can be planned at relatively low cost in this respect. 'The traditional ties of family and face-to-face support can be supported by such steps as cash disability allowances or constant-attendant allowances' for family members or neighbours at a cost less than that of care by a trained professional or total institutionalization of the elder.[22]

An anthropologist working in a small and poverty-stricken shanty town found that 'the desperately poor mobilize ties of real kinship, "fictive" kinship (*compadrazgo*), friendship (. . . *cuatismo*) and the like, into patterns of reciprocity that make up a total "design for survival"'. In terms of older people, the 'patterns of reciprocity' could include such inter-generational schemes as grandparent crèches and grandparent instructional sessions in schools (that is, the grandparent rendering the service to the children, some of whom may lack their own grandparent).[23]

The possibility of establishing surrogate kinships (the 'adopt a gran' type of scheme), will remain important in regions of developing countries where during mass migration the disintegration of the family is more immediate, final and irreversible, due to lack of communications and the vast distances involved. A Czechoslovak commentator also gives this factor as a reason why legislation compelling parents to care for children could not be reversed to compel children to care for aged parents in developing countries, or why, if such a law were promulgated, it would inevitably be ineffective.[24]

The breakdown of the family in some developing countries may be rapid and traumatic, but some commentators see within the development process itself a compensatory factor for the defunct natural family. Durkheim spoke of the 'collective conscience' based on the elaborate interdependencies of the commercially developed world which, if it exists, must eventually work for the reintegration of the great numbers of presently unproductive elderly. Another commentator has noted the universalization of family responsibility in relation to the elderly,

[22] Binstock *et al.* 1982, p. vii.   [23] Lomnitz 1977.
[24] Ladislav Pisca in Gilmore *et al.* 1981, p. 327.

as evidenced in social security systems and public funding of welfare programmes.

Community action

Whether or not these universalized factors are true, the disadvantaged elderly of the areas most affected by mass migration in the developing countries *cannot await* their long-term benefits. The stimulation of 'collective conscience' among local communities and small groups is an immediate tool available to planners.

As far as non-governmental voluntary agencies are concerned, the Brandt Commission as well as other authorities, is on record as appreciating the mobility and adaptability of the ' "vol. ag.", in meeting the needs of the poor at local level, in encouraging self-help and participation, in appreciating the social and cultural sensibilities of all the people involved, in circumventing bureaucratic red tape and getting things done . . .'[25] National governments must encourage NGO enterprise by introducing positive measures such as tax exemptions, family benefits, and graded grants for successful initiatives.

Involving the elderly

Another important consideration in national planning for ageing is the involvement of the elderly themselves at all stages of planning and implementation. Gerontologists remind us that the brain is one of the organs which ages most slowly, and that the powers of conceptual thought and logical reasoning do not suffer with age if the individual has continued to cultivate these powers. It is a waste of potential, therefore, for a nation to omit its elderly from the processes of reasoning out its own future. The waste of the intellectual potential of elders is clearly evidenced in a statistic from Loja Province in Ecuador, where although the elderly constitute only about 4% of the total population, 60% of all illiterates are elderly.[26]

In planning and counselling as well as in more general terms of productivity, national planners need to remember the full potential of the elderly as now evidenced from controlled tests.

---

[25] The Brandt Commission 1983, p. 80.
[26] *Revista* (Feb. 1982), p. 42.

For instance, the ability to learn is equal at ages 12 and 80, and, as the investigators stated not so scientifically, 'the old dog *can* learn new tricks'.[27] In a series of medical tests comparing 30-year-olds with 75-year-olds, in factors such as blood flow to the brain and cardiac output, the potential of the older group was still up to 70%, 80%, or even 90% of the younger group.[28]

Another writer succinctly states the case: 'The elderly have amazing personal resources that enable them to function despite biological and social stresses that intrude upon a satisfying existence. Whatever residual strengths the older person has should be called upon and the emphasis put upon these instead of upon obvious physical and mental deficits.'[29] A Colombian geriatrician quoted earlier states categorically, 'Let us remember that older people, in a significant majority, want to work, are able to work and ought to be allowed to work.'[30]

A recommendation approaching the subject from the economic angle suggests that it is 'of particular importance for policy-makers . . . to recognise that continued employment of the elderly in productive pursuits will help reduce their financial dependency and promote their continued involvement in the community'. Of course this will depend 'on the provision of occupational training and continuing education opportunities that will make it possible for the elderly to function effectively . . .'[31]

This policy of involvement and activity of the elderly must be pursued into the citadels of intransigency in some old people's institutions where activity is an unacceptable option. 'Institutions must establish or increase the occupational activities, for, contrary to the accepted concepts respecting the inability or non-usefulness of the old person for work, it has been demonstrated that he/she is quite capable of carrying out diverse tasks.'

Ownership and integrity

A further recommendation to planners is particularly relevant with regard to an area of programmes which is so heavily community biased and community based, and which concerns a constituency which is so actively concerned with maintaining its

[27] Kaluger and Fair 1974.
[28] Shock 1962.
[29] Shivers and Fait 1980.
[30] Jiménez Gandica 1981.
[31] UN WAA 1982b.

own independence. If it is to succeed, an ageing programme cannot be imposed or foisted upon a community. The local community must have a sense of ownership of the project from the point of conceptualization. People are more likely to carry out a decision that they have had a hand in making than one that has been imposed. If effective implementation is critical, therefore, it is important to involve the implementors as much as possible, and as soon as possible.

A most important aspect concerns the character of the planner and administrator. In many respects, work among the aged is not richly rewarded in terms of salaries or official status. Much of the work relies upon a deep personal commitment. However, particularly since the World Assembly on Aging in 1982, the world is becoming more conscious of the problem of ageing, of the vacuum which exists in certain academic and professional fields relevant to the subject, and of the possibilities of developing a personal career alongside or within the tide of development of ageing programmes.

It is to be hoped that a reasonable balance of professional expertise and personal commitment can be maintained in this field, and that ageing should not become the target for those who perceive it as another nucleus about which to construct a restrictive bureaucracy or upon which to build a lucrative personal fortune.

International Aid

Some reference should be made to the impact which international aid can have on national ageing strategies. In developing a taxonomy of care levels, two American gerontologists have distinguished three 'domains' of caregiving—namely, sites, services, and information/decision-making—with two overarching domains which affect caregiving—financing and regulatory activity.[32] In developing countries, the support of developed countries can be crucial in both these latter domains. Resources in developing countries are not sufficient to cope with the financial requirements of setting up and maintaining an entire

[32] Von Mering and Henretta 1986.

new hierarchy of services to meet the problem of ageing. Nor are the infrastructural, training, informational, and skill resources of some Third World countries adequate to the task of regulating and monitoring standards of the required new programme.

An economist has summed up the total problem of the developing countries very succinctly in four points:

1. In the poor world . . . the problem of unemployment . . . is persistently deteriorating as high rates of population increase throw millions of young people each year into a labour market which . . . cannot conceivably absorb them.

2. Unfortunately it must be recognised that the rich industrialized nations of the world are *not* going to make any significant sacrifices to help the poorer nations of the world.

3. . . . an absurd pattern of development which leads to a Western lifestyle for a small minority and further impoverishment for the vast majority.

4. Old people make for heavier demands upon health services than young people. Hence, despite forecasts of a static total population, *more resources* will need to be devoted to the health services in the 1980s if even the current standards of service are to be maintained.[33]

However, the 'trickle down' theory, in which many economists had so much faith in recent years, now seems to be recognized as at best a fallible tool and at worst a cruel delusion. A British Minister responsible for Overseas Aid wrote that it had been thought 'that a transfer of resources through the investment of foreign private capital in profitable enterprises would, by "trickling down", benefit the poor. But it did not work.'[34]

The whole idea of foreign aid has been criticized by some modern thinkers; Peter Bauer summarizes their objections as follows:

1. Foreign aid is a government-to-government transfer, and therefore not a transfer from the rich in the rich countries to the poor in the poor countries . . .

2. Foreign aid increases the politicisation of the developing countries by providing inefficient governments with greater access to resources . . .

3. Foreign aid has created the Third World. Third World lobbyists and woolly-minded academics have pursued a soft line on Third World

---

[33] Donaldson 1984.
[34] Hart 1978, p. 5.

demands and have created a constituency of aid irrelevant to Third World development . . .[35]

Perhaps it should be noted that Bauer is referring specifically to the type of 'tied' governmental aid which is largely expressed through loan- or grant-extended trade.

Another objection to aid is that 'non-developmental motives still play a major role in aid programmes . . . a high proportion of aid remains tied (to the export trade advantageous to the donor country); if anything, its share is increasing'. Loan-aid can add to the debt burden of weak countries. In 1982, 'the cumulative debt of Central American countries to USAID was US$726 million. And the average price of goods financed by aid funds was 25% above world market prices.'[36]

However, assuming that aid must be given by developed countries to developing countries to ease the imminent problems of the ageing population, how should such aid be given?

The United Nations

It might be assumed that the United Nations would be the appropriate vehicle, especially after the success of the World Assembly on Aging (sponsored by a developing country, Malta), the publication of the Vienna International Plan of Action on Aging, and the establishment of the United Nations Trust Fund on Aging, all as part of the same process. In fact, a number of lobbyists, led by the Ambassador of the Dominican Republic to the United Nations, Sra. Julia T. de Alvarez, have suggested the setting up of an additional special United Nations agency, a kind of UNICEF for the aged.

Unfortunately for that proposal, the United Nations has been experiencing a serious deficit of income against budget estimates and has been in no position to finance expensive extensions of its activities, whether or not these might be desirable. The reduction in the United States contributions to the 1986 budget alone was expected to be in the region of US$100 million, out of a total regular United Nations budget of US$820 million.

---

[35] P. Bauer, as summarized by de Silva 1983, p. 32.
[36] McNamara 1978, pp. 22, 34.

Furthermore, the contributions by the nations of the world to the newly established Trust Fund on Aging were derisory in relation to the needs identified for urgent action. The former Secretary-General to the World Assembly on Aging, William Kerrigan, was forced to express 'deep concern' because, to all practical intents 'the Fund dried up'. Lack of interest on the part of the nations of the world was evidenced when, in reply to an urgent, almost desperate, United Nations questionnaire seeking reinforced action on ageing, only 59 out of 171 governments actually bothered to respond. Among the non-respondents were the United Kingdom, the United States, and the Soviet Union.[37]

It would be incorrect to suggest that the United Nations is entirely inactive in respect of the problems outlined earlier in this study. A number of agencies are actively involved in measures to counteract the causes of migration, one of the root causes of problems of the abandoned elderly. Among these agencies are UNICEF, UNESCO, FAO, WHO, the ILO, the Andean Indian Programme, and others.

The World Health Organization maintains a small ageing programme based in Copenhagen, and this programme has achieved advances in research and information entirely disproportionate to its tiny staff and restricted budget. As a combined initiative of the WHO and the London School of Hygiene and Tropical Medicine, with financial support from HelpAge International, a programme on the epidemiology of ageing has also been initiated, but continues in a precarious state of financial constraints.

Intergovernment aid

Meanwhile, the Aging Unit in Vienna, set up after the World Assembly on Aging, although reduced to less than half its original staff, still acts as a centre for information on the development of ageing programmes world-wide. It also continues to campaign to convince governments of the need to implement the resolutions of the Vienna International Plan of Action on Aging, which was unanimously adopted and ratified by the United Nations General Assembly.

[37] UN Finance Department, 'The Financial Situation of the United Nations', A/C.5/40/16, 1986.

The Brandt Commission recommends in its second report that in order to maximize voluntary effort,

all Northern governments should match on an agreed basis the privately contributed funds of voluntary agencies of recognised effectiveness. Another method . . . would be to establish a new international facility . . . with an annual fund of, say, US$100 million which would be allocated to the private bodies on a matching basis with their own funds.[38]

In fact, a number of governments already make this provision, although in many cases the cause of the aged has very low priority or does not appear as an area for 'co-funding'. With substantial private funds to commit to ageing programmes, Help the Aged (UK), the main fund-raising arm of HelpAge International, has been able to obtain increased priorities for co-funding ageing programmes by a number of governments as well as the European Community. Only in 1985 did the latter feel able to approve a 'block grant' to Help the Aged for ageing programmes. The OPEC Development Fund also gave its first grant for identification of ageing needs in 1984 and its first grant to an ageing project was agreed at the beginning of 1987.

The major 'vol. ag.' role

Voluntary organizations, of whom some are 'non-operational, providing funds for local people to do the work', are an important aspect of international aid to low-key projects, such as most ageing schemes are. 'They are not in the business of funding major dams, fertilizer plants, airports or massive road schemes. . . . Their small size keeps their feet on the ground, and their concern for people, especially poor people, keeps their activities human and directed towards the lessening of poverty.'[39]

In discussing international aid, it is usual to think of governmental aid as being massive and non-governmental aid as being low-key. Yet in the field of age care, the value of aid contributed by the major non-governmental organization on ageing to African countries alone in *one year* (1986) exceeded the world grand total for *five years* of all donations by governments to the United Nations Trust Fund on Aging!

[38] The Brandt Commission 1983, p. 81.
[39] Stamp 1977, p. 35.

A number of voluntary organizations working in developing countries have ageing as a varying priority commitment, rather than a sole or majority interest among their other many social commitments. Many of these organizations have their own, direct routes of international funding, through church and other links. They include such agencies as Caritas, Catholic Relief Services, the Salvation Army, and various Catholic orders such as St Vincent de Paul and Las Hermanitas de los Ancianos Desamparados (the Sisters of the Abandoned Aged). However, the resources available to schemes run by such agencies are often inadequate for necessary development in response to the increasing age problems. Already the international funding organizations are called upon to supplement local resources, and such supplementary funding will need to be extended if even more rapid service developments are to become necessary and possible through existing agencies.

A new area of financial development is the initiative by HelpAge International to support local groups in creating their own organizations for fund-raising. This capability enhances the possibility of international co-funding agencies approving more significant amounts of capital.

Finance is not the only area in which international aid can give support to local programmes. The structural systems upon which excellent schemes can be mounted require considerable infusions of information, training, research, and evaluation. In this field the existing potential of a number of agencies is probably greater than in the area of direct funding.

Information and training

The United Nations Aging Unit in Vienna publishes a regular bulletin on ageing which, because it serves the entire world, contains some matter irrelevant to developing countries but is a useful tool for the carer who wishes to be informed of world developments in ageing. On the non-governmental side, a similar role is performed by the bulletin of the International Federation on Aging, published out of Washington, with cross-cultural information including an up-date of ongoing research as well as practical manuals.

HelpAge International publishes *Ageways*, a quarterly loose-leaf bulletin of practical information and advice aimed at the many carers, professional or volunteer, for whom Third World conditions mean that they have little access to specialist initial training or mid-career refresher courses on ageing. The English version is sent free of cost to caring agencies in some 70 developing countries, while a Spanish version goes free to some 20 countries. Training packs are also produced.

In Bogotá a training centre has been set up by the HelpAge affiliate Pro Vida with the name of CIGAL. This provides brief crash courses on age care and similar matters (such as fund-raising and organization of volunteers) aimed at the same type of constituency as *Ageways*. Under HelpAge bursaries, trainees from other Latin American countries are brought without cost to the local agency and, after training in Bogotá, are expected to return to their own countries and organize seminars in the same subjects. Similar courses have been organized in India, Kenya, Zimbabwe, and elsewhere. Other centres like CIGAL are being planned.

Vast major developments in funding, training, information, and organizational skills for age programmes are needed, at local, national, and international levels, in respect of all countries of the developing world. Certain funding facilities are available through the existing governmental co-funding schemes. If the co-funding idea could be applied also at national levels, this would enable the non-governmental agencies to press ahead with programmes of which they are already capable while governments plan and rehearse more extensive programmes.

Given the very lack of programme structures in developing countries at present, it is within the capacity of HelpAge International, its affiliates, associates, and derivative groups, in both developing and developed countries, to advise and act as a type of entrepreneurial body in the funding field until more realistic funding co-ordination can be established at governmental and inter-governmental levels.

Conference Recommendations

This chapter on general strategies concludes with some further specific strategy recommendations from reports of conferences and studies already alluded to, including the conferences in Dakar, Bogotá, and Nairobi, the Western Pacific study, and the 1987 International Year of Shelter for the Homeless.

Dakar: All-Africa, 1984

The Dakar conference report contains some recommendations which are particularly sensitive to the evolution of an ageing programme in a traditional culture which is being gradually invaded by modernization attitudes and techniques. For example:

. . . an integrated rural development programme should be initiated to revive the countryside by improving living conditions. A special effort should be made to ensure that rural women of all ages take an active part in the development process;

. . . the most simple and most effective techniques should be adopted, since the more sophisticated the means, the more the aging are excluded. On the other hand, aging persons should be taught new techniques which have proved indispensable;

. . . every effort should be made to mobilize different sectors of society so as to ensure African countries nutritional self-sufficiency;

. . . national, regional and international agencies working in the field of agriculture should make as a condition for granting aid, a guarantee that aged agricultural workers and especially women should not be the object of any discrimination whatsoever;

. . . community initiatives for a variety of projects should be encouraged as a means of controlling rural out-migration. Old persons might receive help in the field of animal breeding and market gardening;

. . . the ageing should be encouraged to form groups and take initiatives in setting up small group projects. Technical know-how and the expertise needed to make present and future small enterprises efficient should be made available;

. . . a department should be created to handle economic and social services for the aging and a special sinking fund for projects initiated by the elderly;

. . . a provision should be made to take aged persons into account in all projects so that these men or women may be able to derive benefit individually or collectively from experience accumulated over the years;

. . . for all workers not covered by the existing pension system, an examination should be made of ways to broaden the system on their behalf on the basis of contributions for which practical rules will have to be defined;

. . . pensions should be adjusted to match the real cost of living;

. . . special attention should be given to the older female population, especially widows, by making legal provisions in their favour to ensure them the full enjoyment of the benefits and rights earned by their late husbands;

. . . the aging should benefit from special rates (e.g. transportation) to help them maintain their purchasing power and permit' them to be better able to contribute to the general economic development;

. . . a veritable national policy should be conceived and implemented to eliminate certain ills such as begging;

. . . the aging should be considered one of the main targets for literacy campaigns;

. . . there is a need to supervise the work of traditional healers along with the routine supervision of community health workers. This needs to be done because the domain covered by each system must be defined based on the capacities of traditional healers and community health workers. It also eliminates exploitation by traditional and medical practitioners of the scarce resources of older people;

. . . acceptance of modern health practices by villagers and by many rural residents will be possible only if health workers exhibit good-will with regard to traditional health practices. The secret of success in re-orientating local healers in health education has been by reinforcing traditional practices while also introducing modern methods of prevention and treatment. Notable success using this method has been achieved in the treatment of mental disorders;

. . . the experience of some countries in establishing research institutes devoted to traditional medicine (for example, where the dosages of active ingredients are checked and analysed) appears to be effective in promoting safe and effective treatment using the practices of traditional medicine;

. . . traditional medicine systems exist in other regions of the world—for example, in Asia—and we should ensure exchanges and research at all levels in the fields of traditional and modern medical technologies;

. . . whenever possible, treatment should be at home. Elderly patients should receive care that enables them to lead independent lives and to remain in their natural, familiar environment where their families can participate in their care and treatment. But it is also recognized that families cannot cope alone and consequently home care and home nursing should be organized from community health centres.

Zimbabwe conference, 1986

The report of the Zimbabwe conference is phrased with close

reference to the home country. In fact, the conference included delegates from a number of countries and some of its references have much wider application. A selection of the proposals reads as follows:

   . . . the elderly should always be involved and represented in issues that affect their lives;

   . . . policy makers should include elderly people in planning for their needs;

   . . . elderly people should be involved in cultural education and the socialisation of children and grandchildren. They should also be involved in traditional ceremonies and dances;

   . . . elderly people should participate in the 'education for living' classes in all schools so that they can assist in the teaching of culture and traditions;

   . . . government, local government and NGOs should encourage the elderly to use their dormant skills, e.g. traditional medicine, pottery, basket making, etc. Retired professionals could be used for consultancy;

   . . . public and private institutions should examine their programmes involving the elderly and be encouraged to set up programmes if they are non-existent;

   . . . activities of government and non-government organisations related to the elderly should be co-ordinated for purposes of proper planning;

   . . . comprehensive research is needed to consolidate all the recommendations made for the elderly;

   . . . we call upon the government to declare a day of the elderly on an annual basis;

   . . . curriculum development should take into account the effective aspects as well as technical ones so that children can be exposed to cultural values that recognise the status of the elderly;

   . . . the elderly should be encouraged to form associations which are linked into a national network;

   . . . there is a need for research to find out the educational needs of the elderly;

   . . . policy-makers should include elderly people in planning for their needs through a national association of the elderly;

   . . . the elderly should be encouraged to continue to play an active role in economic development;

   . . . it is recommended that Government:

set up a comprehensive national social security scheme including a pension scheme for all; where, in the agricultural sector, crop levies are accepted as a contribution, community granaries and other food storage systems should be set up by local and responsible authorities as part of such a scheme; increase its vote for public assistance and provide specific rates for elderly recipients;

. . . the elderly should be encouraged to be self-sufficient through community based self-help projects;

. . . It is recommended that non-governmental agencies should increase their role in providing social security and welfare for the elderly:

- churches and service groups [could help the elderly] through material and financial assistance and social visits;
- community-based groups (e.g. Village Development Committees and schools) could provide material and labour to assist the elderly;
- co-operatives could plan for the provision of pensions;

. . . tax rebates for persons looking after elderly people should be increased;

. . . educational programmes should be mounted to encourage people to prepare for their retirement and old age;

. . . there should be planned nutrition education campaigns on the proper feeding of the elderly, using various forms of media such as posters, pamphlets, radio and television;

. . . oral and other aspects of health care of the elderly [should] be given priority and . . . emphasis . . . given to the accessibility, affordability and availability of appliances such as spectacles, hearing aids, dentures, crutches, wheel chairs, etc;

. . . a more comprehensive nutritional survey on the nutritional status of the elderly in Zimbabwe [should] be urgently undertaken to assist policy makers in the formulation of an effective national policy directed at the specific needs of the elderly;

. . . In order to promote mental health among the elderly, it is recommended that the elderly be accepted as important and useful members of the society and that better communication be established between the elderly and members of the community;

. . . It is recommended that the health personnel be reoriented to be aware of the specific needs of the elderly, with emphasis being given to prevention and early detection of medical and psychological problems;

. . . traditional health structures and approaches [should] be used for those elderly who believe in traditional medicines;

. . . there is a need for traditional healers to work hand in hand with modern doctors especially when treating patients with mental and psychological problems.

Kenya conference, 1985

Recommendations from a Kenyan conference include reference to the religious needs of older people and also the supreme importance of independence:

> . . . those looking after the elderly should give all possible spiritual guidance and then let them (the aged) make their own decisions;
> . . . the aged should be cared for materially and this can make it easier for spiritual guidance. They should be taken as individuals whose wishes and decisions are respected.
> . . . it was felt that the elderly should be kept active mentally. This is because when the mind is active the body also becomes active. This can be done by:
> - encouraging the elderly to take part in discussions in the villages or in the home where they live;
> - encouraging the elderly to make creative crafts;
> - involving the elderly in decision making especially when thinking of activities or plans for the aged; they should be left to try and plan for themselves; they should not be made to feel useless;
> - giving the elderly the freedom and choice to do what they want.
>
> . . . it was recommended that all those present be involved in formulating a plan for nationwide education on the elderly and old age, and it was then recommended that education of the rural youth should be part of the National Education on the Ageing and Old Age.

Western Pacific study, 1986

The four-country study in the Western Pacific also made recommendations which could have ready application to many developing countries:

> . . . the most appropriate action for many of the key issues will be a reconceptualization of existing policy and programmes through increasing the awareness and understanding of the key issues; and through focusing attention on the interrelationships between the ageing and the whole community;
> . . . there is a real opportunity in developing countries for recognition of the family's central role, and for policy and planning decisions to reflect the degree to which the caring role of family members is vital to the well-being and independence of the elderly;
> . . . recognition now of the importance of family and community-oriented policy and programme development could help avoid the

mistakes made in the Western developed nations where there has been clear evidence in the past of over-dependence on institutional rather than community solutions to provide support for the aging population, and upon formal rather than informal systems of care;

. . . policy-makers and planners will need to be sensitive to these emerging aspects of community and family life and especially aware of the substantial impact of the changing demographic structure of communities everywhere;

. . . there is now a need to explore the appropriateness and effectiveness of day centre programmes, particularly in urban settings in countries where the growing numbers of the aging in the population and limitations on extended family activities mean that opportunities for social interaction among the elderly are necessarily restricted. The challenge to policy-makers and planners will be to ensure the provision of programmes tailored to the specific societal and cultural characteristics of the populations with which they are dealing in these respects, experimentation and structured evaluation of programmes should be encouraged;

. . . from a policy and programme perspective, it is clear that significant resources should be applied to the maintenance of health and fitness of aging populations. It has been suggested that the apparent robustness of older populations in developing countries should be no cause for complacency for the future. As the population continues to age, the emergence of more, older survivors with chronic disease and disability is likely, and the institution now of preventive measures to minimize the consequent handicaps is important. A positive approach to active promotion and maintenance of physical and mental health will be important;

. . . analysis of mental symptoms revealed generally that forgetfulness, feelings of depression, tiredness, worry and anxiety, apathy and sleep difficulties were not uncommon findings, but overt mental illness was rarely encountered;

. . . more research is clearly needed and attention should be given to the likely impact of increasing numbers of the elderly in the community who will have moderate to severe dementing illness consequent simply upon the increasing number of the very old in the population;

. . . policy and programme implications suggest the need for greater awareness to be promoted of the effects of smoking and the importance of life-style factors generally in maintaining health and fitness even in advanced age.

Malaysia plan, 1986

Whilst the study quoted above included Malaysia, a policy conference in Malaysia added more relevant comment:

. . . labour force implications need to be seriously considered. Steps should be taken to mobilise and enable older persons who are desirous, still economically productive and have skills in demand, to remain in the work force;

. . . another practical solution seems to be the increase of the compulsory retirement age from 55 to 60 and optional employment (be it full or part-time) beyond 60. Malaysia should tap the wealth of experience and wisdom accumulated over the decades by the elderly, especially the professionals and top management personnel;

. . . sheltered employment is an area that merits serious consideration. Generally, elderly workers find difficulties in their work environment due to their diminished capacity to tolerate stress and strains. As such sheltered workshops and cottage industries where the elderly can work at their own pace, particularly those producing traditional arts and crafts, will contribute towards retention of the valued culture of the country while providing income, satisfaction of achievement and companionship for the elderly;

. . . it is crucial that Malaysia begins to institutionalise social support systems directed towards the family rather than towards formal health and social services, the latter of which can never serve as a substitute for the family's informal care and support system;

. . . programmes aimed at keeping the elderly in the family system or at least physically close to their children could be usefully supported by policy makers. For example, in view of the shortage of paid domestic help, increasingly many career women choose to live near their parents or in-law's families so that the elderly can lend a helping hand in child care and perhaps light domestic chores. Future programmes should reinforce this arrangement of convenience and mutual benefit so that the elderly will be economically supported by their families in exchange for child care services rendered;

. . . the implication of the elderly on mental health programmes in Malaysia is the need to modify the training and to retrain health workers and the general public to recognise and cope effectively with these aspects of aging. Hitherto, training has been oriented almost exclusively to dealing with psychotics;

. . . youth and other community groups can render services such as domestic help, visiting, serving meals, counselling, etc. The early elderly who are still mobile and healthy should be encouraged to volunteer their services to the frail elderly in terms of psychological support and companionship. Community-based services for the elderly can be incorporated into the activities of the local community organization.

Indian recommendations

An Indian conference held as long ago as 1975 had its own special recommendations to put forward:[40]

. . . health education should form part of the school curriculum, and this education is more necessary for girls as they are the future mothers of the race. Health education imparted at early age will make one conscious of what is good for health and save one from the future troubles when old;

. . . there is no provision for old age pension in this country and women who have to earn their living through manual labour have to go on working till they die if they have no one to support them. This is a problem which needs as much consideration as the equal pay for equal work for women;

. . . no survey or study seems to have been made so far of the problems of women in old age, either of the women in the urban or of those in the rural setting or of those in the low-income groups;

. . . it is high time that organisations such as this, and the Government institute studies and surveys to measure the depth and extent of the problem and take necessary remedial measures to combat the present financial, health, housing and socio-economic problems as well as to stay the tide of further escalation;

. . . compulsory retirement should be cancelled. No stigma should be attached to a man's age. Men and women should be allowed to retain their jobs for as long as they are able to give efficient outputs;

. . . today's medical practitioners must work hand-in-hand with philosophers. Man is not as old as he feels but as old as others make him feel.

Jamaican meeting

From the Caribbean, a similar range of issues was raised. Jamaican recommendations mentioned, among other subjects,[41]

. . . that all planning for the occupation of the retired and elderly seek to ensure a productive and income-generating basis;

[40] Pathak 1975. See also Bhatla 1986, Sharma 1907.
[41] Jamaica, National Council on Ageing.

. . . that psychological care and attention should be provided for their intellectual and well-being;

. . . that decreased drug costs should be implemented by the appropriate organisations;

. . . that training in geriatrics should be mandatory for all staff employed in institutions for the elderly;

. . . that current individual medical records and necessary referral systems should be maintained in all elderly care institutions;

. . . that mandatory regular medical visits by a physician's assistant, Nurse Practitioner or Community health aide should be scheduled for all elderly in institutions;

. . . that standards of care and hygiene for all elderly care institutions must be established by law. Contravention of such being subject to legal action;

. . . that the news media be mandated to educate the public on the status of the elderly in Jamaican society, and to inform on the aging process in preparation for the latter years of life;

. . . that the public transport system (and the mini-buses association) should provide reduced fares and special seating;

. . . that supermarket proprietors should be encouraged to establish special times when older citizens can come to purchase scarce items and shop with assistance when needed.

Barbados study

A study already mentioned from Barbados (1986) deals with some very basic issues of life for older people:[42]

. . . increase the levels of old age pensions, especially those outside the public service;

. . . make allowances for inflation, such as a more universal usage of cost of living allowances;

. . . rethink the levels at which pensions, especially those of public servants, are taxed;

. . . clearly define a poverty line, and establish some supplement programmes to assist those who fall below this level;

. . . ensure delivery of meals to those who have problems in this area;

. . . teach the elderly about adequate nutrition and its importance;

. . . undertake house repairs to assist those elderly whose homes are in need of repair;

. . . offer more universalised assistance with the payment of utility bills and house insurance;

[42] Braithwaite (ed.) 1986.

. . . introduce programmes of public education about the elderly, their needs and their problems, in the hope that a more objective picture will forestall the problems of labelling and stereotyping;

. . . and social support programmes, and counselling services to help the elderly to deal with their feelings of declining well-being. These may be fostered through the development of community network groups, and the extension of the home help service to include the provision of social psychological support. The latter suggestion will of course presuppose the training of personnel in these skills;

. . . and programmes to reduce the often stated fear of crime among the elderly;

. . . set up programmes to provide companionship, especially for those elderly who live alone and those who complain of loneliness. This may be provided through the establishment of the community network groups suggested above;

. . . promote programmes to encourage greater financial support by relatives. It is possible that this could be encouraged through the increase in dependent relatives allowance under the country's tax laws;

. . . upgrade programmes of information so that old people may know about the social policy programmes which are available to them, and about the terms and conditions of benefits;

. . . initiate training programmes, including information about the elderly, their needs and concerns directed at service delivery personnel, including bus drivers, to enhance the quality of service rendered to the elderly;

. . . facilitate the extension of services under the social assistance and home help schemes since these are areas in which need for assistance was expressed most often;

. . . with respect to health conditions among the elderly, while there is clear evidence that some strides are being made in this area, more attention will have to be paid to:

upgrading the health education service;

implementing and upgrading visits by health personnel so that those in need of care, but who cannot get to the facilities, will have them delivered to them;

a programme of education to stress the importance of compliance with medical prescription;

. . . and on retirement, the findings suggest that there is a need to:

provide occupational opportunities for those who want to continue in active employment—this could probably be partly achieved through encouraging employment in the home;

regulate wages so that the elderly who return to work are not exploited;

implement well-organised programmes of an educational nature which would help those approaching retirement to prepare for the same;

develop a more active programme to enhance the leisure time activities of the elderly.

Bogotá: panamerican

Among the recommendations from the 1986 Bogotá Conference were the following, directed to a large extent at the more highly developed countries of the Third World:

. . . governments should be requested to include special parameters for the development of gerontological research in their national census-taking;

. . . the aged should be encouraged and given incentive to organise themselves so as to represent and defend their own interests;

. . . action to create greater awareness of old age should be increased. This would contribute towards the reaffirmation of positive images and bring about a change in marginalizing stereotypes;

. . . there is a need to promote exchange and co-operation in research especially in comparative studies between different cultures, social classes and ecological contexts, using a multidisciplinary approach;

. . . seminars should be planned for political leaders so that they become aware of the aging process and feel motivated to prescribe the measures necessary for the well-being of old people;

. . . the importance of education should be stressed as a means of changing negative attitudes towards old age, from primary schools onwards;

. . . the main role of the mass media as creators and disseminators of cultural images should be stressed. Massive campaigns should be carried out in order to encourage respect for old people;

. . . epidemiological methods should be developed to evaluate the state of psycho-social well-being of populations, in order to implement appropriate schemes;

. . . there is a need for greater awareness of the possibilities of preventive geriatrics, including the scope of medical care for the aging person;

. . . it would be preferable to speak of pathology 'in' aging rather than 'of aging';

. . . there is an urgent need to introduce courses in gerontology and geriatrics into undergraduate and postgraduate university curricula;

. . . a policy to integrate the old person into the family should be developed in order to support, protect and aid those families who wish and can continue to take care of the aged. Subsidies, networks of community support and structures to lighten the work of the family should be made available;

. . . a 'substitute family' should be provided for those lacking one;

. . . housing policies should be encouraged which build homes of easy access and adapted to the needs of the aged;

. . . in their labour legislation governments should consider specific laws to eliminate any discrimination based on age, to recognise equal rights for the aged worker and flexibility in retirement;

. . . governments and social security institutions should:

find ways of extending horizontal coverage, tending towards the universalization of benefits;

study mechanisms for incorporating old people who do not fulfil the legal requirements for access to existing pension systems;

. . . governments should be urged to promulgate regulations concerning the functioning and establishment of medico-social services, and insist on monitoring of their implementation;

. . . to provide continuity to hospital activity, the establishment of geriatric day centres should be encouraged, so that dependent aged people can receive inter-disciplinary care, and so that the family group can participate in the care of the aged;

. . . any measure for medico-social assistance should be provided on the basis of two principles:

autonomy, so that it can have a maximum level of independence . . . respect for the elderly person's right to control his own environment and his own body . . . includes both the right to be informed and the right to take part in decision-making;

community groups and groups of old people should be stimulated to help each other and to exchange experiences.

Nairobi: Shelter

In the preparation for the 1987 governmental and non-governmental meetings in Nairobi for the International Year of Shelter for the Homeless, I prepared a Charter on Shelter for the Aged in Developing Countries which made recommendations on some of the major points involved:

. . . when housing plans are developed governments and voluntary organizations should recognise the rapidly growing problem of abandoned, destitute elderly people;

. . . in areas which are the target of migration, architects should plan for space in houses to accommodate the grandparent generation, in addition to the nuclear family, and thus enable the extended family to migrate together;

. . . low-cost special housing should be developed on an ownership or lease basis which would enable successive generations of elderly to utilise the same property;

. . . the greatest efforts should be made to locate individual older heads of households within integrated inter-generational communities rather than in ghetto style old people's complexes;

. . . preference should be given to accommodation in which the older person with no family may have a sense of independence, either by way of separate houses or apartments with own front doors, rather than constructing more old people's residential homes or asylums;

. . . consideration should be given to the disablement which occurs more frequently in old age and therefore requires internal adaptations and variations of access to old people's housing;

. . . voluntary organizations should be encouraged to do more to provide accommodation for the aged and to experiment with new types of accommodation provision, and governments should facilitate such voluntary efforts during the interim period of planning for future major developments;

. . . all agencies should combine to provide services including domiciliary health and social care, which will enable the elderly to live comfortably in the shelter available and to improve that shelter;

. . . all agencies concerned, from the United Nations, through governments, and down to small community groups, should clearly recognise and energetically plan for the raising of the necessary finance to give reality to conference resolutions which otherwise would have no impact on the shelter problems of the oldest and poorest.[43]

The plethora of recommendations from these and other conferences and studies since the World Assembly on Aging leaves no excuse for lack of initiatives. At the same time they underline the massive financial and human material resources which will be required to implement even a minority of the ideas expressed.

[43] HelpAge International 1987.

10

SPECIAL GROUPS OF ELDERLY

THIS chapter will look briefly at the circumstances of three groups of elderly who may diverge somewhat from the general pattern of ageing expected in their culture and environment. These groups are the elderly refugees, older women in the Third World, and grandmothers of AIDS stricken families.

The Elderly Refugee

There is some debate as to what constitutes a refugee or a displaced person. The term is used in this instance simply to denote any group of people which has been forcibly removed from its natural and chosen locality, by either natural or man-made disasters.

In view of my own association with Help the Aged, it is relevant to mention that this voluntary organization was founded in London in 1961 with the original intention of catering for the needs of elderly refugees in disaster situations 'overseas'. Its first responses to disasters included European catastrophes as well as various emergencies in developing countries.

Help the Aged was founded by a group of British businessmen, headed by Cecil Jackson-Cole, who had been closely associated with the general development agency Oxfam since its origins as the Oxford Committee for Famine Relief during the Second World War. In 1960 the group had noted that no agency existed to meet the needs of elderly people in disaster situations, and discussions with the United Nations confirmed this lack of service. Some other agencies engaged in relief operations tended to believe that few elderly people survived through natural disasters into the refugee stage, that those few elderly survivors had no significant specific needs which could not be met by general services, and that after such experiences the older people would die very quickly anyway, so that money and personnel expended in serving the elderly refugee was a waste of always inadequate resources.

In spite of these doubts Help the Aged prospered, raising such substantial amounts of funds that it was able eventually to move into general welfare programmes—and later development schemes—both in Britain and in developing countries. Some of the doubts persisted. Twenty years later, Help the Aged's Dr Christopher Beer visited refugee camps after major influxes into both Somalia and Sudan. More than once he was assured by other observers that there were virtually no elderly refugees in the camps. Undeterred, he persisted in visiting individual shelters of refugee families in order to see for himself.

Dr Beer found, in shelter after shelter, an elderly person, or perhaps an elderly couple, sitting quietly in a dark corner of the shack or tent. These people rarely came to the light of day. There were three main reasons for this. It was an unspoken rule that any food or supplies went first to the children, nursing mothers, and any working men who might be present, so that the elderly did not venture to the relief centres. There also appeared to be a cultural expectation that the elderly should not push themselves forward but should patiently wait for whatever fate had in store. And as a result the elderly spent their days conserving what little energy they had by avoiding any unnecessary exercise. Needless to say, Dr Beer and later Help the Aged teams were able to identify specific needs of those elders which could be met.[1]

A striking description of the development of a refugee crisis has been provided by Peter Strachan, who has shared in many of the ideas expressed in this chapter:

At all stages older refugees may have specific problems arising from the coincidence of . . . age and refugee problems. Striking suddenly, or building to a head over a period of years, the originating crisis results in a mass displacement and migration to a haven of relief. The relief phase merges into one of care and maintenance in a state of limbo which may last for many years. . . . Eventually one or a combination of the three

---

[1] As indicated, this section relies heavily on Help the Aged field reports from Drs Chris Beer, Ann Rose and other staff, as well as Nancy Godfrey who carried out a survey in Sudan; see Godfrey 1986.

classic solutions will become possible: the refugees will be able to return voluntarily to their own homes, or they will be enabled to settle and integrate into their country of asylum, or a third country resettlement will be arranged. But the two latter solutions do not end the situation, for the refugees will most probably consider themselves as such for decades after.

The first problem to confront the elder in a disaster situation is that he or she may be left behind by the mass migration. When refugees flooded into Sudan from Central Tigray, an Oxfam report estimated that up to 40,000 elderly people had been left behind without adequate support. Most of these old people were incapable of walking for perhaps two months across rough country to reach the 'haven of relief'. Others would have preferred not to be uprooted from ancestral villages in order to plunge into an unknown future. Starvation and death would have seemed a less fearful option. Yet others of the older population began the trek and collapsed by the wayside. I retain for ever the memory of an aged Chilean woman crouching in a shattered cottage which was gradually disintegrating into a vast earthquake crater. Her problem was not so much the utter paralysis of fear as a determined decision not to desert her treasured home and possessions, come what might.

The second problem in a sudden flight from catastrophe is the inevitable splitting up of families, due to varying speeds of flight, transport difficulties, official intervention, and other unaccustomed factors. This is linked to the lack of organization and tracing services at the reception points, and the lack of co-ordination between different reception points, so that the elderly person is unable to resume contact with younger members of the family. In such a situation more mobile, younger people are much more likely to link up again than older people whose frailty has been exacerbated by added disablement of disaster injury or travel weariness.

In certain displacement situations, the destination of the elders may differ entirely from that of the younger family. This is noted in a situation such as the disturbances in El Salvador. An elderly person displaced by destruction of the home or village may find refuge after walking an hour or two. The younger family members may be disposed, because of political affiliation or economic realities, to migrate out of their own country altogether, perhaps into neighbouring Honduras or even crossing entire territories to the havens of Belize or Mexico.

A further problem which tends to affect the elder more than the youngster, in respect to mobility and adaptability, is the double disaster and evacuation by steps. A classic example of this situation developed recently in El Salvador. A number of older people, who had been displaced by war damage and whose younger relatives had left the country, were found accommodation in San Salvador, the capital. The available accommodation was extremely poor, but at least provided living quarters in which the rural elder might try to come to terms with the realities of urban living. Then San Salvador was struck by a major earthquake. Prominent in the ruins of city centre housing were the old people who, once again and as a result of a different horror experience, were rendered homeless and totally disorientated.[2]

Material lack is a common factor in disaster situations, but again one which is temporarily more easily accepted by the younger person. In the Khmer refugee camps of Thailand, as well as in Sudan, the poor state of clothing has been a recurrent complaint of older refugees. In the Khmer camps this complaint has been met by the sensible tactic of distributing cloth and sewing materials so that older people can be usefully employed in making clothing, rather than simply queuing for hand-outs.

Relief teams have identified specific health needs of the elderly. Help the Aged's first surveys in the camps of northern Somalia found 67% of older refugees suffering from serious eye conditions, some of them caused by refugee flight and camp conditions. This justified the recruitment of a specialist ophthalmic team to treat the refugees as well as to train local medical staff in the specialty.

A researcher in Sudan reported that information on the health needs of elderly members of refugee populations is scarce. Most of what is known has been derived from studies involving the entire population of these communities. To date, the few studies that have focused solely on the aged refugees have been restricted to the identification of disease-specific morbidity in camps or settlements. Consequently the health status and needs of elderly refugees are not well known.

General studies, such as those of Dr Pathak in Bombay,

[2] The Catholic Social Secretariat co-operated with Help the Aged to care for elderly refugees in El Salvador.

mentioned earlier, which make a strong case for the development of geriatrics in developing countries, indicate a variant pattern of health potential and disease susceptibility in the ageing population. These suggest that such variant patterns could be repeated or even accentuated in disaster conditions.

Overcrowding is another factor which, even in normal conditions, may lead to the elder being rejected by the family, or subjected to the most degrading of physical provision. This factor becomes particularly acute in an area like Hong Kong, which is one of the most overcrowded countries in the world, with a population of six million people crowded into just over 1,000 square kilometres, an average density 200 times that of the United States.

Into overcrowded Hong Kong came the waves of Vietnamese refugees. At first they were accommodated in open camps with access to employment. Since July 1982 it was considered necessary to enclose the camps in order to cope with the continued increase in numbers of refugees. When many refugees were accepted into resettlement schemes in the United States, Canada, Australia, and elsewhere, a further cruel factor came into play. Resettlement criteria on the part of the welcoming governments favoured skilled and employable younger people with their children, which often resulted in the grandparents being rejected and split from their families.[3]

A single such case, illustrating all the agony of the refugee's plight, is portrayed by Liz Juggins:[4]

One such person is Luong Thi Hung Thuong, whose story is typical of many Vietnamese refugees in Hong Kong. Thuong's son and daughter and their respective families have been resettled in Canada, and Thuong is desperately afraid that she might never see them again. She and her 80 year old sister, Tam, arrived in Hong Kong by boat in 1982, together with her daughter, son-in-law and two grandchildren. Her son, Thanh, with his wife and three children, had managed to reach Hong Kong in 1979, and Thuong was able to see him once before he left for Canada—just three days after her arrival. Her daughter, son-in-law and their two children were resettled in Canada in April 1983.

Since their arrival in Hong Kong, Thuong and Tam have lived in

---

[3] Helping Hand of Hong Kong has carried out excellent work among elderly refugees.

[4] Liz Juggins, of the Help the Aged Press Office.

three different refugee camps. They are currently living in the geriatric ward of the Hong Kong Christian Service Hostel . . . counting the days (now months and years) until they can join their loved ones. Thuong is afraid that time is running out and that, even if she is ever permitted to join her son and daughter in Canada, she and her sister, who has lived with her for many years, will be parted and resettled separately.

A detrimental aspect of retirement, which is further aggravated in refugee situations, is that of loss of role and purpose. The disintegration of communities and the dislocation of services leaves even younger people disorientated and unoccupied—even drifting into a state of dependency on relief hand-outs—in some refugee camps. The impact on the older person is even more intense. To a senior citizen used to exercising authority and receiving honour among the community, this almost invisible indignity may be the cause of more acute suffering than the visible conditions which attract the cine and television camera. The condition calls for special consideration such as the system set up by Norwegian Redd Barna in a camp in Thailand where committees are chosen from among the older people to plan and administer their own special activities.

There are many psychological after-effects of disaster and also of residence in even the best supplied refugee camp, or resettlement area. After more than 40 years, Polish survivors of the Nazi holocaust, long settled in Britain, are four times more likely than their British-born peers to suffer dementia and breakdown needing psychiatric treatment. The Colombian organization Pro Vida cared for some 150 elderly survivors of the Armero disaster who had lost their families. One elderly woman had survived for nearly three weeks in a freak cave within her house after it had been submerged by the 40 feet deep tide of mud which had covered Armero after the eruption of the volcano and the melting of snow on the summit. Pro Vida discovered that, after binding the physical wounds and providing alternative accommodation, there remained the almost permanent task of sensitive attention to the psychological aftermath of horror, bereavement, and isolation, which affected the elderly more than younger survivors.

My own experience includes the aftermath of a major earth-quake where, while I was able to sleep and sit within a partly ruined building during continuing earth tremours, the disaster survivors would only stand around the inner walls of the building, ready to rush out into the street at the first sign of another tremor. In those circumstances, the less mobile of the elderly chose not to enter a building at all but to take the risk of pneumonia in the constant freak monsoon-type rain caused by a vast terrestrial disturbance.

A rather different, but equally tragic experience concerned a recent mission to Palestine refugee camps in Jordan.[5] After many years of efficient administration by UNRWA, the Jordanian camps are in fact reasonably equipped, if rather cramped housing estates, rather than the tented encampments which the term 'refugee camp' tends to evoke. There was no evidence of malnutrition, and basic health services were available. The particularly sad circumstance was that, from the mountains nearby, an elderly refugee could look across at the West Bank and at the more remote areas of Israel and probably identify the place where his farm or house was situated. Afforded, like Moses, only a sight of that distant land, and knowing that by a legal freak the new tenant of the farm had not yet supplanted him as the owner, the refugee faced death with the thought that never more would he again tread his own land. Whatever the political implications and complications of the case, the individual personal suffering of very old, long-term refugees was very apparent to the observer.

One of the few in-depth surveys of the elderly in a refugee camp took place in Sufawa, Sudan, and concerned the refugees from Tigray province of Ethiopia.[6] Some conclusions are worth noting. As regards general conditions,

mothers had often been left behind in Tigray. Reasons given included illness, tending the farm or tending other ill family members . . . death was frequently reported in the very young and the very old. Many families had experienced death, suggesting a high mortality in this population . . . adolescent men *and* women frequently had returned to Tigray after living in Sufawa [leaving elders in the camp] . . . persons living in the same tent were *usually* limited to nuclear family members. Other tent residents included extended family members and occasionally

[5] In Dec. 1986, UNRWA, WHO, and HelpAge combined to send a team to investigate growing problems of ageing in the UNRWA camps in Jordan. The team included Professor Gary Andrews. Dr Hana Hermanova (both representing WHO), Dr Moussa (UNRWA), and myself.

[6] Godfrey 1986.

friends of the head of the house; the majority of the family moved together. Rarely did an individual move separately from his/her family [presumably referring to the nuclear family, as distinct from the first and third comments above].

On disabilities of the elderly within the camps the following observations were made:

many elderly were independent and reported few disabilities [possibly there was some element of survival of the fittest elderly who had managed to complete the long journey to Sufawa] . . . family or community support systems were often present for those with disabilities . . . reported levels of functioning were often the same for both Sufawa [the present] and Tigray [just prior to moving]; economic dependency in respondents was frequently reported. (Personally interviewing a few elderly refugees made it clear that employment was desired and that the elderly were capable. Discrimination by camp agencies and by Sudanese landowners favoured younger workers.)

Nutritional assessment of the older population led to the following not entirely negative findings:

the majority of elderly weighed over 40 kg—which is the current cut off point for supplementary feeding . . . many elderly weighed over 50 kg [cut off point favoured by some authorities] although the HtA team anticipated that few would weigh over 50 kg; . . . although the majority appeared thin, few appeared severely malnourished . . . most elderly persons were able to come to a central location independently. Few were assisted by other persons.

While some of the above findings appear reassuring, the commentator falls into the trap of using the normal majority for main reference instead of concentrating on the minority need. It is relevant to observe the frequently of qualifying terms such as 'often', 'the majority', 'frequently' and so on. Had the report been couched in negative terms referring to the minority, it would have reflected needs for specialist services for those who were not managing to adapt to camp conditions. Indeed, this minority justified the presence of a specialist team over a period of two years.[7]

---

[7] An interesting facet of the Sudan operation was the excellent co-operation between different non-governmental agencies. Thus, in Sufawa the health services were run jointly by the Save the Children Fund and Help the Aged, each of which was able to bring some specialist skills to bear.

A strange by-product of the refugee situation is that, in some cases, efficient relief and rehabilitation services rushed in by international agencies result in the camp inmate being better served than the indigenous inhabitant tilling the arid soil outside the camp's limits. Some of the international agencies are learning to give consideration to this peripheral problem, as in the case of the ophthalmic team in Hargeisa, Somalia, which, in addition to tending the needs of the refugees, trained local medical staff to give a permanent expert service to the local population after the refugees have departed.

This section can best be concluded by another quotation from Peter Strachan:

> although recognised as a vulnerable group, the elderly are often not treated as such. Screening and morbidity data may not subdivide adults by age, meaning that widespread malnutrition in the upper brackets may not be recognised, unlike that among children or pregnant and lactating women. Communities may have excellent reasons for de-prioritising older people, and the paramount requirement is for a basic needs approach to ensure that the refugee community can adequately feed all its members. However, during an emergency the institution of therapeutic feeding programmes may save lives among the very old as well as the very young.

Given the reduced number of very old refugees, the cost of delivering the additional therapeutic supplies would not be excessive in order to achieve so humane a goal.

The Older Woman

Many references have already been made to the tendency of the female to survive longer than the male, and also to circumstances which adversely affect the widowed or single elderly woman. In my own experience of some 40 years' work with older people in many countries, developed and developing, the saddest individual plight tends, in fact, to be that of the widowed aged man, particularly where incompetence in domestic matters aggravates his abandonment. But in mass it is elderly women who are more likely to suffer problems accruing not only from a current state of abandonment but also from earlier disadvantages. Tables 2.10 to 2.13 have already illustrated typical sex ratios, with pronounced female survival rates. Tables 6.3 and 6.4 further point up the bleak story of widowhood with the vast preponderance of disadvantage to the older woman.

A Kenyan commentator has summed up some of the women's disadvantages:

a large number of elderly and ageing women are left in the villages. This situation has been created by the effects of rural–urban migration, seeking job opportunities, urbanization, etc. Food production . . . is largely in the hands of the elderly rural woman who is also largely illiterate and ignorant of modern farming methods and technology. Health services are inadequate in the rural areas. . . . The rural woman's counterpart, her urban sister is not very much better. She has to reckon with employment seeking, health hazards (vehicles, elevators, noise), competition for services, age barriers, etc., in the urban areas.[8]

She continues to enumerate some of the traditional roles of the older woman which are being eroded by modernization, although official efforts are being made in Kenya to retard or reverse that trend.

First, she [the older woman] was the traditional midwife through whose hands many of us passed . . . secondly, traditional medicine was the domain of elderly men and women . . . thirdly, counselling and bringing up of young girls was the duty and expected responsibility of the elderly woman. Young girls slept in their grandmother's house. From these elderly women they learned to be of age, societal norms and values were instilled in them, and from them they learned the respected motherhood . . . fourthly, traditional crafts were learned from the elderly people. For instance the Kikuyu *kiondo*, the Luo *agulu* and *tawo* and many more examples that could be given, were the works of elderly women . . . fifthly, some rituals and rites were performed by elderly men and women. These are rituals like circumcision, dowry issues, etc. . . . for some rites ritual alcohol was a necessity and it was the elderly women who brewed it . . . this is being overtaken by modern breweries . . .

In sub-Saharan Africa, the emergence of female-headed households caused by migration, widowhood, and divorce is reportedly a major problem in rural areas. Whereas in parts of Africa, widows traditionally remarried into the deceased spouse's

---

[8] From the HelpAge Kenya Conference already quoted, and also from *Women and Ageing*, report of Kenya NGO Organizing Committee for 1985 World Conference of the UN Decade for Women.

family or were integrated into his kin structure, this custom is now breaking down.

Massive out-of-country migration is adding to the troubles of elderly widows who, during the lifetime of the spouse, elected to stay on in the home country. In Malta it is now the case that more Maltese people live outside the country than inside it. In an Egyptian study, one-third of elderly Egyptians who were institutionalized had children living abroad. Reference was made in an earlier chapter to a grandmother caring for a number of dependent children encountered by me in Belize. This factor of grandmother remaining with young grandchildren in country of origin while the parent generation seeks, and often fails to find, fortune in a far country, is a frequent modern phenomenon of all Caribbean lands as well as of countries in other continents.

A further root of disadvantage for older women is the higher level of illiteracy among women as compared with men. Although female illiteracy is declining among younger people, the gap persists and will persist in the upper age groups for the next two decades at least. A report of the Secretary-General of the United Nations stated that 'female illiteracy is one of the priority problems in developing nations'.[9]

In a meeting related to the United Nations Decade for Women, women from several countries, including African nations, India, Pakistan, and Indonesia, agreed that

although tradition in their societies requires young family members to care for the old, this is becoming more and more difficult to accomplish because of the migration of the young from rural to urban areas and the poor living conditions in urban centres . . . elderly . . . are often left alone and destitute in their villages with no one except small children to help them fetch wood and carry water.

For most old men there is a spouse to share the duties, but for most women there is no partner.[10]

At the same meeting another woman, this time from Korea, underlined 'the dilemma confronting many older women in South Korea and in fact around the world. They experienced tension when living with their children and grandchildren because of differences in values and lifestyles between the

[9] IFA 1985.   [10] AAIA 1985.

generations. Yet they lack the financial resources to live independently and fear the loneliness implicit in living away from their families.' In Western Europe those value and life-style differences may have taken 200 years to evolve, compared with the eruption of change in developing countries over perhaps 20 or 30 years.

Summarizing the problems of the older woman, the Korean delegate ended 'therefore we are in a situation where we cannot live and we cannot die'. However she was able to mention programmes of mutual support which brought shared experience leading to strength, support, and happiness. An Indian delegate stated that 'grandmothers, traditionally the caretakers and teachers of the children, are now considered by younger Indians to be out-of-date. This discrepancy in values and ideas causes tensions to develop among different generations of women in the family.' At the same time, the Indian speaker thought that modernization itself was producing new opportunities for involvement of grandmothers, with increasing numbers of urban young women moving into permanent jobs, leaving their children with grandmothers in a trend which 'may pressage a return to joint families'.

The researches of Dr Pathak in Bombay, quoted earlier, point to a need for urgent research into the special health problems of elderly women. He mentions the psychological problems arising from equating the menopause with the onset of terminal ageing, an aspect also identified by a Colombian team, which pointed out that, whereas older women in North America viewed the menopause as a very positive occurrence, women beyond the menopause in developing countries saw it as negative and detrimental.[11]

Further distinctive problems of older women's health emerging from Pathak's educated assumptions are the high proportion of gynaecological complaints (specifically, deterioration of the female reproductive organs, compared to the incidence of common complaints shared by both sexes), an incidence of eye diseases 50% more frequent in women than in men, effects of

[11] J. Pathak, surveys and symposium, 1975–85. Reference should also be made to the report of a round table discussion held by the International Conference on Health Policy on 6–8 Dec. 1986 in New Delhi, and published as Bhatla 1986. See also Dulcey-Ruiz 1985.

earlier malnutrition where traditionally men eat first or choose the better cuts, the low number of women seeking hospital admissions (30% over 60, compared with 70% men), contrary to the proportion that would be epidemiologically correct, and the social effects of trying to care for aged female paralytics in congested modern accommodation (28 women with paralysis and 21 with hemiplegia, out of a sample of 514). To this could be added the positive factor of the marked willingness to reintegrate rehabilitated blind grandmothers as housekeepers in a Guatemala scheme. Where the grandmother is viewed mainly as a carer, ill health can be a vital and tragic factor.

Among the particular needs of women in development programmes, the following are some of the recommendations from various conferences:[12]

more research and data collection on specific needs, especially regarding health . . . programming of housing to provide space for the grandmother; literacy and retraining programmes (especially for daily living in a new environment) for older women . . . rehabilitation services after stroke, injury, operations, other traumas, as well as retraining for the permanently disabled . . . equality of nutrition at all ages . . . love and care; if necessary the arrangement of surrogate families and peer groups where families are irrevocably parted . . . governmental measures to preserve the family, including allowances for carers in the home . . . utilization of the skills of older women, including persuading professions to allow use of certain skills such as midwifery (single trained nurses and aides) and traditional medicine; courses to adapt traditional health skills to modern reality . . . legal security for women working the land or setting up small industries, individually or as cooperatives . . . governmental encouragement of voluntary organization pilot schemes and councils of elders . . . dissemination of information of all kinds and networking of women's organizations and those working with women . . . revival of tribal values and/or education of younger generations to revive respect for the aged woman . . . equality of marriage rights and customs.

A note of warning is sounded by a woman involved in development programmes, as to the dangers of segregating or isolating older women by imposing well-intentioned programmes which are too exclusive. She says that 'the needs of older women are generally those of the rest of the community . . . if the need is

----

[12] Mainly those referred to in nn. 9–11.

water, then an elderly woman in the area also needs more pure water, easier access to it and better sanitation, just as the rest of the community needs it. The older woman may have exaggerated needs because of her age or physical disability, but essentially her needs are the same.' Where programmes for the older woman are developed, she believes, these should be so structured that benefit will come to the entire community, so that the older woman will acquire added respect and stature and 'it is less likely that families will consider the care of elderly relatives a burdensome problem'.[13]

Grandmothers and AIDS

There has been some reluctance on the part of a number of developing countries to encourage open debate on the subject of the incidence of AIDS or HIV in their countries. At a conference organized by the London School of Hygiene and Tropical Medicine at the Barbican Centre in London in 1987 an African medical representative stated categorically that AIDS did not exist in Africa. This kind of reluctance to acknowledge facts is probably understandable in the light of the tendency on the part of more sensationalist commentators to 'blame' Africa for the emergence of this new and deadly disease.

It is therefore significant that the Ugandan Ministry of Health has approved circulation of statistics from that country. If this leads to more open debate generally, without imputation of blame, in developing countries it may lead to more urgent and positive measures to meet the rapidly developing pandemic crisis. As AIDS is generally associated with younger and sexually active age groups it is instructive to see what the Ugandan data reveal before discussing why this disease has such awesome significance for older people, and particularly for African grandmothers.[14]

In Latin America, AIDS appears to be conforming to the North American patterns, that is, tending to affect mainly homosexuals. The disease is already present in several areas, and

[13] Katie Kelly, founding editor of *Ageways*.
[14] Ugandan and other data on grandmother and HIVS edited by Dr Winston Carswell, Consultant Surgeon, New Mulago, Uganda, 1987.

Brazil has probably the second or third largest accurately recorded proportional incidence of AIDS of any country (which does not necessarily mean the largest *actual* proportional incidence, in view of the lack of accurate recording in countries which may have much higher actual incidence rates). Until the first half of 1987 it was still being stated that AIDS was not identifiable in certain West African or Asian countries. The mobility of modern populations is leading to a moment when a number of countries will probably have to admit cases, epidemic areas, and even national pandemics.

A report circulated in 1987 of a survey of blood donors in Kampala, Uganda, recorded that testing for AIDS/HIV of 2,340 young men in apparent good health found 296 to be seropositive for AIDS antibodies, that is, 12.6% of the sample. Seropositive donors 'do not have AIDS but have been exposed to HIVS and may pass it on to others, either sexually or by blood transfusion'. Among a group of 1,011 young women attending an antenatal clinic, 136, or 13.5% revealed 'evidence of infection'. It is pointed out that these women 'can pass on the virus to their sexual partners or to the child they are carrying'. In other Ugandan tests among 200 children, only 2 (one of them having recently had a blood transfusion) were seropositive. Of 71 adults in West Nile there was only one positive. Of 96 old people in Kampala and Jinja none was seropositive. On the other hand, of 81 adults at an out-patient clinic, 30% were positive (this may have been a skewed sample due to reasons for attending the clinic). More significantly, of 186 bar girls, no less than 76% were positive. Of long-distance truck drivers, 33% had evidence of HIV infection.

It should again be stressed that the people in the samples were still in good health and not suffering from AIDS yet. It is to be assumed that 'many of those infected are liable to develop AIDS'. The low incidence of AIDS so far in comparison to HIVS is related to the very recent arrival in Uganda of the disease. However, patterns of infection are already obvious, both in Uganda and other countries. The significant features are a clear geographical route of development, related to sexual promiscuity, and a heterosexual pattern of infection rather than homosexual. The evidence shows that

rates of infection are extremely low or absent in those who are below the years of sexual activity or who are beyond the years of sexual activity . . .

high rates of infection among those who are sexually active . . . very high
rates of infection among those who are very active sexually, i.e. bar girls
. . . AIDS [= infection plus disease] is commonest in those at peak
sexual activity and is seen in equal numbers in men and women . . .
absence of infection plus disease in children between 4 years and 13
years, and in persons over 60 years.

A particularly sad aspect is the infection of unborn babies by the
mother. 'The third most important mode of transmission is from
infected mother to child *in utero*. This mode of transmission is
likely to become proportionately more important as the number
of infected women in the community rises.'

Although considerable expense is involved, the Ugandan
Ministry of Health announced the screening of all donated blood
for HIV antibodies, and a first laboratory training course was
organized in November 1986.

The impact of AIDS is already being described as threatening
to be 'the greatest crisis in the recorded history of Africa', and
'with the threat of many millions of deaths before the end of the
century alone, the depopulating effect is likely to cripple the
economies of even relatively prosperous countries'. The same fate
may await other regions of Asia and Latin America.

All that has been said so far points to mortality among the
sexually active age groups. It is easy in this atmosphere of almost
hysterical pessimism to regard the problems of the elderly as
relatively lesser and unimportant. In fact, much of the real
impact of AIDS mortality will not fall upon the sufferers, who, to
put it bluntly, face death within a relatively short period. The
impact will affect none more than the surviving grandmothers,
rather than the bewildered but uninfected surviving infant
children.

A typical scenario develops as follows: a man travelling
through an infected area has promiscuous sexual relations (not
necessarily a reprehensible act in his particular culture),
contracts AIDS, and infects his wife. The wife, in turn, infects the
unborn child. Each follows the tragic programme of disease and
death, possibly suffering from three months to a year from
unfamiliar symptoms of the disease. Over a certain period all
three die.

During that period, in the absence of adequate domiciliary and
hospice services, it is the grandmother who will have to care for

the terminally ill relatives. Without full understanding of what HIVS and AIDS are all about, ignorant of the risks, and with no skills to cope with the unfamiliar course of the disease, the grandmother will have to try her best to alleviate the sufferings of the dying and then arrange their burial. In the meantime she will have to assume full responsibility for the remaining children of the family.

In her particular community the grandmother may find that a considerable number of the productive members of the community have also died or are terminally ill. The entire weight of productivity, commercial activity, transport, and even local government in the community may have devolved upon a random group of grandmothers like herself. In view of the tendency for older men to marry younger additional wives in a community where mobility of partners is accepted, some of the older husbands will also develop AIDS, probably much more frequently than the sexually inactive senior wives.

In this kind of scenario, the grandmother's future existence is compounded of grief; struggle with an unknown disease of horrific potential; continuing guardianship of a small family until the children become old enough to learn about (and avoid) AIDS, and begin to work; perpetual, unalleviated hard labour of production and income earning, and sharing in the rehabilitation of desolated communities. On the grandmothers—as on the international community—will depend whether entire regions of some developing countries are doomed to become starvation areas beyond anything seen in the recent major drought emergencies, or whether some form of survival can be worked out until a new generation is able fully to share in productivity and preservation of the environment.

In such an emergency, certain support can be given to the grandmother generation. Direct personal support is imperative as the size of the crisis is likely to make it impossible for the development of hospitals, laboratories, pharmacies, hospices, domiciliary nursing schemes, and professional training programmes to keep pace with the development of the disease, much less compensate for existing service deficiencies.

Among the most important elements of a support programme are the provision of AIDS counselling and instruction in basic nursing skills. Without these, elder carers will be unable to offer the optimum comfort to the dying members of family, or to apply the relatively simple preventive measures which are so necessary. Another means of support would be helping the older people to set up income-generating projects, either of an individual nature or in co-operatives. This would need minor injections of capital and training as well as ongoing support for organizational and marketing problems.

One significant measure would be the development of new appropriate technology which would enable elderly people to continue tasks previously performed manually or with simple tools by younger and physically stronger workers, as also the provision of refined types of crops or varied small industries, again requiring the injection of external capital in order to set schemes in motion.[15]

While basically the local problem can only be tackled by local mobilization and utilization of the now undervalued skills and experience of the elderly, on the wider scale national and international agencies will need to act as intermediaries and initiators, especially where the signs of future peril are more obvious to the external observer.

[15] The scenario and proposals are based on internal HelpAge International discussions related to meetings to co-ordinate general non-governmental agency response to the problems of AIDS.

QUESTIONS THAT REMAIN

BLUEPRINTS now exist for action on ageing in developing countries. The Vienna International Plan of Action on Aging constitutes a global strategy by which detailed plans can be measured. A number of subsequent recommendations have served to reduce the world plan to regional dimensions. Among these are the recommendations of conferences covering Africa, Latin America, and the Caribbean as well as those included in a study of the Western Pacific. In 1988, the PanAmerican Health Organization, PAHO, completed a considerable study of the health of the elderly in 15 countries, while a number of countries now have national studies of some kind.

No further reference is necessary to these carefully edited and easy-to-read blueprints, to which must be added other publications listed in the bibliography, except to comment that in general they lack in one respect: how can the excellent recommendations be put into practice?

A Latin American technical meeting preparatory to the World Assembly on Aging in 1980 recognized that total social security, as introduced in some European countries, would not be feasible in most developing countries for the remainder of this century. The meeting therefore recommended that attention should be given to spreading the available resources as widely as possible, even though this might reduce some individual benefits in the first instance.

Elsewhere it has been stated that it is 'clearly predictable that the costs of institutionalization cannot be borne even by developed countries . . . it is essential [in developing countries] to develop policies that keep the elderly within some socially supported situation'.[1] Studies need to be initiated to determine

[1] UN WAA 1982*f*, p. 7.

what particular forms of 'socially supported situations' may be appropriate to, and successful in, different cultures and environments. Special attention needs to be given to the woman member of a family who accepts the responsibility of nursing an older family member in an era when many younger women must go out to work. Equally, such studies must refer to the special needs of the older woman, including the need to fulfil a meaningful role in life, as mentioned in the last chapter.

Perhaps the most urgent area of study is that of the family and how its faltering structure may be strengthened or restored. Certain assumptions have been made in the present work as to the observed breakdown of the extended family, but more detailed research is needed into the extent of this breakdown, its causes, its geographical and socio-economic patterns, and its effect on various members of the disintegrating unit. Perhaps the most significant assumption made by gerontologists and non-gerontologists alike is that the extended family in developing countries typically 'cares' for its older members. To date there are very few studies of the *quality* of that care, and as to whether it includes such elements as love, true mutual esteem, accurate awareness of the realities of ageing, and skills to enhance the quality of the old person's life to the fullest extent.

There are suspicions—indeed, some workers on ageing programmes have very clear perceptions on this subject—that in some instances, reliance on the traditional extended family may not be the normally acceptable panacea, but may for the old person be a gruesome and cruel experience of dependence, dearth, and degradation. Following a survey in São Paulo in 1987, Luis Ramos listed residence of an older person within a multi-generational family as a detrimental factor in slum conditions.[2] More research is urgently needed, particularly to identify the reasons for such uncaring accommodation of the elderly within the family and to propose measures to enable the family to improve its care.

Closely related to any idea of improvement of social services, whether they be rendered by government-maintained professional workers or by community volunteers or by family members, is the provision of adequate training, and access to updating of

[2] Luis Ramos, working with Alex Kalache on the Epidemiology of Ageing out of London School of Hygiene and Tropical Medicine.

information. It has been said that in some developing countries 'most training programmes . . . reflect values and orientations that were current in the major approaches to ageing in the industrial world of twenty years ago', approaches which have been criticized and rejected in industrial countries and which should not be foisted upon countries with newly developing ageing programmes.[3] Where satisfactory approaches to indigenous problems have been implemented, there is a most urgent need to accelerate the 'training of trainers' so that skills may be developed more rapidly in more areas. Often the elderly may be a part of such development—as in Jamaica, where new pools of expertise are being discovered among teachers and nurses who are retired but still healthy and willing.

Moving into the health field, there is need for a 'better understanding of just what constitutes proper nutrition for older people. Currently the recommendations on dietary allowances for all people beyond the age of 50 are based on studies done on younger adults.'[4] A new area of nutritional studies relates to the problems of older people (often the cooks for the entire family) who have migrated into urban or differing rural settings where their traditional foodstuffs are not available, or those who, although still in the home village, find the food supplies are being varied because of the exodus of the heavy agricultural labour force.

Another area of the health field requiring attention is public beliefs and attitudes about health. 'We do not know enough about elderly people's beliefs and attitudes regarding health . . . In some cultures, for instance, it is assumed that illness results from sin or witchcraft . . . the myth that illness and disability are the inevitable results of growing old is prevalent in developed and developing countries alike.' In the face of such attitudes, it may be more feasible in the short term to vary the treatment rather than hope to educate older people quickly into new attitudes.[5]

Bearing in mind the incidence of some kind of weakness or disability in many older people, priority must be given to the question of alternative types of work for the elderly, especially in

[3] Tapia-Videla and Parrish 1981.
[4] Williams 1985, p. 31.
[5] Coppard 1985, p. 49.

those places where the normal systems of production are breaking down due to migration, AIDS mortality, and so on. As important as the evolution of new forms of income-generating occupations for the elderly, and viable organizational and marketing structures to ensure permanence for initiatives when launched, is the possibility of adapting and replicating those pilot projects which have demonstrated a measure of success to date, some of which have already been referred to in earlier chapters. While a perfectionist might wish to await further trials and further in-depth assessment of needs and responses, there is enough evidence already to warrant a certain level of investment by governments and international agencies in low-key, grass-roots programmes.

The question of housing has already received some attention, and HelpAge India merits some mention for its work in this respect. In the interests of independence, the main impetus should be in the provision of independent homes for older people who have no family, with many possible variations of sharing and warden provision. Where possible the requirement for an extra room in urban houses should be considered by town planners as a preferred way of enabling families to continue to support their elders.

The intellectual aspirations of older people should not be forgotten. This is sometimes considered a luxury addition to the supply of basic needs, but in fact it can be a vital element in an individual's programme, helping to preserve purpose and health-ful living and postpone expensive psychiatric and somatic treatment at almost all levels of cultural development.

The more academic student in search of new territory to explore may become concerned about the lack of standardization of methodologies in all aspects of ageing research and practical programmes. A particularly barren area is that of evaluation of existing programmes. Whilst researchers from the North can make a conspicuous contribution to knowledge in the South, the contribution must never disturb the cultural flow of the host country being investigated. A Latin American writer has com-mented that imported research techniques often fail to 'capture the essence' of the Latin American situation 'not only because these techniques were elaborated for different societies and contexts but also, chiefly, because their basic assumptions are inappropriate'.[6] The vastness of the problem calls for maximum application of the best brains available in all societies, while respecting the cultures and practices of each developing nation.[7] And a most urgent demand will be for publication of general and specific texts; such texts are at present almost non-existent.

Having discussed many aspects of this developing world phenomenon of a greying population, recognizing the positive elements that exist, and being closely involved in current problems and potential solutions, I find myself returning to one basic factor which underlines all else. The question is, 'Who pays the bill?'—for research, awareness campaigns, planning, training, mobilization of volunteers, organization of the elderly themselves, capital costs of building and equipment, ongoing revenue expenditure, evaluation, and interchange of experience. None of the blueprints give a hint as to how this might be done.[8]

A vast increase in governmental contributions to the United Nations Trust Fund on Aging would be excellent, if it could be realistically envisaged. Ambassador Julia Alvarez of the Dominican Republic has a vision of a UNICEF for the elderly which should materialize one day, but not soon enough for many elderly now alive. A massive transfer of resources from the developed to developing world as described by Brandt still appears a long way off. And governmental priorities tend to relegate the social and health concerns of the aged to the bottom of aid lists. Many developing countries clearly lack resources sufficient to mount massive programmes on ageing.

It is not as a last forlorn hope, but as a viable tactic already proven in particular locations, that recourse is recommended to the mobilization of community response. The example of HelpAge India, or Pro Vida Colombia, with considerable indigenous ability to mobilize volunteers, raise funds, influence local thinking, promote innovative practical programmes, maximize the skills of local elderly, and liaise successfully with international agencies, is one which, if multiplied a thousand times, could have a very considerable impact on the fortunes of older people world wide. And to multiply this type of operation a

---

[6] Quijano 1975, p. 109.   [7] Warnes 1986, pp. 3–5.

[8] That is to say, excluding HelpAge 'blueprints' (such as Tout and Tout 1985), which, being directly programme- and project-oriented, inevitably gave major consideration to the question of provenance of finance.

thousand times is not so much wishful thinking when it has already been multiplied twenty times or more by a small staff of a dozen people working out of a London office on extremely modest funding.

It is not wishful thinking if the world will recognize in practice what the United Nations recognized in theory in 1982: that the ageing of the world's population is potentially one of the most serious socio-economic problems of the next decades. It is not wishful thinking if international organizations, as well as national organizations in industrial countries, would allocate to the subject a very modest amount of thought, capital, training resources, and moral support.

The teeming ageing population of the year 2000 can be a vital and thrilling human resource, rather than a root of economic disaster, if society will restore to the elderly the prestige, independence, mobility, and challenge which so-called civilized attitudes have virtually destroyed.

REFERENCES

AAIA, *Conversations in Nairobi: Report on the 1985 World Conference of the UN Decade for Women*, Washington, DC: 1986.

Aldritch, C. K., and Mendkoff, E., 'Relocation of the Aged and Disabled', *Journal of the American Geriatrics Society*, 11 (1963), pp. 185–94.

Amaya, Sor Clara, Paper for pre-World Assembly on Aging workshop at Villa Levya, Colombia, 1981.

Anderson, A. A., Jr., ' "Old" Is Not a Four-Letter Word', in H. E. Fitzgerald (ed.), *Human Development*. Guilford, Conn.: Michigan State University and Dunskin Publishing, 1981.

Andrews, F. M., and Phillips, G. W., 'Case Study: The Squatters of Lima', in Renner (ed.) 1982.

Andrews, G., Esterman, A. J., Braunack-Mayer, A. J., and Rungie, C. M., *Aging in the Western Pacific*. Manila: WHO Regional Office, 1986.

Anzola-Pérez, E., 'Aging in Latin America and the Caribbean', in PAHO 1985, pp. 9–23.

Apt, N. A., *Aging in Ghana*. Legon: University of Ghana, 1981, rev. edn. 1985.

Barca, R. (ed.), *Conferencia Latino-Americana y del Cáribe de gerontología* (Latin American and Caribbean conference of gerontology), Bogotá, June 1986. CIGS: Paris, 1986.

Beer, C., *The Politics of Peasant Groups in Western Nigeria*. Ibadan: Ibadan University Press, 1976.

Belize, Ministry of Education, *Belize Today*. Belize: 1984.

Bhatla, P. C. (ed.), *Proceedings: Care of the Elderly: A Round-table Discussion of the International Conference on Health Policy*. New Delhi: ICHP, 1986.

Binstock, R. H., Chow, W-S., and Schulz, J. H. (eds.), *International Perspectives on Aging Population and Policy Challenges*, UNFPA Policy Development Studies No. 7. New York: UN, 1982.

Bourne, R., *Political Leaders of Latin America*, London: Pelican, 1969.

Braithwaite, F. S. (ed.), *The Elderly in Barbados*. Barbados: Carib Research and Publications, 1986.

Brandt Commission, the, *Common Crisis: North–South Co-operation for World Recovery*. London: Pan, 1983.

Brazil, Bishops of, *Liberate the Land*. London: CIIR, 1986.

Brazil, Ministry of External Relations, *Brazil*. Brasilia: 1976.

Brody, E. M. *Health and Its Social Implications*, in Gilmore *et al.* 1981, pp. 189–201.

Burland, C. A., *Peoples of the Sun*. London: Weidenfeld & Nicolson, 1976.

Butler, R., *Aging and Mental Health: Positive Psychosocial and Biomedical Approaches*. St Louis, Miss.: C. V. Mosby, 1982.

Carbal Prieto, J. M., *La tercera edad* (The Third Age). Buenos Aires: Ediciones Troquel, 1980.

CERIS (Centro de estatistica religiosa e investigações sociais). Report on Old People's Homes in Brazil. S'Hertogenbosch: Caritas Neerlandica; Rio de Janeiro: CERIS, 1981.

Chinoy, E., in *Automobile Workers and the American Dream*. New York: Doubleday, 1955.

Choucri, N., *Population Dynamics and International Violence*. Lexington, Ma.: Lexington Books, 1974.

CIGS (Centre International de Gerontologie Sociale). *Report on African Conference on Gerontology, Dakar*. Paris: CIGS, 1984.

Colson, E., and Scudder, T., 'Old Age in Gwembe District, Zambia', in Amoss and Harrell (eds.), 1981.

Contreras de Lehr, E., 'Long-term Care Services in Mexico: The Nursing Home'. Paper presented at Kellogg International Work Group on the Quality of Long-term Care, Utrecht (1986).

Coppard, L., 'Self-health Care and the Elderly', in PAHO 1985, pp. 42–53.

Cortina, J., *The Faith of Archbishop Romero*. London: CIIR, 1986.

Combrugghe, G., Howes, N., and Nieukerk, M., *An Evaluation of CEC Small Development Projects*. Brussels: COTA, 1985.

Danon, D., Shock, N. W., and Marois, M. (eds.), *Aging: A Challenge to Science and Society*. Vol i *Biology*. Oxford: Oxford University Press (for L'Institut de la Vie and WHO), 1981.

Denton, C., *Costa Rica et Amerique central*. In series '*Les Personnes agées dans le monde*', Paris: CIGS, 1982.

—— and Acuña, O. M., *La Población de 60 años y más: Sus problemas y necesidades* (The population aged 60 years and over: Their problems and needs). Costa Rica: IDESPO, National University, 1985.

Diaz, Ralph, 'Development in Primary Health Care in Urban Areas', paper presented to the Annual Congress of the Medical and Dental Association of Botswana, Gaborone, 1986.

Dobrizhoffer, M., 'Account of the Abipones', in Sara Coleridge (ed., trans.), *Historia de Abiponibus*. London: 1704–32.

Donaldson, P. *Economics of the Real World*. London: Pelican, 1984.

Driest, Piet, 'Social Services and the Elderly in the Netherlands', unpublished monograph. The Hague: Netherlands Federation for Policy on Ageing, 1985.

Dulcey-Ruiz, E., *Imagen de la vejez percibida en medios de comunicación social en Colombia* (Images of old age perceived through social communications media in Colombia). Bogotá: Centro de Psicología Gerontológica, 1985.

Ekpenyong, S., Oyeneye, O. Y., and Peil, M., 'Reports on study of Elderly Nigerians'. Centre of West African Study, University of Birmingham, 1986.

Flores Colombino. A., 'Psychology of the Third Age', in Morelli *et al.* 1982.

Foner, N., 'Old and Frail and Everywhere Unequal. Care for the Aged in Nonindustrial cultures', *Hastings Center Report*, New York, April 1985.

Francis, S. E., *Roles, Programmes and Projects for the Elderly in the Caribbean which Combat Loneliness and Isolation*, Kingston: University of the West Indies, 1987.

Fraser, S. H., *Medical Needs of the Elderly*, Report on Commonwealth Caribbean Medical Research Council meeting, Barbados, 1982. PAHO Microfiche LO 30045.

Garcia, E., 'Legislation: Situation of the Elderly in Colombia'. Speech to Opera Pia pre-World Assembly Workshop on Aging, Villa Leyva, Colombia. Bogotá: Pro Vida, 1981.

Gilmore, A. J. J., Svanborg, A., Marois, M., Beattie, W. M., and Piotrowski, J. (eds.), *Aging: A Challenge to Science and Society*. Vol. ii, *Medicine and Social Science*, Oxford: Oxford University Press (for L'Institut de la Vie and WHO), 1981.

Glascock, A., and Feinman, S., 'Social Asset or Social Burden: An Analysis of the Treatment of the Aged in Non-Industrial Societies', in C. L. Fry (ed.), *Dimensions: Aging, Culture and Health*. New York: Praeger, 1981.

Goffman, E., *Asylums*. Garden City, New York: Anchor Books, 1961.

Godfrey, N., *Research on Sudan Refugees Programme*. London: HelpAge International, 1986.

Goldstein, A., and Goldstein, S., 'The Challenge of an Aging Population: The Case of the People's Republic of China', *Research on Aging*, 8/2 (1986), 179–97.

Golladay, F., and Liese, B., *Health Problems and Policies in the Developing Countries*, World Bank Staff Working Paper No. 412. Washington, DC: World Bank, 1980.

González-Aragón, J., *Qué es el envejecimiento?* (What is ageing?). Mexico City: Costa-Amic Editores SA, 1984.

Griffiths, J., *The Caribbean in the Twentieth Century*. London: Batsford Academic and Editorial, 1984.

Grunwald, J. (ed.), *Latin America and the World Economy*. Beverly Hills, Calif.: Sage, 1978.

Hampson, J., *Old Age: A Study of Ageing in Zimbabwe.* Gweru and Harare: Mambo, 1982.

Hart, Judith, *Realities: Development, Basic Needs and Human Rights,* MOD Paper No. 12. London: HMSO, 1978.

HelpAge International, *Report on Zimbabwe Training Course.* London: HAI, 1986.

—— *The Aged and the International Year of Shelter.* London: HAI, 1987.

Help the Aged, *Vilcabamba Research,* London: HtA, 1983.

Hill, E., and Tomassini, L. (eds.), *América Latina y el nuevo orden económico internacional* (Latin America and the new international economic order). Santiago de Chile: Corporación de Promoción Universitaria, 1979.

Ibrahim, M., *Tradition and Modern Development in Bangladesh Society.* Dhaka: Bangladesh Association for the Aged, 1985.

IFA, *Women and Aging around the World.* Washington, DC: 1985.

Iliovici, J., 'Aging and Development: The Humanitarian Issues'. Background paper for the World Assembly on Aging, 1982. Vienna: CSDHA, UN, 1982.

International Centre of Social Gerontology. See CIGS.

Jiménez-Castro, W., 'Economic Implications of the Aging of the Population in Latin America and the Caribbean', in PAHO 1985, pp. 87–96.

Jiménez Gandica, J., Paper for pre-World Assembly on Aging workshop at Villa Leyva, Colombia: Pro Vida, Bogotá: 1981.

—— 'La Familia y su desempeño en la atención y cuidado del anciano colocado en centros hospitalarios', (The family and its role in the attention and care of the old person placed in hospital centres). Unpublished report of CIGAL, Pro Vida. Bogotá, 1986.

Johnson, B. C. L., *Development in South Asia.* London: Penguin, 1983.

Jordão Nétto, A., 'Agressão e segregação: As relaçoes entre idoso e sociedade em S. Paulo' (Agression and segregation: The relations between the old person and society in Saõ Paulo). Unpublished notes of speech to Brazilian Society of Geriatrics and Gerontology, Saõ Paulo, May 1982.

—— 'Tabus medico-sociais que envolem o idoso', (Medical and social taboos affecting the aged). Speech at Pontificia Universidade Catolica de Sorocaba, August 1982b (mimeo).

Kalache, A., 'Ageing in Developing Countries: Are we Meeting the Challenge?' *Health and Planning,* 1/2 (1986).

—— 'The Epidemiology of Aging', *The Lancet,* 5 April 1986.

Kalish, R., 'The New Agism and the Failure Models', *The Gerontologist,* 19 (1979).

Kaluger, G., and Fair, M., *Human Development: the Span of Life.* St Louis, Miss.: 1974.

Kieffer, J. A., in *Generations*, 6/4 (1982), pp. 7–9.

Lal, D. *The Poverty of Development Economics*. London: Institute of Economic Affairs, 1983.

Lambo, T. A., 'Psychiatric Disorders in the Aged: Epidemiology and Preventive Measures', in Gilmore *et al.* (eds.), 1981, pp. 74–81.

Leaf, A., discussant on 'Islands of Immunity', in Danon *et al.* (eds.) 1981, pp. 218–22.

Levy, H., 'Migration in Brazil'. M.Sc. thesis, University of Wisconsin, 1973.

Liebowitz, B. 'Background and Planning Process', *The Gerontologist*, 14 (1974).

Lietaer, B., *Europe and Latin America and the Transnationals*. Farnborough: Saxon House, 1979.

Light, D., Jr., with Keller, S., *Sociology*, 3rd ed. New York: Alfred Knopf, 1982.

Lindgren, G., 'Aging, health and social policy: problems of communication and utilization', in Gilmore *et al.* (eds.), 1981, pp. 231–42.

Litwak, E., 'Geographical Mobility and the Extended Family Cohesion', *American Sociological Review*, 25 (1960).

Loja, University of, Research into aging in Vilcabamba, November 1982, for Help the Aged, London.

Lomnitz, Larissa A., *Networks and Marginality: Life in a Mexican Shantytown*. London: Academic Press, 1977.

Loughran, D., Research for Help the Aged in Peru, 1986. London: HelpAge International, 1987.

McNamara, R., *Address to the Governors: Nairobi, Kenya, 24 September 1973*. Washington, DC: World Bank, 1973.

—— *Address to the Governors: Washington, DC, 25 September 1978*. Washington, DC: World Bank, 1978.

Mahar, Dennis J., *Frontier Development Policy in Brazil: A Study of Amazonia*. New York: Praeger, 1979.

Malta, Centre for Social Research, *A Study on the Aged*. Malta: Social Action Movement, 1982.

Mangin, W., 'Latin American Squatter Settlements: A Problem and a Solution', in Renner (ed.), 1982.

Maxwell, R. J., and Silverman, P., 'Geronticide'. Paper prepared for American Anthropological Association, Los Angeles, 1981.

Merchan, R., *Estado gerontológico ecuatoriano: La población adulta y anciana* (Gerontological update on Ecuador: the adult and aged population). Quito: Ministry of Social Well-being, 1984.

Mira y Lopez, *Hacia una vejez joven* (Towards a youthful old age). Buenos Aires: Editorial Kapeluz, 1962.

Morelli, A. C. *et al.* (eds), *Tercera edad bio-psico-social* (Bio-psycho-social Third Age). Montevideo: Libreria Medica Editorial, 1982.

Myers, G. C., 'The Aging of Populations', in Binstock *et al.* (eds.), 1982.

—— and Nathanson, Constance, 'Aging and the Family', *World Health Statistics Quarterly*, 35 (1982).

Neugarten, B., *The Psychology of Aging: An overview*. Washington, DC: American Psychological Association, 1976.

—— (ed.), *Middle Age and Aging*. Chicago: University of Chicago Press, 1986.

Notestein, F. W., *Proceedings of the American Philosophic Society*, 98 (1954).

Oberai, A. S., and Manmohan Singh, H. K., *Causes and Consequences of Internal Migration: a study in the Indian Punjab*, copyright 1983, International Labour Organisation, Geneva, published on behalf of ILO by Oxford University Press, New Delhi, 1983.

Opera Pia International, *Castelgandolfo Document on Active Ageing*. Report of Catholic Church pre-World Assembly on Aging, September, 1980. Vienna: UN Aging Unit, 1982*a*.

—— *Pre-World Assembly on Aging workshop at Villa Leyva, Colombia, October 1981*. Bogotá: Pro Vida, 1982*b*.

Owen, N., Talks, J., and Goldsmith, S., 'Health Care of the Aged', Cambridge Study Group in Ecuador, Cambridge University with HelpAge International, 1985.

PAHO, *Hacia el bienestar de los ancianos*. Washington, DC: 1985. (Also in Eng, as *Towards the Well-being of the Elderly*.)

Pathak, J. D., 'Elderly Women, Their Health and Disorders'. Bombay Medical Research Centre, 1975.

—— 'Our Elderly', Bombay Medical Research Centre, 1978.

—— 'A Report on the Incidence of Main Diseases and Disorders in Women Patients of Upper Age', Bombay Medical Research Centre, 1985.

Posadas, E., *Reducing Social Isolation and Promoting the Health of the Elderly in Argentina*. Kellogg Program, 1987.

Posnansky, A., *Tiahuanacu, the Cradle of American Man*. La Paz, Bolivia: Ministry of Education, 1896.

Quijano, A., in J. E. Hardoy (ed.), *Urbanization in Latin America: Approaches and Issues*. New York: Doubleday Anchor Books, 1975.

Renner, J. (ed.), *Source Book on South American Geography*. Auckland: Longman Paul, 1982.

Roemer, R., *Basic Principles and Legislative Strategies to Promote the Health of the Elderly*, WHO/AGE/82.2, 9181B, 1982.

Rosenmayr, L., 'More than Wisdom: Research and Reflection on the Position of Old Age in Traditional and Changing African Society', University of Vienna, 1986.

Rubin, Z., and McNeill, E. B., *Psychology: Being Human*. New York: Harper and Row, 1985.

Sauvy, A., 'Social and Economic Consequences of the Ageing of Western European Countries', *Population Studies*, 2 (1948).

Schaie, K. W., 'The Seattle Longitudinal Study', in K. W. Schaie (ed.), *Longitudinal Studies of Adult Psychological Development*. New York: Guilford Press, 1982.

Sepp, A., 'Voyages' in P. Caraman, *The Lost Paradise*. London: Jackson, 1975.

Shahrani, M. N., 'Growing in Respect: Aging among the Kirghiz of Afghanistan', in Amos and Harell (eds.), 1981.

Sharma, M. L., and Dak, T. M., *Aging in India*. Delhi: Ajanta, 1987.

Shivers, J. S., and Fait, H. F., *The Elderly*. Philadelphia: Lea and Febiger, 1980.

Siegel, Jacob S., and Hoover, Sally L., *International Trends and Perspectives: Aging*. International Research Document No. 12, US Department of Commerce, Bureau of the Census, Sept. 1984.

Simmons, L., *The Role of the Aged in Primitive Societies*. New Haven, Conn.: Yale University Press, 1945.

Shock, N. W., *The Physiology of Aging*. New York: Scientific American, 1962.

Silva, L. de, *Development Aid: A Guide to Facts and Issues*. Geneva: Third World Forum, 1983.

Smith, R. V., and Thomas, R. N., 'Population Crisis and the March to the Cities', in A. Taylor (ed.), *South America*. Newton Abbot: David and Charles (New York: Praeger), 1973.

Soles, R., 'Confessions of a Peace Corps Volunteer'. Field Report, Land Tenure Center, University of Wisconsin, 1980.

Stamp, E., *Growing Out of Poverty*. Oxford: Oxford University Press, 1977.

Strachan, P., 'Problems of Older Refugees: An Overview', in G. Crisp, (ed.), *New Dimensions in Displacement*. London: Independent Commission on International Humanitarian Issues, 1987.

Swensen, C. H., 'A Respectable Old Age', *American Psychologist*, 38 (1983).

Tapia-Videla, J., and Parrish, C. J., *Ageing, Development and Social Service Delivery Systems in Latin America*. Washington, DC: PAHO, 1981 (Microfiche LO 30024).

Tout, K. J., *Journey to Latin America*. London: HtA, 1983.

—— and Tout, J. R., *Perspectives on Ageing in Belize*. London: HAI/OPEC, 1985.

Trujillo, A. M., and Moreta, A. V., *Vilcabamba: Valle de la eterna juventud* (Valley of eternal youth). Loja, Ecuador: Editorial Don Bosco, 1972.

UN, *Living Conditions in Developing Countries*. E/85/IV/3. New York: United Nations, 1985.

UN CEPAL (Comisión Económica para América Latina), *Envejecimiento de la Población en América Latina* (Ageing of the Latin American Population), ECOSOC, UN, New York, 1982 (and PAHO microfiche LO 30062).

UNCTAD, *The Least Developed Countries*. New York: United Nations, 1985.

UN General Assembly, Agenda Item 58, on A/9126 of 28 Aug. 1973. Basis for papers for World Assembly on Aging, 1982.

UN WAA, *NGO Forum, Vienna, March–April 1982*. Vienna: UN Aging Unit, 1982a.

—— *Opera Pia International Meeting at Castelgandolfo, Italy, September 1980*. Vienna: UN Aging Unit, 1982b.

—— *Regional Preparatory Meeting, Haifa 1980*. Vienna: UN Aging Unit, 1982c.

—— *Regional Technical Meeting for Latin America, San José, Costa Rica, December 1980*. Vienna: UN Aging Unit, 1982d.

—— *Vienna International Plan of Action on Aging*. Vienna: UN Aging unit, 1982e. Various languages.

—— *World Health Organization Preparatory Meeting, Mexico, December 1980*. Vienna: UN Aging Unit, 1982f.

UN WAA ECOSOC, *First Review and Appraisal of the Implementation of the International Plan of Action on Aging*, F/1985/6. New York, 1984.

University of Florida, Center for Gerontological Studies, 'Aging, Demography and Well-Being in Latin America', University of Florida, Gainesville, 23–25 Feb. 1988.

US Bureau of the Census, *An Aging World*, International Population Reports Series P.95, No. 78, 1987.

Von Mering, O., and Henretta, J. C., 'Developing a Taxonomy of Care Levels in "Continuum-of-care" Retirement Situations'. University of Florida, Center for Gerontological Studies, 1986.

Ward, R. A., *The Aging Experience: An Introduction to Social Gerontology*. New York: J. B. Lippincott, 1979.

Ward, T., 'Housing the Elderly in Barbados', MSc. thesis, Michigan State University, 1988.

Warnes, A. M., 'Social Welfare Implications of Ageing in Less Developed Countries: A Geographical Perspective'. Paper presented to Institute of British Geographers, University of Reading, Jan. 1986a.

—— 'The Elderly in Less Developed Countries', in *Ageing and Society*, 6 (1986b), 373–80.

—— 'Geographical Locations and Social Relationships among the Elderly in Developing and Developed Countries', in M. Pacione (ed.), *Progress in Social Geography*. Beckenham: Croom Helm, 1987.

—— and Horsey, A., 'The Elderly Population of Third World Cities: Projections . . .' (Thailand), Kings College, London, 1988.

WHO Kuala Lumpur, Curricular Changes to Meet the Health Needs of the Elderly: Report of the Workshop. 1986.

Williams, T. F., 'The Scientific Challenge: Health Care and the Elderly', in PAHO 1985, pp. 28–34.

Williams, D., The Specialized Agencies and the United Nations: The System in Crisis. London: C. Hurst and Co., 1987.

Wilkening, E. A., 'Some Problems of Development in the Central Plateau of Brazil', in Renner (ed.) 1982.

World Bank, World Development Report, Washington, DC, annually.

ADDITIONAL READING

Further Sources of Information

General information on health matters can be obtained from the WHO world headquarters in Geneva. Specific references to the health of the aged can also be obtained from the office of the WHO Aging Programme in Copenhagen.

Further information on any of the publications listed can be requested either from the UN Aging Unit in Vienna, or from the office of AGEWAYS, HelpAge International, St James's Walk, London EC1R OBE.

Other sources of information include the International Association on Gerontology; the International Center of Social Gerontology (CIGS) in Paris; the International Federation on Aging in Washington; the International Gerontological Exchange at the University of South Florida; and other regional and national gerontological and geriatric associations.

While this book was in preparation the International Institute on Aging (INIA) was inaugurated in Malta as a joint venture of the United Nations and the Government of Malta, thus affording another centre for information, training, and exchange of ideas.

Additional Reading

Abélès, M., and Collard, C. (eds.), *Age, pouvoir et société en Afrique noire*, (Age, power and society in Black Africa). Paris: Kathala, 1985.

Adi, R., *The Aged in Homes for the Aged in Jakarta: Status and Perceptions*. Indonesia: Pusat Penelitian Universitas Katolik, 1982.

Agate, J., *Taking Care of Older People at Home*. London: George Allen and Unwin, 1979.

Ageways, (quarterly loose-leaf bulletin of practical information for age-care workers in developing countries (English and Spanish)). London: HelpAge International.

Amoss, T., and Harrell, S. (eds.), *Other Ways of Growing Old: Anthropological Perspectives*. Stanford, Calif.: Stanford University Press, 1981.

Anderson, F., 'Preventive Medicine in Old Age', in J. Brocklehurst (ed.), *Textbook of Geriatric Medicine and Gerontology*. London: Churchill Livingstone, 1978.

Argentina, Ministerio de Salud y Accion Social de la Nacion, *Situacion de los ancianos en Argentina* (Situation of old people in Argentina). Buenos Aires, 1985.

Barnett, H. G., *Being a Palauan*. New York: Holt, Rinehart and Winston. 1960.

Barrowclough, C., and Fleming, I. *Goal Planning with Elderly People*. Manchester University Press, 1986.

Beattie, W. M., Jr., 'Aging: The Developed and Developing World' and 'Aging: A framework of characteristics and considerations for cooperative efforts between the developing and developed regions of the world'. Paper for the Expert Group Meeting sponsored by L'Institut de la Vie and UNFPA, New York, 1978.

Bergener, M., *Psychogeriatrics: An International Handbook*. New York, 1986.

Binstock, R. H., and Shanas, E. (eds.), *Handbook of Aging and the Social Sciences*. New York: Van Nostrand Reinhold, 1976.

Birren, J. E. (ed.), *Handbook of Aging and the Individual*. Chicago: University of Chicago Press, 1959.

—— and Schaie, K. W. (eds.), 'History of Gerontology', in D. Woodruff, and J. Birren (eds.), *Aging: Scientific Perspectives and Social Issues*. New York: D. Van Nostrand, 1975.

Brazil, Saõ Paulo State Government, *Secretaria da Promoção Social, Investigação preliminar sobre a situação do idoso internado em establecimientos particulares na Cidade de São Paulo* (Preliminary investigation into the conditions of the old person resident in private institutions in the City of Sao Paulo), Technical document No. 6. Saõ Paulo, 1976.

Cambridge (UK) Industrial Training Research Unit, in R. M. Belbin (ed.), *Training the Adult Worker*. London: HMSO.

Canal Ramirez, G., *Envejecer no es deteriorarse* (Getting old is not deterioration). Bogotá: Canal Ramírez-Antares, 1980.

Cassen, R., *et al.*, *Does Aid Work?* Oxford: Clarendon Press, 1986.

Caston, D., *Easy-to-make Aids for our Elderly*. London: Souvenir, 1985. (Also several booklets on design for developing countries from UNICEF.)

Chebotarev, D. F., 'About Standardization of Terms and Definitions and Research Methodologies in Gerontology'. Kiev: Institute of Gerontology of the USSR Academy of Medical Sciences, 1985.

Chen, P. C. Y., *The Health of the Elderly Malaysian: Findings and Policy Implications*, University of Malaya, Kuala Lumpur, 1986.

Chen, Y. P., 'Demography and Aging in Less-developed Countries: Trends and Policy Implications'. Paper for 13th Congress of the International Association on Gerontology, New York, July 1985.

CIGS (Centre International de Gerontologie Sociale), *Report on Latin*

American and Caribbean Conference on Gerontology, Bogotá. Paris: CIGS, 1986.

CIGS, *Gerontologie Africaine/African Gerontology*, periodical published in French and English. Paris: CIGS, from 1984.

Clark, W. A. V., *Human Migration.* London: Sage, 1986.

Collado-Ardon, R., 'La Tercera edad: Problema o recurso?' (The Third Age: problem or resource?). Paper presented at University of Florida Conference, 1988 (q.v.).

Conable, C. W., *Aging and the Global Agenda for Women: Conversations in Nairobi.* Washington, DC: AAIA, 1986.

Contreras de Lehr, E., 'Psicología de la senectud' (The psychology of old age), *Revista española de geriatría y gerontología*, 16/3 (1981), 225–44.

—— *Zum Altenbild in Mexiko und Deutschland* (Profile of ageing in Mexico and Germany). Munich: Wilhelm Fink, 1984.

—— 'Altern in Mexiko' (Old people in Mexico), *Zeitschrift für Gerontologie*, 19 (1986a), 112–15.

Connors, M. M., *Community-based Initiatives to Reduce Social Isolation and Protect and Improve the Health of the Elderly: An Extensive Bibliography.* Kellogg International Program on Health and Aging, University of Michigan, 1987.

Cox, F., and Mberia, N., *Aging in a Changing Village: A Kenyan Experience.* Washington, DC: IFA, 1977.

Danish Medical Bulletin, Copenhagen. Special numbers on gerontology and geriatrics: *The Contribution of the Primary Care Doctor to the Medical Care of the Elderly in the Community* (1985); *Alzheimer's Disease* (1985); *Hearing Problems and the Elderly* (1986). *Quality of Long-term Care* (1987). In preparation with Kellogg International Program on Social Isolation of the Elderly.

Datta, S. K., and Nugent, J. B., 'Are Old-age Security and the Utility of Children in Rural India Really Unimportant?', *Population Studies*, 38 (1984).

Davis, K., 'The Effect of Outmigration on Regions of Origin', in A. A. Brown and E. Neuberger (eds.), *Internal Migration: A Comparative Perspective.* New York: Academic Press, 1977.

Desai, K. G., *Aging in India.* Bombay: Tata Institute of Social Sciences, 1982.

De Souza, A., *The Social Organisation of Aging among the urban Poor.* New Delhi: Indian Social Institute, 1982.

De Vos, S., *The Old-age Economic Security Value of Children in the Philippines and Taiwan.* Honolulu: East–West Center, 1984.

di Gregorio, S. (ed.), *Social Gerontology: New Directions.* Beckenham, Kent: Croom Helm, 1987.

Dwyer, D. J., *People and Housing in Third World Cities: Perspectives on the Problem of Spontaneous Settlements*. New York: Longman, 1975 (2nd edn., 1979).

Eldemire, D., 'The Role of Government and Nongovernment Organizations in Service Planning and Delivery for the Elderly in Jamaica'. Paper presented at University of Florida Conference, 1988 (q.v.).

Feuerstein, M-T., *Partners in Evaluation*. London: Macmillan, 1986.

Fitzpatrick, J. P., *Puerto Rican Americans: The Meaning of Migration to the Mainland*. Englewood Cliffs, NJ: Prentice-Hall, 1971.

Foner, N., *Ages in Conflict: A Cross-cultural Perspective on Inequality between Old and Young*. New York: Columbia University Press, 1984.

Goldstein, C., and Beall, C. M., 'Modernization and Aging in the Third and Fourth World: Views from the Rural Hinterland in Nepal', *Human Organization*, No. 1, p. 48.

Grell, G., *The Elderly in the Caribbean*. Kingston: University of the West Indies, 1987.

Hampson, J. (ed.), *Ageing and the Elderly*. Harare: Strang Multiprint, 1982*b*.

Heath, A., *The Aged in Developing Countries: A Review of Literature*. Washington, DC: IFA, 1981.

Heisel, M. A., 'Aging and the Developing World', *Populi*, 11/2 (1984).

—— 'Aging in the Developing World: The Time to Plan is Now'. Paper for the Northeast Gerontological Society, Boston, 1985.

—— 'Population policies and aging in developing countries'. Paper for 13th Congress of the International Association on Gerontology, New York, July, 1985.

Help the Aged, *The Pallepalem Report*. London: HtA, 1980.

—— *Declaration to World Assembly on Aging*. London: HtA, 1982.

Heok, K. E., Chye, A. P., and Merriman, A., *Health Care in Old Age*. Singapore: Gerontological Society, 1986.

Hodgkinson, J., *Home Work: Meeting the Needs of Elderly People in Residential Homes* (pack of nine booklets). London: Centre for Policy on Ageing, 1988.

Holmes, L. D., *Other Cultures: Elder Years. An Introduction to Cultural Gerontology*. Wichita, Kans.: Wichita State University, 1983.

Horizontes de la Tercera Edad, *Primer seminario nacional sobre la problemática de la Tercera Edad en el Perú* (First national seminar on the problem of the Third Age in Peru). Lima: Horizontes de la Tercera Edad with Ministry of Health, 1982.

—— 'III Seminario Nacional', H. de la T. E., Lima, 1983.

HORIZONTES Pro Vida. Spanish version of *Ageways* (HelpAge International, London), quarterly.

Hugo, G. J., 'Population Ageing: Some Demographic Issues in

Developing Countries'. Paper presented at the 13th Congress of the International Association on Gerontology, New York, 1985.

Husaini, M. A., and Karyadi, D., 'Nutrition of the Elderly in Indonesia'. Paper presented at a WHO Workshop, Hyderabad, November 1986.

International Federation on Aging, *Ageing International*, Washington, DC.

—— '*An Ageing Population: Focus on Day Centres*' (also available in French, Portuguese, Spanish). IFA: Washington, DC, 1984.

Jones, A. B., 'The Relations of Human Health to Age, Place and Time', in Birren (ed.), 1959.

Kabwasa, Nsang-O'Khan, '*La Personne agée dans la cosmogonie africaine: Concept, place, rôle et problèmes de vieillesse et du troisième age en Afrique*' (The old person in African cosmogony). Paper presented at 4th Congress of Fondation van Clé, Brussels, 1982.

Kaplan, R., 'Care for the Elderly in South America: Who is Going to Take Up the Challenge?'. Paper presented at the University of Florida Conference, 1988 (q.v.).

Kendig, H. (ed.), *Ageing and Families: A Support Networks Perspective*, Sydney: Allen and Unwin, 1986.

Kinsella, K. G., *Aging in the Third World*. Center for International Research staff paper no. 35. Washington, DC: United States Bureau of the Census, 1988.

Kumekpor, T. K., 'Fact Finding from Rural People', *Current Research Report*, No. 1, University of Ghana, 1971.

Lawton, M., 'Environments and Living Arrangements', in Binstock *et al*. (eds.), 1982.

Little, V. C., 'Social Services for the Elderly (with special attention to Asia and the West Pacific region)', Paper presented to the Gerontological Society, Portland, Oreg., October 1974.

—— 'For the Elderly: An Overview of Services in Industrially Developed and Developing Countries', in Teicher *et al*. (eds.), 1979.

Litwak, E. and Szelenyi, I., 'Primary Group Structures and Their Functions: Kin, Neighbours, and Friends', *American Sociological Review*, 34 (1969).

McAuslan, P., *Urban Land and Shelter for the Poor*, for the International Institute for Environment and Development. London and Washington, DC: Earthscan, 1985.

McNamara, R., *Address to the Governors, Belgrade 1979*. Washington, DC: World Bank, 1979.

Maddox, G., and Busse, E. (eds.), *Aging: The Universal Human Experience*. New York: Springer, 1988.

Maeda, D., 'Aging in Eastern Society', in D. Hobman (ed.), *The Social Challenge of Aging*. New York: St Martin's Press, 1978.

Mangen, D., and Peterson, W. A. (eds.), *Research Instruments in Social Gerontology*, 3 vols. University of Minnesota Press: Minneapolis, 1984.

Middleton, J., *The Lugbara of Uganda*. New York: Holt, Rinehart, and Winston, 1965.

Misra, R. P. (ed.), *Million Cities of India*. Delhi: Vikas, 1978.

Morales-Martinez, F., *Long-Term Care Services in Costa Rica*, Kellogg International Program on Health and Aging, University of Michigan, 1987.

Morgan, J. H., *Aging in Developing Societies* (2 vols.). Bristol, USA: Wyndham Hall Press, 1985.

Mubbashar, M. H., *Diagnosis and Therapy in Psychogeriatrics*. Rawalpindi: Psycho Publishers, Pak American Commercial, 1985.

Myers, G. C., 'Future Age Projections and Society', in A. J. J. Gilmore, A. Svanborg, M. Marois, W. M. Beattie, and J. Piotrowski, J. (eds.), *Aging: A Challenge to Science and Society*. Vol. ii, *Medicine and Social Science*, Oxford University Press (for L'Institut de la Vie and WHO), 1981.

Nair, K. T., *Old People in Madras City*. University of Madras, 1972.

—— *Older People in Rural Tamil Nadu*. University of Madras, 1980.

Nusberg, C. (ed.), *Home Help Services for the Aging Around the World*, Washington, DC: IFA, 1975.

—— *The Situation of the Asian Pacific Elderly*. Washington, DC: IFA, 1981.

—— *Aging International*, IFA, Washington DC, quarterly.

—— and Sokolovsky, J., *The International Directory of Research and Researchers in Comparative Gerontology*. Washington, DC: IFA, 1987.

Odonne, M. J., 'Anciano y sociedad' (The old person and society). Paper presented at the University of Florida Conference, 1988 (q.v.).

Osaka, M., 'Increase of Elderly Poor in Developing Countries: The Implications of Dependency Theory and Modernization Theory for the Aging of World Populations', *Studies in Third World Societies*, 22 (1982), 85.

PAHO—PanAmerican Health Organization, *Gerontological Update*, No. 1. Washington, DC: 1985.

Paillat, P., 'Influence de l'evolution demographique sur la constitution de la famille et sur la place des personnes agées' (Influence of demographic evolution on the constitution of the family and on the role of aged persons), in Gilmore *et al.* (eds.), 1981, 279–84. (*See under Myers, 1981.*)

Paulme, D., *Classes et associations d'age en Afrique de l'ouest* (Classes and age associations in West Africa). Paris: Plon, 1971.

Raj, B., and Prasad, B. G., 'A Study of Rural Aged Persons in Social Profile', *Indian Journal of Social Work*, 32 (1971).

Revista Latinoamericana de Psicología, Bogotá, three times a year.

Roberts, B., *Cities of Peasants: The Political Economy of Urbanisation in the Third World*. London: Edward Arnold, 1978.

Roberts, H., *An Urban Profile of the Middle East*. London: Croom Helm, 1979.

Rosenmayr, L., *Die späte Freiheit. Das Alter—Ein Stück bewusst gelebten Lebens* (Elderly freedom). Berlin: Severin and Siedler, 1983.

Rubinstein, R. L., and Johnsen, P. T., *Toward a Comparative Perspective of Filial Response to Aging Populations. Aging and the Aged in the Third World*, pt 1. *Studies in Third World Societies*, No. 22. Dept. of Anthropology, College of William and Mary, Williamsburg, 1982.

Schweeger-Hefel, A., *Masken und Mythen. Sozialstrukturen der Nyonyosi und Sikonse in Obervolta* (Masks and myths: Social structure of the Nyonyosi and Sikonse in Upper Volta). Vienna: Schendl, 1980.

Sen, A., *Poverty and Famines*. Oxford University Press, 1981.

Shelton, A. J., 'Igbo Child-raising, Eldership and Dependence: Further Notes for Gerontologists and others', *The Gerontologist*, 8, (1968), 241.

Sheppard, H. L., and Streib, G., *Aging in China*. Tampa: International Exchange Center on Gerontology, 1985.

Simeone, I., 'The Evolution of the Family and the Health of Elderly People'. Paper presented to WHO preparatory conference for World Assembly on Aging, Mexico City, December, 1980.

Simmons, L., 'Aging in Preindustrial Societies', in C. Tibbits (ed.), *Handbook of Social Gerontology*. Chicago: University of Chicago Press, 1960.

Sjoberg, G., 'Familial Organization in the Pre-industrial City', *Marriage and Family Living*, 18 (1982), 30.

Sokolovsky, J., *Growing Old in Different Societies: Cross-cultural Perspectives*. Acton, Mass.: Coply Publishing, 1986.

Solomons, N. W., Mei-Ling, S., and Mazariegos, M., 'Gerontological Research Expanding in Guatemala', *Ageing International*, (Spring, 1987), 17–21.

Sottas, E., *The Least Developed Countries*. New York: UNCTAD, 1985.

Sow, I., *Psychiatrie dynamique africaine*. Paris: Payot, 1977.

Ssenkoloto, G. M., *Social Development and Aging in Developing and Developed Countries: A Background Document for Policy Makers*, Buea, Cameroon: Panafrican Institute, 1981.

Stearns, P. N. (ed.), *Old Age in Preindustrial Society*. New York: Holmes and Meier, 1982.

Teicher, M., Thursz, D., and Vigilante, J. (eds.), *Reaching the Aged: Social Services in Forty-four Countries*. Beverly Hills, Calif.: Sage, 1979.

Tout, K. J. 'The Community against Ageing Problems in the Third World', in *COMM*, 26 (Nov. 1985), 252–61 (European Clearing House for Community Work, Marcinelle, Belgium.)

—— *Perspectives on Ageing in Developing Countries of America*. London: HAI, 1986.

—— *Social Isolation of the Aged in Developing Countries*. Kellogg International on Health and Aging: University of Michigan, 1987.

Traore, Gaoussou, 'Famille traditionelle, famille rurale'. Paper presented at expert meeting on the Role of the Family in the Processes of Development in Africa, Bujumbura, Burundi, 1985.

UN, *Urban, Rural and City populations, 1950–2000*, ESA/P/WP/66, New York, n.d.

—— *The World Population and Its Age–Sex Composition*, ESA/P/WP/65, New York, 1980.

—— Finance Department, *The Financial Situation of the United Nations*, A/C.5/40/16, briefing meeting, March, 1986. UN Headquarters, New York.

UN DIESA, *Selected Demographic Indicators* . . . , ST/ESA/SER.R/38, New York, 1980.

—— —— *Periodical on Aging*, 1/1 (1984).

—— —— *The World Aging Situation: Strategies and Policies*, E/85/IV/5, UN, New York, 1985.

UNESCO, *The Fullness of Time*. Special issue of *Unesco Courier*, No. 10 (Oct. 1982), devoted to old age.

UN WAA, 'Aging and Development: The Humanitarian Issues'. Background paper for the Assembly. Vienna: UN Aging Unit, 1982. (And other background papers.)

—— *World Assembly Full Report*, E/82/I/16. Vienna: UN Aging Unit, 1982.

WHO, *Aging in Developing Countries: Final Report of International Symposium*, Hamburg, July, 1981.

—— *World Health Statistics*, 35/3–4 (1982).

—— *Long-term Planning for Health Care of the Elderly*, IRP/HEE 115–01. Copenhagen, 1984.

—— *Co-ordinated Action on Aging*. Reports of NGO/WHO Collaborative Group on Aging, Geneva (annually from 1984).

—— *Reunión de los paises del cono sur programa de control de las enfermedades crónicas* (Meeting of the Southern Cone countries on control of chronic illnesses). 1984.

WHO, *Health of the Elderly: Intercountry (Western Pacific Region) Workshop.* Manila, 1985.

—— *Nutrition in the Elderly.* Washington, DC, 1985.

—— *The Effectiveness of Health Promotion for the Elderly,* 1986 Advisory Group, Hamilton, Canada (IRP/HEE 115), 1987.

—— *Nutrition, Aging and Epidemiology in Asia and Oceania,* 1986 Workshop, Hyderabad (IRP/HEE 115.1.4), 1987.

Yap, P., 'Aging in Underdeveloped Asian Countries', in C. Tibbits and W. Donahue (eds.), *Social and Psychological Aspects of Aging.* New York: Columbia University Press, 1962.

Yeh, S. H. K., and Laquian, A. A., *Housing Asia's Millions.* Ottawa: International Development Research Centre, 1979.

Yung-huo, L., 'Retirees and Retirement Programs in the People's Republic of China', *Industrial Gerontology,* 1 (1974).

Zahan, D., *The Bambara.* Leiden: E. J. Brill, 1974.

INDEX